LANGUAGE IN BEHAVIOR
Second Edition

LANGUAGE IN BEHAVIOR
Second Edition

Richard W. Howell, Ph.D.
Department of Anthropology
University of Hawaii at Hilo
Hilo, Hawaii

Harold J. Vetter, Ph.D.
Department of Criminal Justice
University of South Florida
Tampa, Florida

HUMAN SCIENCES PRESS, INC.
72 FIFTH AVENUE,
NEW YORK, N.Y. 10011

Printed in the United States of America
987654321

Library of Congress Cataloging in Publication Data

Howell, Richard W.
  Language in behavior. (Second Edition)

  Bibliography: p.
  Includes index.
  1. Linguistics. 2. Language and languages.
3. Communication. I. Vetter, Harold J.
II. Title.
P121.H73 1985   401′.9   84-6557
ISBN 0-89885-215-3
ISBN 0-89885-219-6 (pbk).

CONTENTS

ACKNOWLEDGMENTS

We should like to acknowledge our indebtedness to Daniel E. Brown, Craig Severance, Andrew Terker, and Ron Amundson of the University of Hawaii at Hilo for their helpful readings of several chapters of the manuscript; to Ziff-Davis Publishing Company for graciously permitting us to reprint material originally prepared for them under contract; and to Mr. Thomas R. LaMarre and Mr. Ted Peacock of F. E. Peacock Publishers for their kindness in allowing us to reproduce material for which they hold the copyright.

In addition, our thanks are due to the following authors, editors, and publishers for granting the right to quote from or reproduce copyrighted material: *American Anthropologist; American Journal of Psychology*; Dr. John Atkins; Dr. Jean Berko; Dr. John B. Carroll; Dr. Joel Davitz; Harcourt Brace Jovanovich; Little, Brown and Company; Liveright Publishing Corporation; McGraw-Hill; Dr. Wilder Penfield; Philosophical Library; Prentice-Hall; Princeton University Press; *Speech Monographs*; Dr. Anthony F. C. Wallace; and *Word*.

Finally, we are especially grateful to our editor, Ms. Norma Fox, for her patience and counsel in helping to develop the manuscript for the original edition and for suggesting that a second edition would be in order.

R. W. H.
H. J. V.

PREFACE TO THE SECOND EDITION

This new edition of *Language in Behavior* follows the basic plan
of the original while, we trust, showing improvement through extensive rewriting, updating and the consolidation of several chapters and
the expansion of others.

The first chapter (Linguistics in Historical Perspective) has been
augmented by a discussion of the current controversy over the "cor-
ruption" of English through "wrong usages" and excessive redundancy. To the dismay of purists, perhaps, we suggest that this
lamentable trend actually reflects the language in the process of
change. The order of the second and third chapters has been reversed on logical grounds, while the present Chapter 3 (The Origin
and Diversity of Languages) now includes a brief sketch of major
language groupings around the world.

Expressive uses of language and sound symbolism are now included in Chapter 4 (Nonverbal Communication). A similar econ-
omy has been achieved by including material on the biological bases
of language in Chapter 2 (Antecedents of Language). The chapter
on descriptive linguistics (Theory of Language) is now dealt with in
two chapters, the first (Chapter 5) treating phonetics and phonology,
the second (Chapter 6) treating morphology and syntax. The original single chapter was simply too compact for most beginning students.

The more important material on multilingualism has been incorporated into the present Chapter 7 (The Ontogenesis of Language).

The present Chapter 10 (Pidgins and Creoles) has been extensively revised to reflect some of the wealth of research in this rapidly growing area. The original materials on language and social identity and language and social change are now reflected in Chapter 11 (Language and Society), to which some new materials have also been added. As in the original edition, the book concludes with a chapter on Language and Culture, with some necessary updating.

We have been helped appreciably in the task of revision by comments and criticisms from our readers. We hope that the changes, additions, and revisions have resulted in a book that achieves all of the objectives we had set for the original volume—in a more attractive and readable fashion.

R.W.H.
H.J.V.

PREFACE TO THE FIRST EDITION

For most social scientists, it is not the study of language as such that is of special relevance, but rather the use of language as a means of getting at other kinds of information on social science. Thus the sociologist wants to know how language can help him to learn about social structure or interpersonal relationships; the psychologist looks at language as a key to some of the ways people learn, perceive, and interpret the world around them; and the ethnologist depends on language to reveal how culture categorizes and orders experience.

Inconvenient though it may be, however, language cannot be utilized naïvely with much profit. In order to investigate social science phenomena effectively through the clues provided by language, it is necessary to know something about the nature of language and of linguistic analysis. There is an obvious analogy between linguistics and statistics, in that both are legitimate disciplines in their own right and yet are widely used as tools by scholars whose primary interests are in other areas. There is also a second analogy: both are likely to be considered rather painful hurdles in the path of academic success for the graduate student.

Since we do not feel that the acquisition of a basic knowledge of linguistics need be painful, we hope on the one hand to present some fundamental linguistic concepts with sufficient clarity to instill confidence into the reader, and on the other hand to motivate him, through an exposition of the kinds of research that are possible, to acquire some of the skills of linguistic analysis.

Some understanding of linguistics is important, not only because the use of language is likely to be misguided without it, but also because the methods of linguistic analysis have been applied to essentially nonlinguistic events. Thus the use of the contrast within a frame was used by Conklin (1955) to analyze Hanunóo color categories, and by Frake (1961) to describe Subanun disease categories, while componential analysis has been widely used to deal with other semantic domains, including kinship systems (Lounsbury, 1956; Goodenough, 1956; Wallace and Atkins, 1960).

While basic techniques and concepts were being borrowed from structural linguistics to be used in the analysis and description of various semantic domains, a major shift in emphasis was taking place within the field of linguistics itself. To summarize this briefly (and no doubt too simply): before 1957, linguists had treated language as if it were a static semantic domain. A great deal of attention was devoted to the definition of relatively low-order events such as phonemes, which would be grouped into larger components such as morphemes, but virtually no attention was paid to the high-order sequencing of events that we call syntax. Today most linguists are primarily concerned to develop the rules that generate the possible utterances of a language. The older skills are still necessary, but they are no longer an end in themselves. Similarly, it is likely that an increasing number of anthropologists will try to apply ideas of generative grammar to culturally patterned sequences of behavior. This has scarcely begun, but the techniques are promising and the interest is there. Goodenough (1971), for instance, has noted the relevance of Eric Berne's *Games People Play* (1964), and has added his own discussion of *recipes* for certain cultural patterns. The older ethnographers did of course attempt to describe behavior patterns, but did not systematically attempt to render the descriptions in terms of what is significant for the practitioners themselves. Now, on the other hand, we are starting to see such formal studies as Colby's partial generative grammar of Eskimo folk narratives (1973).

Generative grammar involved a step away from the Bloomfieldian abhorrence of meaning, at least in the matter of linguistic analysis. The new respectability of meaning, long a concern of many psychologists and philosophers, has indeed led to an extension of generative grammar to the loftier level of generative semantics. According to Werner (1972), at this point we can trace the convergence of ethnoscience (or ethnolinguistics), computer simulation of semantic information-processing, the ethnography of speaking, and generative semantics. It is too early to judge how far the concern with meaning will go before methodological difficulties will induce a backlash and a return to problems that are operationally more gratifying.

As early as 1951, the psychologist Karl Lashley was referring to "the syntax of action," and was discussing serial order with specific reference to language, but the real development of psycholinguistics began at about the same time, when a number of psychologists began to display linguistic sophistication (Miller, 1951; Brown, 1958). By the time Chomsky's *Syntactic Structures* appeared (1957), a cadre of psychologists was ready to apply the new look in linguistics to such problems as the acquisition of the first and second language. Indeed, the importance of the generative-transformational approach to language was so great for psychology that Judith Greene's *Psycholinguistics* (1972) is really a detailed exposition of Chomsky's views as they pertain to psychology. This may be an extreme position, but it does suggest that linguistic theory is very important to our understanding of the psychology of language.

Sociolinguistics is the other main area in which linguistics has penetrated the social sciences. The field actually developed when linguists realized that they could not adequately describe speech varieties independently of their social contexts. The other side of this coin, the focus on contexts rather than speech varieties, has given rise within sociology to the closely related subdiscipline of ethnomethodology, in which problems of sequencing in conversations have already begun to draw serious attention (Schegloff, 1968, 1972; Schegloff and Sacks, 1969).

In summary, then, we are concerned with the linguistically oriented approaches to human behavior, including sociolinguistics, psycholinguistics, and ethnolinguistics. In addition, we are also interested in placing language within its behavioral and historical context. Thus we shall touch on the antecedents of language, including nonverbal communication and sound-symbolism, the biological basis of language, and derived systems such as the manual communication of the deaf, drum language, and secret languages. We cannot touch all bases, but we hope to range widely enough to suggest the myriad directions that language-based studies can take.

REFERENCES

Berne, E. 1964. *Games People Play*. New York: Grove Press, Inc.

Brown, R. 1958. *Words and Things*. New York: The Free Press.

Chomsky, N. 1957. *Syntactic Structures*. The Hague: Mouton & Co.

Colby, B. N. 1973. A partial grammar of Eskimo folktales. *Amer. Anthropol.* *75:* 645–662.

Conklin, H. C. 1955. Hanunóo color categories. *Southwestern J. Anthropol.* *11:* 339–344.

Frake, C. C. 1961. The diagnosis of disease among the Subanun of Mindanao. *Amer. Anthropol.* *63:* 113–132.

Goodenough. W. H. 1956. Componential analysis and the study of meaning. *Language 32:* 195–216.

Goodenough, W. H. 1971. *Culture, Language, and Society*. Reading, Mass.: Addison-Wesley Publishing Co., Inc.

Greene, J. 1972. *Psycholinguistics*. Baltimore, Md.: Penguin Books, Inc.

Lashley, K. S. 1951. The problem of serial order in behavior. In L. A. Jeffress (Ed.), *Cerebral Mechanisms in Behavior*, pp. 112–136. New York: John Wiley & Sons, Inc.

Lounsbury, F. 1956. Semantic analysis of the Pawnee kinship usage. *Language 32:* 158–194.

Miller, G. A. 1951. *Language and Communication*. New York: McGraw-Hill Book Company.

Schegloff, E. A. 1968. Sequencing in conversational openings. *Amer. Anthropol. 70:* 1075–1095.

Schegloff, E. A. Notes on a conversational practice: Formulating place. In David Sudnow (Ed.), 1972. *Studies in Social Interaction*. New York: The Free Press, pp. 75–119.

Schegloff, E. A., & H. Sacks. 1969. Opening up closings. Paper delivered at annual meetings of the American Sociological Association, San Francisco, Cal., September 1969.

Werner, O. 1972. Ethnoscience 1972. In *Annual Review of Anthropology*. Vol. 1. Bernard J. Siegel (Ed.), pp. 271–308. Palo Alto, Cal., Annual Reviews, Inc.

Chapter 1

LINGUISTICS IN HISTORICAL PERSPECTIVE

It is probably not possible to trace in intimate detail the intricate network of interrelationships between our increasing linguistic sophistication and our broad social attitudes and programs, but a general connection is easily demonstrated. For example, when high-school and college students in Hilo, Hawaii, recently formed a group for the study and promotion of "Hawaiian pidgin," they had considerable moral support from the Hilo academic community. While the interest faded as the original student founders of the group went their several directions, it had risen in the face of a continuing tradition that regards the use of "pidgin" as a severe developmental handicap, if not an outright evil. Indeed, not too many years ago there were schools on Hawaii where instruction was in Standard English for the elite minority, but in "pidgin" for the majority (who would presumably pass their lives as plantation workers).

Obviously the student group was responding to a desire to strengthen or re-establish its local identity; and this is part of more general ethnic identity movements in Hawaii and on the mainland. It is doubtful, however, that "pidgin" would have been singled out for such serious attention without the dissemination of the contemporary linguistic attitude that all speech varieties are equally worthy of study and equally "legitimate." Of course, the same influence is seen to an even greater extent among other groups, most notably, perhaps, among those who identify as Chicano or Black. In some cases, the language selected for identification is not a serious part of the group's personal experience. Thus the recent interest in Swahili is a little arbitrary, because there are probably very few Black Americans who can reliably trace their genealogies back to Swahili-speaking ancestors. In Hawaii, many students who are enrolling in Hawaiian language courses have had little previous experience with the language beyond a few dozen floral, faunal, personal, and place-names. Third- and fourth-generation Japanese in Hawaii usually have an even more limited acquaintance with their ancestral tongue, yet they now swell Japanese classes.

In all these cases, the language symbolizes a group identity. The "pidgin" case is particularly instructive for two reasons: first, it is spoken by people of diverse origins, and thus is not directly related to ethnic origins (as in the case of Japanese, Hawaiian, or Spanish) or to racial origins (as in the case of Swahili); and second, it differs from the other languages in that it lacks even their mythical "purity," and thus their respectability.

LANGUAGE STUDY IN ANCIENT GREECE

While the idea of legitimizing a pidgin or creole language may seem socially dubious to some critics, even nonlinguists today accept the validity of such languages as Hawaiian, Spanish, Swahili, and Japanese—at least as suitable objects of study and as perfectly respectable media of communication. But until rather recently, students of language were quite narrow in their conceptions of academic respectability. According to Bloomfield (1933), the ancient Greeks "studied no language but their own; they took it for granted that the structure of their language embodied the universal forms of human thought or, perhaps, of the cosmic order" (p. 5). This lack of modesty no doubt restricted the kinds of statement that the philosophers could make about language, but they were the first European language theorists; their work began somewhere around the latter part of the sixth century B.C. They discovered the parts of speech for Greek, and also such syntactic constructions as that "of subject and predicate, and its chief inflectional categories: genders, numbers, cases, persons, tenses, and modes. They defined these not in terms of recognizable linguistic forms, but in abstract terms which were to tell the meaning of the linguistic class" (p. 5).

Hellenic interest in language was an outgrowth of philosophical pursuits. It was essentially in response to philosophical questions that Greek scholars speculated on the origin of language, the relationship between words and their meanings, and the application of principles of logic to grammar. Philosophical discussions were often directed toward linguistic problems. One of these discussions, as Ivič (1965) points out, is quite famous—the argument over whether the connection between the meanings of words and their sounds is logical and direct, or arbitrary and capricious. The "analogists" maintained that language is not dependent upon man-made conventions, but is a gift of nature. There was perfect correspondence between the sound of a word and its meaning, in their view; any imperfections that had arisen in this relationship in the course of time could be explained by etymological research, by systematic studies of words and their origins and derivations. The "anomalists," on the other hand, rejected the notion that there was perfect harmony between the sound and meaning of words. They drew on the existence of synonyms and homonyms, the demonstration of linguistic change over time, and the irregularity of grammar to show the imperfect nature of language.

Note that in studying the nature of their language the Greeks were engaging in linguistic activity. That is, the linguist is concerned with the science of language and may or may not be able to display practical competence in the use of any language other than his or her native tongue. The linguist may or may not be a *polyglot*, who can handle several languages. Polyglots often develop a kind of general language sense that helps them add to their repertoire, but may never learn much about language in the sense that the linguist does, any more than the rest of us become linguistically sophisticated by virtue of being native speakers of our language.

LANGUAGE STUDY AMONG THE ROMANS

As in so many other spheres of activity, the Romans borrowed liberally from the Greeks in matters pertaining to language. Thus, when a formal grammar was required with which to unify the Roman Empire and to compose a Latin literature (ca 100 B.C.-200 A.D.), the model they chose was Greek. The most famous of the Latin grammars remained as textbooks through the Middle Ages, while spoken forms of Latin developed into what we recognize today as the Romance languages. The medium of written communication, however, remained classical Latin.

The medieval scholar, accordingly, in both the Latin countries and others, studied only classical Latin. The scholastic philosophers discovered some features of Latin grammar, such as the distinction between nouns and adjectives and the differences between concord, government, and apposition. They contributed much less than the (Greek) ancients, who had, at any rate, a first-hand knowledge of the languages they studied. (Bloomfield, 1933, p. 6)

THE DEVELOPMENT OF NORMATIVE GRAMMARS

Somewhat later, the notion developed that general grammars could be written on the basis of universally valid canons of logic. Bloomfield attributes to this idea the subsequent development of normative grammars, in which authorities presume to dictate the way people *ought* to speak. This tradition is still very much with us, of course, in the form of concern over what is "correct" English.

Lamberts (1972) has recently documented some of the absurdities that the quest for correctness has added to our language. Chaucer, for example, probably pronounced "perfect" as /pǽrfit/ and spelled it *parfit*, but grammarians introduced the present spelling to make the word look Latin. Eventually the spelling dictated the pronunciation. *Comptroller* is a re-spelling of "controller"; and while the standard pronunciation for both is the same, the spelling pronunciation for the former /kâmptrówlər/ is common, and may well replace /kəntrówler/. Cases in which the artificial pronunciation never caught on include "victuals" (from *vittles*), "debt" (from *det*), and "doubt" (from *doute*).

> Similarly, names like *Matthew*, *Thaddeus*, *Bartholomew*, *Dorothy*, *Martha*, *Katherine*, *Elizabeth*, and *Theodore* have the shortened forms *Matt*, *Ted*, *Bart*, *Dot*, *Marty*, *Kate*, *Bet*, and *Ted*, reflecting the time when the *th* spelling symbolized the stop /t/.
> The full forms were subjected to spelling pronunciation, presumably as being more dignified, but the nicknames have been left untouched. Thomas is an exception; so is the Thames in England and Canada. The Thames in Connecticut is gradually becoming /θéymz/. (Lamberts, 1972, p. 82)

The modern grammarians are the linguists, and it is hard to imagine that a contemporary professional linguist would abet the pedantic absurdity of such "improvements" on the basis of an alien model. This is part of the meaning of our earlier statement that all speech varieties are academically legitimate. This does not mean, of course, that all speech varieties are socially appropriate. What is socially appropriate constitutes "good" English. As Lamberts (1972) expresses it, " 'good' English in any given situation is the kind of English that certifies a person's competence to deal with the subject he is speaking or writing about. It is believable language" (p. 23). Professorial eloquence is no more appropriate in an infantry barracks than extremely salty speech is in church.

VERBOOM!

Those of us who have gradually and perhaps painfully learned to deal with the language in a way that elicited smiling approval from our mentors are likely to feel some sympathy for Edwin Newman and others who lament at length on the abuses to which the language is being subjected. But many of the apparent abuses are simply reflections of the language in the process of change, whether we endorse those changes or not.

One kind of change is in the pronunciation of words, though we often fight the change by citing dictionary guidelines. Most of the time the dictionaries reflect contemporary pronunciations by the more educated segments of the population, but because the lexicographers want to be sure new pronunciations are becoming typical rather than a passing fad or practiced by a limited number of educated speakers in a local region, they tend to be conservative, and in some cases are too slow to reflect changes that have taken place. Thus, 20 years ago a well-regarded professor at UC Berkeley rebuked a graduate student for not pronouncing the final vowel of "rationale." He was able to cite the most respected dictionaries in support of his pronunciation, but among university people in the United States, at least, he was a member of a very small minority and the hallowed dictionaries were simply out-of-date on that point. It is well to remember that the purpose of dictionaries is to reflect usage, not to dictate it.

One kind of rather general change that seems to be taking place involves an increase in redundancy. Thus, we now hear such things as "nine a.m. in the morning," or "plenty of ample parking," which may be irksome to some of us, but are so common now that they may slip right by us. The unnecessary addition of "situation," for example, as in a "poor field position situation" (Howard Cosell, cited by Newman, 1975/1976) has become quite fashionable.

To cite two more examples from the sports world, Jim Simpson of NBC noted before a Miami/Baltimore football game that:

> Miami was driving for its sixth consecutive playoff in a row. Many sports broadcasters now believe that consecutive is shorthand for consecutive in a row, just as eight straight wins seems incomplete to them alongside eight straight wins without a loss. . . . (Newman, 1975/1976:81).

Another contemporary development is an increasing fondness for pretentious expression. In some cases the purpose is to obfuscate, as when representatives of the Nixon administration would not acknowledge having lied: the earlier statements were "no longer operative." In other cases, the purpose is to make an office or product sound more important. Sanitation engineer is a relatively old example. More recent examples include "individual flotation devices," for life jackets or the more colorful Mae Wests. Libraries are giving way to learning resources centers; glasses are out, eyeware is in.

Pompous language presumably enhances the prestige of the user. Thus, a faculty member of a university received a memorandum from an administrator which advised him that "Having prioritized available funding, your request for staff-support facilities cannot be actuated at present. Student throughput indicators show marked declining motivational values in subsequent enrollment periods in elective liberal arts choices" (Newman, 1975/1976:69–70). Newman's correspondent interpreted that to mean that his request had been turned down.

Two other trends today involve an increased use of grammatical devices that have been available for a considerable time. Thus, the suffix –wise, meaning "manner," has been around for a long time ("likewise," for "in a similar manner"), but it seems to have been redefined and made more productive. Thus "we are told about the team with the worst record won and lostwise" (Newman, 1975/1976:83), where the –wise has the sense of "in regard to." Note that this is different from the older suffix of "streetwise," or "ringwise," which means "wise in the matter of."

Finally, we seem to be in the midst of a verb boom (verboom!), in which new verbs are being coined from nouns. In some cases the noun is simply treated as a verb (parenting, for instance), or a specific device may be applied, as the suffix –ize (prioritize).

We may see these tendencies as reflecting an impoverishment in language ability, but it may not be long before many of the tendencies will become established practice. They will constitute the new norm; they will be "correct" English for the most educated segment of the population.

HINDU GRAMMARIANS

Before continuing with European developments, we pause briefly for another glimpse into antiquity, this time in India. Roughly contemporaneously with the classical Greek philosophers, Hindu grammarians (traditional guardians of such sacred texts as the Rig-Veda, parts of which, according to Bloomfield, date back at least to 1200 B.C.), began to turn their attention to the language of the upper caste. This language, Sanskrit, was subjected to minutely detailed analysis, probably for generations; the eventual result was the grammar of Pāṇini. Bloomfield (1933) describes it thus:

> This grammar, which dates from somewhere around 350 to 250 B.C., is one of the greatest monuments of human intelligence. It describes ... every inflection, derivation, and composition, and every syntactic usage of its author's speech. No other language, to this day, has been so perfectly described. It may have been due, in part, to this excellent codification that Sanskrit became, in time, the official and literary language of all Brahmin India. Long after it had ceased to be spoken as anyone's native language, it remained (as classical Latin remained in Europe) the artificial medium for all writing on learned or religious topics (p. 11).

In many respects, this ancient Hindu work may have been worth more than all other language studies combined until around the beginning of the nineteenth century. Thanks to the Greeks and the Latinists, Europe did have a linguistic tradition; but when Pāṇini's grammar came to light, it presented Europeans with their first complete and accurate description of a language based on observation. Not only does it remain a model since unmatched, but it seems probable that it may never be matched—not because we lack those who have sufficient skill to accomplish the task, but rather because we do not have a group of scholars sufficiently motivated to produce a comparable *tour de force*. The task is something on the order of extending the value of π another dozen or so decimal places. Theory does not require such detail, and although it might be desirable for the development of good mechanical translation systems, it seems likely that the cost of achieving such detail would reach prohibitive levels long before perfection could be closely approximated. Also, while we are naturally interested in linguistic descriptions, they are not an end in themselves; they test theory and provide material for theory, but the theory is not ultimately aimed at establishing more perfect descriptions. The current generative approach is exciting not because it will feed the computer better (although it may), but rather because it may bring us closer to an understanding of human mentality.

There are other, related reasons why we may not find it worth our while to emulate Pāṇini's magnificent achievement. We now understand what a tremendous variety of codes is described by a label such as "English." The codes are related, of course, but do we determine by a toss of the coin which variety to describe? We drive trucks, while the English drive lorries; we ascend in elevators, while the English avail themselves of the lift. It is often as difficult to account for such lexical differences as it is for grammatical differences, such as our need to go "to *the* hospital," while the English simply go "to hospital." Since we go "to school" and "to church," it might seem that such high frequency events lose the definite article, but is is not clear that the English spend more time in hospitals than we, and we go "to college" but "to *the* university," while the English also go "to university." This particular difference seems also to distinguish American and Canadian varieties, though the lexical differences are fewer. Other nationally identified varieties have similar differences; even in American English we have abundant regional and social variations, and English is but one general bundle of closely related codes. We could raise the same problems with other European languages, with Japanese, with Chinese, and probably with any other language. The point here is not to disparage the Hindu achievement, but simply to show that we have more urgent and more theoretically interesting tasks to occupy our attention and our efforts.

COMPARATIVE LANGUAGE STUDIES

Besides showing European scholars what a proper grammar looks like, the discovery of the Sanskrit work revealed the possibility of comparative studies. Of course, some obvious relationships had already been noticed; as Bloomfield (1933, p. 9) pointed out, the English *drink*, Dutch *drinken*, German *trinken*, Danish *drikke*, and

Swedish *dricka* comprise one of the many sets that suggest there is a close relationship among the Germanic groups of languages. There were also obvious similarities among the Romance group and among the Slavic group, but the discovery of the Sanskrit forms made the correspondences of these groups to the Greek forms more obvious. After the first great European Sanskrit scholar, Sir William Jones (1746-1794), had hypothesized that Sanskrit, Latin, Greek, and so forth, must have come from a common source, which might no longer exist, there followed a century of enthusiastic study that resulted in highly detailed comparative analyses. The excitement was not caused exclusively by the aesthetics of comparative or historical linguistics; it also arose because the newly discovered relationships implied the idea of tribal migrations, and raised the hope of deducing information on the origin of peoples and customs.

While the European and Hindu scholars provided the basis for our current linguistic researches, there were also other notable efforts, which have not, however, contributed directly to the discipline. Bloomfield (1933) noted that the Arabs worked out a grammar of the classical form of their language as it appears in the Koran; this provided a model for Jews in Mohammedan countries, who constructed a Hebrew grammar. In both these cases, the linguistic interest was related to religious concerns. In China, excellent lexical research was performed by the Han scholars (206 B.C.–220 A. D.), who were concerned to reconstruct the great classics after the enthusiastic book-burning of Shih Huang Ti in 213 B.C. The unifier of the Chinese Empire and founder of the Ch'in Dynasty had ordered the mass destruction largely because his literary opponents kept fighting him by means of allusions to the methods of government embodied in the classics (Karlgren, 1923).

In Japan, the great scholar Motoori Norinaga (1730-1801) was inspired to produce prodigious studies of Japanese by his extreme distaste for the high esteem enjoyed in his country by Chinese culture and Chinese language studies (Miller, 1967). Before the end of the eighteenth or by the early nineteenth century, then, virtually all serious language study was motivated by a desire to maintain the "purity" of a particular language, usually for religious or nationalist reasons. Gumperz (1965) credits the French with being the first to study dialects, which they did early in the nineteenth century; but their objective was to eliminate vulgar manifestations of the language, and even in modern India it is still inconceivable that anyone would want to know about the speech of illiterates.

THE NINETEENTH CENTURY

To return to the point made at the beginning of this chapter, it should be clear by now that the current dictum that all speech varieties have equal legitimacy is a relatively new idea. Even aside from their social and academic legitimacy, there were effective restrictions on the kinds of speech varieties that were subjected to serious scrutiny. In the nineteenth century, the pursuit of comparative and historical problems almost necessarily centered on written forms of language, although this was not always done as a matter of principle.

Nevertheless, descriptive linguistics did develop increasingly during the nineteenth century. In particular, students of American Indian languages had no choice but to focus on spoken forms, because there was no pre-Columbian script to rely on. Since there were many dozens of apparently unrelated languages north of Mexico alone, displaying the most varied types of structure, the challenge was enormous. There was no room for self-deception about the need for descriptive data; as Bloomfield (1933) expressed it, "In the stress of recording utterly strange forms of speech one soon learned that philosophical prepossessions were only a hindrance" (p. 19).

Lehmann (1976) suggests that an increasing awareness of the complexity of language in the course of the nineteenth century promoted the view that all languages might be described as variants of a single language, much as football, baseball, etc., could be considered variants of a single, abstract game. Presumably certain relationships, such as that of the phonological component to the syntactic component, or the syntactic component to the semantic component, would be the same for all languages.

Treating languages this way entailed dealing with external features only, rather than underlying patterns, so that, for instance, Japanese nouns were discussed as if they were inflected in the way that corresponded to Latin case forms. But the approach encountered too many problems for the Latin framework as more and more exotic languages came under scrutiny (Lehmann, 1976:35-36).

Pāṇini's Sanskrit grammar, on the contrary, was radically different from those produced in the Latin tradition because it provided rules for the underlying semantic, syntactic, morphological, and phonological patterns in a sequence that permitted a concise description of the language, though the elegance of the approach went largely unappreciated (Lehmann, 1976:36-37).

One nineteenth century scholar who was concerned with theory and who anticipated the twentieth century focus on deep versus surface structure (his "form" and "substance," respectively), was the Swiss linguist, Ferdinand de Saussure. Thus he noted the ambiguity of French [sižlaprã] which can be either *si je la prends* "if I take it" or *si je l'apprends* "if I comprehend it." He insisted on language as a system of arbitrary signs, the meanings of which are determined by relationships. Efforts to determine the various kinds of relationships possible in language led to a productive concern with language in all its variety (Lehmann, 1976:37).

For all his importance to contemporary linguistics, Saussure never actually formulated a model of language. Indeed, except for his classic study of the vocalic system of Indo–European, he published little and had an unfortunate tendency to destroy his lecture notes. So what we do have of his observations is based on the lecture notes of his students, compiled in the posthumous publication in 1916 of his *Cours de linguistique generale* (See Saussure, 1959).

THE TWENTIETH CENTURY

For the first 30 years or so after 1916, the notion of language as an abstract system underlying the various speech forms was applied mainly to the phonological component of language. Thus, the concept of the phoneme is an abstraction and the actual sounds may vary widely. We have a phoneme /t/ that can even show up as a glottal stop (ʔ) in some pronunciations of "bottle," for instance. Subsequently the distinction between Saussure's form and substance was applied to the syntactic component, where we speak today of deep and surface structure, or even of the difference between competence and performance (1976:37).

In American linguistics, landmark publications include Edward Sapir's *Language* (1921), which is still available and is still of inestimable value as a general treatise on language; Bloomfield's *Language* (1933), which held the center of the stage for a quarter of a century; and Chomsky's *Syntactic Structures* (1957), which launched the current concern with generative grammar. His *Aspects of the Theory of Syntax* (1965) is yet another landmark, because it distinguishes deep and surface structures, and includes an explicit semantic component (inspired largely by the various works of Katz, Fodor, and Postal). And yet another landmark publication by Chomsky (with Morris Halle, 1968), is *The Sound Pattern of English*, which is the starting point of concern with generative phonology. While there is no single publication of comparable stature to mark the subsequent emergence of generative semantics or other spin-off theories, this new focus was perhaps predictable from the direction the linguistic field was taking under Chomsky's leadership (even though Chomsky himself takes issue with the generative semanticists).

CHOMSKY

While the development of the prescriptive attitude toward grammar, which is now viewed as reprehensible, has been widely attributed to the philosophical grammarians who were overly enchanted by their Latin model, the most influential linguist in the post-Bloomfield era, Noam Chomsky, feels that the older scholars have been much maligned. He does not account for the normative attitude which has indisputably prevailed for some considerable time in our own schools, but he does note, with obvious justification, the *Grammar* and *Logic* of Port-Royal (1660), were written in French, "the point being that they formed part of the movement to replace Latin by the vernacular" (1968, p. 13).

In an important sense, Chomsky traces his own academic heritage back to René Descartes (1596-1650), but this is almost certainly a belated recognition, since his views developed more immediately from modern structural linguistics. There was in effect an important discontinuity between the views of Descartes and his followers on the one hand, and the contemporary view of language on the other. However much Chomsky may care to read into Descartes, and however warm he may feel in recognizing a kindred spirit, it seems likely that Chomsky's brand of genius would have led him pretty much to his present theoretical position even if he had never heard of Descartes. In a similar sense one could see the origins of psycholinguistics in Descartes, or even in the Greek philosophers; but this is a dubious course if one selects as landmarks those discoveries that others have built on more or less directly.

An important development from the middle of the present century is the efflorescence of "hyphenated linguistics," perhaps beginning with psycholinguistics. Studies on the psychology of verbal learning stem from the work of Ebbinghaus (1885) on memory, and even today they depend to some extent on a thread of theory that can be traced back to the associationism of Locke (1632-1704). Since verbal learning theorists were almost totally lacking in linguistic sophistication, it might be said that they represented precisely what psycholinguistics was not. Psycholinguistics can be said to originate as far back in the history of philosophy as one cares to trace psychology, but the widespread use of the term and the development of psycholinguistcs as a distinct discipline goes back only to the early 1950s, when George Miller (1951) and other psychologists introduced a knowledge of linguistics into the psychological study of language. This was long before the concept of meaning was given its new respectability in linguistics. Now, with the advent of generative semantics, it appears that there is a potential union of linguistics and verbal learning, with the latter's heavy involvement in word associations and "meaningfulness."

But the students of "verbal learning" are not, for the most part, the same individuals identifying as psycholinguists. The latter are interested in language and mind, usually as manifested in problems of first-language acquisition (by children, of course).

Ethnolinguistics, or ethnoscience, is essentially another development of the 1950s, but the immediate forebear of the science was a most remarkable fire-prevention inspector named Benjamin Lee Whorf. His essential idea, or at least the idea for which he is best known, is that patterns of thoughts and perception are molded by our language forms. In his work he had noted, for example, that people tend to be quite careless with matches and cigarettes around "empty" gasoline drums, even though they are probably more dangerous than full drums, around which great care is exercised. The label "empty" implies a lack of danger, and the people respond to the label as if there were indeed no danger around the "empty" drums (Carroll, 1956, p. 135). Eventually Whorf came under the influence of Edward Sapir, who held similar views on the way language influences perception and behavior. Sapir, in turn, seems to have been influenced by the earlier conceptions of Wilhelm von Humboldt (1767-1835), whom Bloomfield (1933) credits with the first great book on general linguistics. In brief, ethnolinguistics is concerned with the relationship of language and culture, including culturally defined cognitive domains.

Sociolinguistics is more a development of the 1960s, an outgrowth of the problems encountered by linguists in describing dialect and other speech varieties, but the key point of departure is perhaps the distinction made in 1961 by Saussure (Saussure, 1959). He distinguished *la langue*, the linguistic code of a group, from *la parole*, the actual speech performances of an individual. In English we usually refer simply to "language versus speech." Traditionally, we may say, linguists have been primarily concerned with language rather than speech, and they still are to the extent that they are concerned with what Chomsky calls linguistic *competence* (what an individual must know in order to engage appropriately in verbal interaction). Thus we must have rules by which to produce utterances intelligible to the other party. Now, there is a gap between language and speech; hence we may hear or produce "errors," without seriously interfering with the communication. For example, if we are told that "He can't make a—formulate that problem," the same rules that led the speaker to alter his sentence halfway through lead us to edit out the phrase "make a." The performance was faulty, but our linguistic competence permits us to endure such problems with minimal difficulty.

This rather sketchy review will be filled out a little more as we discuss specific problems and study specific areas, but for the moment we should try to bear in mind the idea that there is a great deal of overlapping interest in the fields of psycholinguistics, ethnolinguistics, sociolinguistics, and linguistics proper. Thus von Humboldt has a proper place in the history of linguistics, is often specifically mentioned as the ancestor of ethnolinguistics, and appears in some discussions of the history of psychology, at least in its more philosophical aspects. Similarly Whorf has been mentioned in connection with ethnolinguistics, but he is probably equally well known in psycholinguistics, and he was a solid descriptive linguist. Likewise, studies of bilingualism are often read equally easily as sociolinguistic or as psycholinguistic. The reason for the overlap is obvious: language is the key to most human thought, social behavior, and culture.

REFERENCES

Bloomfield, L. *Language.* New York: Henry Holt and Co., 1933.

Boring, E. G. *A history of experimental psychology.* New York: Appleton-Century-Crofts, 1950.

Carroll, J. B. *Language, thought, and reality: Selected writings of Benjamin Lee Whorf.* New York: John Wiley & Sons, Inc.; Cambridge, Mass.: Technology Press, 1956.

Chomsky, N. *Syntactic structures.* The Hague: Mouton & Co., 1957.

Chomsky, N. *Aspects of the theory of syntax.* Cambridge, Mass.: The M.I.T. Press, 1965.

Chomsky, N. *Language and mind.* New York: Harcourt, Brace & World Inc., 1968.

Chomsky, N. & Halle, M. *The sound pattern of English.* New York: Harper & Row, 1968.

Ebbinghaus, H. Übuer das Gedächtnis. Leipzig: Dunker & Humblot, 1885.

Gumperz, J. H. Unpublished lecture of Anthropology 120, 24 September, 1965. University of California, Berkeley, California.

Ivič, M. *Trends in linguistics*. The Hague: Mouton & Co., 1965.

Karlgren, B. *Sound and symbol in Chinese*. London: Oxford University Press, 1923.

Lamberts, J. J. *A short introduction to English usage*. New York: McGraw-Hill Book Co., 1972.

Lehmann, W. P. *Descriptive linguistics* (2nd ed). New York: Random House, 1976.

Miller, G. A. *Language and communication*. New York: McGraw-Hill Book Co., 1951.

Miller, R. A. *The Japanese language*. Chicago: University of Chicago Press, 1967.

Newman, E. *A civil tongue*. New York: The Bobbs-Merrill Company, Inc., 1975/1976.

Sapir, E. *Language*. New York: Harcourt, Brace & World, Inc., 1921.

Saussure, F. de. *Course in general linguistics*. New York: Philosophical Library, Inc., 1959.

Chapter 2

ANTECEDENTS OF LANGUAGE

Communication in the broadest sense is the process whereby two or more entities are joined. Thus communication between cities may be accomplished by means of railroad lines, air routes, highways, river systems, and so forth. We may nudge and by means of a nod direct a companion's attention to an event in a specific location. Facetiously, perhaps, we may note that a Peeping Tom counts on one-way communication while an exhibitionist seeks two-way communication.

Within the broad frame of communication, *language* is the distinctively human form of communication upon which not only civilization but culture itself depends. As we shall see, at present efforts are being made to test the extent to which other species have a language capability, but only language in the human context provides the means by which we are able to accumulate knowledge, to build upon that knowledge, and to transmit it from one generation to the next.

There are nonhuman societies of considerable complexity which lack culture and there are some rather elaborate systems of communication that are qualitatively different from language. But the infrahuman societies and modes of communication are essentially the products of what we think of popularly as instincts, in contrast to language and culture, which are not instinctual, but rather are learned. Given these differences, it is still useful to examine some of the features of communication among infrahuman species, both for the perspective it provides on language and because some of the features may be found in our own nonlanguage communication.

COMMUNICATION AMONG INSECTS

Kroeber (1948, p. 34f.) has provided a useful discussion of the essential difference between insect and human societies. Many species of social insect live in communities that may number hundreds of thousands or even millions of individuals, and thus compare with our largest cities in population. In some respects such insects are more socialized than we are, since the individual tends to subordinate his own welfare more or less completely to the welfare of the group. Typically there is a thoroughly developed caste system; some species of ants and most termites have subdivided or added castes, especially a soldier caste.

> This professional army again may be differentiated into an aggressive corps with powerful jaws; a sort of flame-throwing or gasthrowing service that squirts a dangerous liquid; a defensive or shield-bearing division that blocks the gate with an enormous impermeable forehead. Workers, in turn, may come in two or even three sizes for indoor and outdoor labor. . . . Nor are the castes always inflexible. Certain ants use their large-jawed soldiers to crush for them hard-shelled seeds that the workers can bring in but cannot crack. When autumn comes on and the harvest of these seeds is over, when the community goes into winter retreat and ordinarily need fear no further insect enemies, these warrior-millers have become useless and would be a drain on the hoard of the hive. Like the drones among honeybees, they are therefore killed by the workers . . . not only individuals but even classes are sacrificed for the good of the society. [Kroeber, 1948, p. 35]

Pheromones

When an insect society is examined in detail, the complexity of the behavior patterns that serve to sustain the group is awesome, and it may be difficult to realize that there is no conscious intelligence of the kind that is so important to the maintenance of our own societies. A great deal of the communication that governs insect behavior depends on secretions called *pheromones*. The fire ant, for example, makes a trail to a food supply or to a new nest site by releasing minute quantities of a particular pheromone through its sting, which intermittently touches the ground. When workers encounter the substance, which serves as an attractant, they move automatically up the gradient to the source of the emission. So long as the food supply holds out, the ants will secrete the pheromone. Thus the greater the supply of food, the more ants will follow and intensify the trail. But as the supply diminishes, the ants cease to emit the pheromone, and the number of individuals attracted to the trail quickly decreases. The pheromone itself is rather volatile, and the trail laid down by a single individual becomes too weak to attract after about 2 minutes. As Wilson (1963) points out, the effectively short life of the individual trail is useful as an index to the abundance of the supply, and it also means that trails do not linger beyond the time of their usefulness to confuse hunting workers later.

Pheromones have a wide range of functions in the insect world, perhaps about as many as there are activities that require some sort of communication (though there are, as we shall see, other ways of communicating). They enter into the formation of migratory locust swarms, for example, and are widely observed as sex attractants. The female gypsy moth has about 0.01 μg of gyplure, which under optimum conditions would be potent enough to excite more than a billion males! The responses to the pheromones are not learned, however, but are automatically released. This is seen quite clearly when experimenters manipulate such situations artificially. An ant that has just died, for instance, will be groomed by other ants as if it were living, but after a day or two products of chemical decomposition accumulate, and this stimulates workers to bear the dead ant away from the nest, to the refuse heap. This sounds quite sensible to us, of course, but the process continues thus (Wilson, 1963):

> When other objects, including living workers, are experimentally daubed with these substances, they are dutifully carried to the refuse pile. After being dumped on the refuse the "living dead" scramble to their feet and promptly return to the nest, only to be carried out again. The hapless creatures are thrown back on the refuse pile time and again until most of the scent of death has been worn off their bodies by the ritual. [p. 8]

Human Pheromones?

While there is some reason to suspect that human pheromones may exist (Wilson, 1963), the question is complicated by cultural factors. Hall (1966), for example, contrasts U.S. and Arab olfactory systems. It is common in Arab nations for people to breathe on each other, but Americans are distressed when within olfactory range of people with whom they are not on close terms, especially in public settings. We are likely to find the intensity and sensuality overwhelming to the extent that we may have difficulty even attending to what is being said to us under such circumstances.

Television commericals in particular teach us to dread human smells, though the artificial odors of colognes or after-shave lotions are to be considered desirable. It is difficult to determine whether human waste products were ever used for communication purposes within human populations, but the Canadian writer Farley Mowat (1963) once studied wolves on behalf of the Dominion Wildlife Service. He had established himself in a tent near the lair of a family of wolves. While they never showed much interest in him, he was not entirely comfortable with the situation. So he was inspired to follow the example of his subjects by marking his own territory. He spent most of one night, while the wolves were out hunting, moving from his teapot to the periphery of his territory to urinate on stones, clumps of moss, and patches of vegetation every 15 feet or so around his parcel, which he defined to include about a 100–yard section of the path normally followed by the wolves when leaving or returning to the lair. Mowat was greatly relieved, as it were, to see that his lines were to be respected. The returning wolf

> began a systematic tour of the area I had staked out as my own. As he came to each boundary marker he sniffed it once or twice, then carefully placed *his* mark on the outside of each clump of grass or stone. As I watched I saw where I, in my ignorance, had erred. He made his mark with such economy that he was able to complete the entire circuit without having to reload once, or, to change the simile slightly, he did it all on one tank of fuel. [p. 84]

The "Dancing" Bees

Pheromones are also important to honeybees, to regulate the reproductive cycle of the colony and to mark the target when a worker stings an intruder (this accounts for the tendency of angry swarms of workers to sting at the same spot). In addition, when a worker discovers a new food source, it may release a type of alcohol that attracts other workers and thus communicate some information about the food source. But the bees are much better known for another means of communicating this kind of information.

The studies of the German naturalist von Frisch (1955) have shown that bees are able to convey the location and direction of food discoveries to others in the swarm by means of a series of maneuvers which are as stylized, in some respects, as the figures in classical ballet. Von Frisch constructed a hive with glass walls, which permitted him to observe the behavior of the bee tenants when they returned from a food-seeking flight. When the source of the nectar was close, say within 100 feet or less, the finder bee would perform a "dance" consisting of a circular movement. To indicate longer distances, the bee would run in a straight line while moving its abdomen rapidly from side to side, then would make a turn and repeat the maneuver. For distances in excess of 200 yards, the number of turns made by the bee decreased. A run followed by only two turns, for example, might indicate that the food source was several miles away.

After observing this behavior, the other bees were able to fly directly to the food. It was apparent that they received cues to the location of the food from the direction of the "run" made by the finder bee. An upward vertical run in the hive indicated that the food source would be found by flying into the sun, whereas a downward vertical run indicated that the food source was away from the sun. Von Frisch found that if they were restricted to a horizontal surface and deprived of sunlight, bees were unable to communicate the direction of their finds.

In addition to pheromones and the information conveyed by the dances, the smell of the food substance itself is important, if Wenner and Johnson (1967) are correct. While scent may be useful, Esch (1967) and von Frisch (1967) point out that the dance still conveys the relevant information when scent is experimentally removed as a variable.

THE DOLPHIN

The bottle-nosed dolphin, or porpoise, has received considerable attention over the past decade or so because it may have an aptitude for linguistic behavior. Equipped with a brain larger than ours, the dolphin has a remarkable capacity for complex learning and has an elaborate and variegated set of sound-making capabilities. Most specialists, however, do not share Lilly's (1961, 1967) conviction that dolphins are capable of language. The status of the problem has been neatly summarized by Herman and Tavolga (1980):

> The concept of an extant natural language in dolphins . . . is unsupported by analytic or experimental evidence, though the idea remains a part of the dolphin popular mystique and is hard to extinguish. There is no solid evidence for any unusual degree of complexity (information content) in the whistle sounds of dolphins, which are presumed to have an important communicative function. [p. 181]

Herman and Tavolga (1980) also find no support in experimental efforts to establish the capability of one dolphin intentionally to transfer information to another about arbitrary events in the environment. Whether dophins may be successfully trained in language fundamentals in the laboratory remains under study, however (see Herman, 1980). The door is not closed to the possibility of a dolphin language or to the possibility of being able to establish some sort of language-type communication with dolphins, but a serious breakthrough does not appear imminent.

APES

The animal that seems in all ways to be closest to ourselves is the chimpanzee, though the gorilla and orang-utan are also very close and all three of these great apes have demonstrated some ability to learn sign language.

While there is no evidence that chimps in the wild use either gestures or sounds in a way that would qualify as language, a prolonged attempt to teach a chimpanzee normal spoken language was attempted by Keith and Cathy Hayes (Hayes, 1951). They tried to raise the chimp, Viki, in their home as if she were a human child. Beginning when the ape was only 3 days old, Hayes and Hayes tried for $6\frac{1}{2}$ years to teach Viki to speak, but they were rewarded with only three or four words: papa, mama, cup, and maybe "up." Indeed, all such attempts to teach nonhuman primates to "speak" have failed (see Kellogg, 1968).

Washoe

The basis for a dramatic breakthrough in interspecific communication was laid in June, 1966, when R. Allen Gardner and Beatrice T. Gardner of the University of Nevada undertook to teach a young female chimpanzee the gesture language of the deaf (American Sign Language, or ASL). To this end they began an essentially operant technique of rewarding the animal's own gestures when these happened to resemble the gestures in ASL.

The experiment began when Washoe, named after the county in which the University of Nevada is located, was between eight and fourteen months old. After 22 months of training and other interaction with the investigators and their assistants, Washoe had a repertory of more than 30 signs and had begun to combine them into elementary "sentences" (Gardner and Gardner, 1969). A year later, when Washoe was about four years old, she had about 85 signs and the process of combining them had advanced slightly (Gardner & Gardner, 1971). By the time the Gardners ended their work with Washoe she was five years old and had about 250 vocabulary items; while the combinations continued to develop, her progress with "grammar" lagged badly by comparison with human children (the lag was clearly evident by the age of three) (Gardner & Gardner, 1974, 1975).

Combining signs in a patterned way constitutes a grammar, however primitive, so it is not surprising that critics have concentrated on the patterning in order to judge Washoe's language ability. The loudest nay-sayer to date is a psychologist at Columbia University named Herbert S. Terrace. Terrace (1979) has described his own efforts to train a chimp under circumstances reminiscent of a Marx Brothers scenario. His account is highly entertaining and so candid that he leaves himself utterly vulnerable on methodological grounds. Still, the chimpanzee, named Nim Chimpsky in honor of Noam Chomsky, seems to have learned to sign in much the same way as Washoe (and many other later apes).

The essence of Terrace's argument is that videotape analyses indicate that most of Nim's utterances were prompted by the teacher's prior utterance and that Nim interrupted his teachers more than children interrupt adults. That is, he argues that the "sentences" are not really linguistic events so much as they are nonlinguistic stimulus–response events (Terrace, Petitto, Sanders, & Bever, 1979). Terrace and associates also looked at relevant materials for other signing apes.

Gardner and Gardner (n.d.) have accused Terrace of using a rubber ruler, using one set of criteria to judge chimp signs and another to judge the early language development of children, and they deny that prompting accounted for Washoe's utterances. Francine G. Patterson (1981), who has been working with a gorilla, accuses Terrace of being selective in his comparative efforts, and in some cases inaccurate and misleading, not only with regard to the gorilla but even with regard to Nim. Terrace, Petitto, Sanders, and Bever (1981), however, stick by their original conclusions. Most recently, Gardner and Gardner (1983) have been engaged in research which seems designed to minimize their vulnerability on methodological grounds.

Other Approaches to Ape Language Ability

A different approach to the language capacities of chimpanzees has been through the use of artificial languages. Premack and Premack (1972) taught their chimp Sarah to manipulate plastic pieces of various colors, sizes, and shapes; each piece represents a different word. In 1972 Sarah had a vocabulary of 130 terms and had learned to use and understand the negative and interrogative markers, wh–questions, and such concepts as "name of," dimensional classes, prepositions, the conditional, and hierarchically organized sentences. One of the men working with the Premacks, Dick Sanders, subsequently joined the Nim project and is currently among the Terrace skeptics.

The other major project concerning chimp language capacities is located at the Yerkes Regional Primate Center in Atlanta, Georgia. Sometimes the project is called the Lana project, after the most promising of the simian students there. Lana has been taught to read and write simple sentences by using an odd–looking computer–typewriter. The training relies on essentially the same kind of conditioning techniques that have been employed in the other chimp experiments. The artificial language is called "Yerkish," after the name of the Primate Center. Some people feel that the use of artificial languages and the use of gadgetry reduce misinterpretations of behavior by removing the experiment from the social context required by signing. That is, it may be a purer way of testing the ability of the apes to deal with abstract symbols. But in any event, the Sarah and Lana projects seem to raise the same questions and doubts in the minds of Terrace and his associates. Terrace (1979) provides a fairly simple description of the major projects, even if he does question the interpretation of the findings. Rumbaugh (1977) has a more technical survey of the artificial language projects, particularly that of the Lana project, with which he has been personally associated. And even Terrace (1979) concedes that the simian ability to acquire extensive vocabularies of arbitrary words represents a tremendous break-through in our understanding of the intelligence of the apes.

LANGUAGE AND SYMBOLS

It is customary to treat language as basically a vocal system and distinctively human. So far as we have as yet determined, no other species left to its own resources has developed a language in the sense that we use the term to describe the essence of human communica-tion.

Communicative Preadaptations

Largely inspired by Lamendella's (1976) careful effort to use the development of language in the child as a possible model for the de-velopment of language in the species, Bickerton (1981) offers an ex-tended discussion of cognitive and communicative preadaptations. Assuming that language could not have suddenly appeared on the cultural scene as an intact system without any preliminary genetic groundwork having been laid, Bickerton considers the increase in the capacity of creatures to analyze the environment and predict out-comes.

One of the most primitive cognitive developments, for instance, is the ability to distinguish light and dark, but even at the level of the mollusk (*Aplysia*), with a nervous system containing but a handful of ganglia with a few hundred neurons each there is evidence of *habit-uation*.

> . . . the sensitive organs are extruded from a mantled cavity and consist of a gill for breathing, a siphon for eating, and a purple gland. The last two serve as primitive organs of perception. If anything touches the siphon or gland, the gill retracts into the cavity. However, if you touch either gland or siphon at regular, brief intervals, the withdrawal response will diminish in both speed and intensity until eventually it is extinguished. *Aplysia* has done its equivalent of deciding that your actions are nonthreat-ening and thus it is wasteful to respond to them. [Bickerton, 1981: 282]

It is difficult to provide a few simple examples without giving the impression that the argument is simple and the evidence sketchy, which would be quite unfair in the present case. But the simple examples are helpful for showing the basis of Bickerton's hypothesis that

> *those semantic distinctions whose neural infrastructure was laid down first in the course of mammalian development will be the first to be lexicalized and/or grammaticized in the course of human language development.* [Bickerton, 1981: 242, original emphasis]

Thus the most elementary distinction to be made in color terminology among the cultures of the world is between light and dark. That is, if there is a culture that employs only two basic color terms, they will be labels for light and dark. Berlin and Kay (1969) have worked out an evolutionary sequence of the development of basic color terminology (beginning with the light/dark distinction) that seems to have gained wide acceptance.

In other words, according to Bickerton's argument, the light/dark distinction is one that is made very early in evolution (long before the emergence of mammals, certainly), and it is a distinction that should be labelled very early in language development—and current thinking is that the distinction was made early. Bickerton argues that habituation is perhaps the first feature of a tense-mode-aspect system to be grammaticized. Eventually, he tries to demonstrate that this sort of approach is quite consonant with his findings for the development of creole languages, which seem to reflect very elementary features of language origin and development.

While Bickerton's discussion is wide-ranging, it is not aimed at setting a particular point in time for the emergence of language.

SYSTEMS APPROACHES

An earlier and more exclusively "systems" approach to the origin of language was offered by Charles Hockett (1960; Hockett & Ascher, 1964). By comparing the communications systems of many species of animal, it is possible to see which features are peculiar to language. Thus language is culturally transmitted and we can communicate with reference not only to objects and events that are in the past and out of sight, but also to purely imaginary events. These are more the characteristics of man than of the system he employs, but important features of the system itself are *arbitrariness*, *productivity*, and *duality of patterning*.

Arbitrariness refers to the fact that there is no necessary relationship between an event and its linguistic representation. We must *learn* to use the label "cat" to refer to the animal in question; a quite different sound sequence must be learned by the Japanese, for whom the label for the same creature is *neko*. The essence of the symbol is its arbitrariness, in that anything can stand for anything else, so long as we agree on the representation. We may, for instance, use bottles to stand for cities and then discuss transportation routes as if the bottles were actually the cities. In this case the bottles symbolize cities in about the same way that the words we use—the sound sequences or labels—symbolize them. A nonarbitrary relationship would be *iconic*. We impose iconic features on our speech when we make loudness an expression of our emotional state: softly cautioning a child about to bump into something but perhaps shouting the same warning if there is apparent danger. The dances of the honeybee are arbitrary in that the movements are indepedent of the food substance—a waggle is not a picture of sugar—but to the extent that the movements are direct representations of the distance and direction of the food source, they are iconic.

Language is productive in that it can generate an infinite number of utterances, including messages that have never been transmitted before. Most animal messages that are transmitted by sound represent a rather limited inventory and are used mainly to express what we might term "emotional states," such as alarm or rage. The sound segments of such messages cannot be freely extracted and recombined to produce new messages.

Duality of patterning means that we have a set of sounds that we regard as significant and these significant sounds (which we call phonemes) are combined into meaningful patterns. Thus we must distinguish a *t* from a *k* in English, but there is a measure of variation that is permitted and fairly predictable for each. When the *t* or *k* come at the beginning of a word they are pronounced with a puff of air, but when they come after an *s* they are pronounced without that puff of air. Thus "till" has the puff of air and "still" does not; "kin" has it and "skin" does not. Other variations involve the precise placing of the tongue, which will depend on the kind of sounds that precede or follow the one in question. The variations, being patterned, are predictable for a given language. Such variations constitute one kind of patterning; the other kind has to do with meaningful arrangements of the significant sounds. While the sounds themselves lack meaning, the patterns they form do have meaning. The sounds we represent as *o*, *d* and *g*, for example, do not have any meaning in themselves, but they may be arranged in two ways that are meaningful in English: d–o–g and g–o–d.

Systems approaches help us to focus on what is truly distinctive about language and to decide where in our evolutionary progression we developed the initial capacity for language. The features of arbitrariness, productivity, and duality of patterning place language at a considerable distance from the signal systems of other creatures.

BIOLOGICAL BASES OF LANGUAGE

While each language must be learned, and while humans are the only creatures that develop language in the normal course of events, our discussion in terms of evolution indicates that we believe there is a biological basis for language. We seem to be "programmed" for language learning, though the specific language(s) we learn depends on the nature of the linguistic community in which we are raised.

The most substantial evidence at present for the biological basis of language lies in certain universals: all human societies have languages that share certain general features; every normal member of the human species acquires language; language development in children unfolds in quite regular ways; special evolutionary adaptations seem to have fitted humans for language; and injuries to particular parts of the nervous system can result in abnormalities of language (Miller & Lenneberg, 1978, p. 2).

Speech habits emerge as a function of maturational changes within the growing child; a great variety of environmental conditions leave the age of onset unaffected, and there is no solid evidence that training procedures can substantially advance the rate of language learning. Further, there is much evidence that language development is interlocked with other maturationally-based behavior, such as stance, gait, and motor coordination, although it is independent of these other processes (i.e., it is neither caused by nor is a cause of these processes). The question thus becomes: when in our phylogenetic history had we developed to the point that such maturational processes could come into play to trigger language learning? More generally, when in our evolution did we acquire our language learning capacity?

Language and Evolution

We have seen that modern apes have a rudimentary ability in language which can be brought out under patient human tutelage. Modern apes may be brighter than their precursors some 10 million years ago, when the human line seems to have diverged from that of the apes (Campbell, 1974), but our own apelike ancestors were almost certainly brighter than modern apes. That is, it is reasonable to seek the origins of language rather early in our evolution, when we were more apelike than we are today.

The distinctively human type of adaptation that depends on culture seems to have been launched some 5 million years ago with the appearance in Africa of a small, bipedal, tool-making man–ape with the generic name of *Australopithecus*. According to one influential school of thought, some of these fossil fellows (and females) actually constitute an advanced type of hominid more appropriately identified with our own genus, *Homo*. More specifically these fossils are called *Homo habilis* (handy man). It may be that *habilis* is actually our ancestor while the others, the Australopithecines, faded by the wayside. The paleonanthropological disputes over the taxonomic issue and more generally the interpretation of the fossil evidence has been told in lively and entertaining fashion by Johanson and Edey (1981). Here, we may follow Campbell (1974), Washburn and Moore (1974), and others in considering all of the relevant materials to represent the Australopithecines because the general considerations relative to language are essentially the same no matter how the taxonomic issues are resolved.

Brain Size

In a general way we expect to find brain size positively correlated with mental ability (and, presumably, potential language ability). Thus chimpanzees have a mean brain size of a little less than 400 cc, orang-utans slightly more than 400 cc, gorillas just over 500 cc, while the relatively smaller Australopithecines average just under 600 cc, or about 50 per cent more than the chimps and orangs. By comparison, contemporary humans (*Homo sapiens*) enjoy a weighty 1330 cc, while the intermediate form *Homo erectus* sported a respectable 950 cc (Campbell, 1974).

We cannot assume a direct correlation between absolute brain size and mental ability, however. One kind of whale, for example, has a brain of more than 10,000 cc. While we cannot usefully gauge the mental ability of such a creature, we have no reason to think it is within the human range, let alone six times as great. Relatively, the whale has only one gram of brain substance for each 8500 grams of body; modern humans have about one gram of brain for each 44 grams of body weight. Relatively, then, we fare well, but this is not a reliable index of mental ability either, because the capuchin monkey has one gram of brain for each 17.5 grams of body (Washburn & Moore, 1974).

While neither absolute brain size nor brain size relative to total body weight is a reliable indicator of mental ability, there remains a general correlation. So it is likely that the Australopithecines were at least a little brighter than their simian contemporaries, and they did leave behind evidence of culture, however rudimentary. Speculation on the language capability of our fossil ancestors depends largely on how far we think cultural forms could develop in the absence of language. It is at least conceivable that Australopithecus had some elementary form of language. And it is much more likely that the intermediate form, *Homo erectus*, who was found in most parts of the Old World from about a million years ago until perhaps 300,000 years ago, had fairly well developed languages.

Homo sapiens neanderthalensis and Homo sapiens sapiens

By 300,000 years ago, if Campbell is correct, the people living in Eurasia and Africa (that is, the Neanderthals, *H. sapiens neanderthalensis*) were physically distinguishable from modern populations mainly by their relatively longer skulls (which contained a slightly larger brain than we enjoy) and by heavily built faces and jaws. It is possible that language only developed with the Neanderthals, but Lieberman (1973, 1975; Lieberman, Crelin, & Klatt, 1972) and his associates claim that Neanderthal lacked the supralaryngeal vocal tract necessary for speech as we understand it today. At best, they feel, any Neanderthal language would be greatly restricted, slow, perhaps supplemented by a gestural system and appropriately considered to be an intermediate form of language (Lieberman, Crelin, & Klatt, 1972). Lieberman's argument has been rebutted on technical grounds by Carlisle and Siegel (1974) and Falk (1975) has argued that Lieberman's reconstruction of the laryngeal area would not have permitted Neanderthal to swallow! George A. Miller (1981) offers a particularly lucid discussion of the controversy and seems provisionally receptive to Lieberman's argument.

If Lieberman turns out to be correct, then language in the modern sense probably developed with the reduction of the massive jaw and the slight reshaping of the skull that took place between 50,000 and 30,000 years ago as the Neanderthals were replaced by modern forms (*H. sapiens sapiens*).

One problem with Lieberman's approach is that it focuses too strongly on the specific quality of a very few sounds. There is no obvious reason why any language should have to depend on a specific sound or even a limited set of sounds. People who have had various of the "speech organs" surgically removed are often able to compensate for the loss sufficiently to speak more or less intelligibly. Lenneberg (1962) demonstrated that a child with a congenital speech defect that made any speech impossible was still able to comprehend language more or less perfectly. And manual systems, such as those used among the profoundly deaf from birth (who have thus never had any experience with spoken language) clearly demonstrate the secondary importance of speech mechanisms as such. Most language is spoken, but the essence of the ability is in brain mechanisms.

NEUROPHYSIOLOGICAL ASPECTS OF SPEECH

From a neurophysiological standpoint, the expressive and symbolic qualities of language are merely manifestations of what Head (1926) considered to be the basic processes of symbolic formulation and expression. Brock and Krieger (1963) point out that in its most complete form, this symbolic thinking and expression becomes a function of the entire cerebral cortex. It is largely through the work of Penfield, however, that the true complexity of the speech mechanism has been revealed.

Penfield and Roberts (1959) have demonstrated that no two human cerebral hemispheres are ever the same in form and in the pattern of convolutions and fissures. At the time of birth, the motor and sensory areas of the brain are beginning to take on their function as transmitting stations. At that time the speech areas are "blank slates on which nothing has been written" (p. 198). Generally three cortical speech areas, shown below in Figure 2.1, will be developed in the left hemisphere. The right hemisphere may become dominant with respect to localization of the speech centers, but this is quite rare. In addition, a small lesion in infancy may produce some displacement of the expected location of the areas within the left hemisphere. A large lesion in the posterior speech area may cause the whole speech

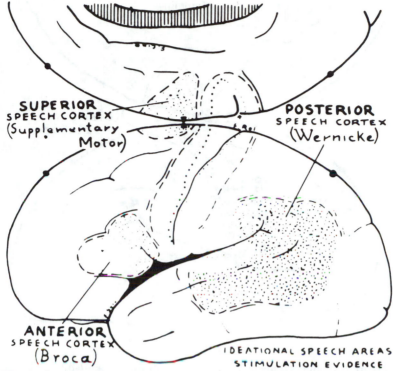

Figure 2.1. Summarizing map of the areas of cortex in the dominant hemisphere which are normally devoted to the ideational elaboration of speech. Conclusions derived exclusively from the evidence of electrical speech mapping. (Reprinted by permission of Princeton University Press and the authors. Source: W. Penfield and I. Roberts. *Speech and Brain Mechanisms*. Princeton: Princeton University Press, 1959.)

apparatus to be developed in the right hemisphere, where the cortical areas will take up homologous positions.

In the cerebral cortex of the human adult certain areas are devoted to the control of speech musculature, and certain areas are devoted to the ideational processes of speech. Each of these areas will be discussed separately.

Information about the motor mechanism of speech has been obtained by Penfield and others through the electrical stimulation of the cortex of conscious subjects. Vocalization (Penfield & Jasper, 1954) has been found to be the response of a small area between those

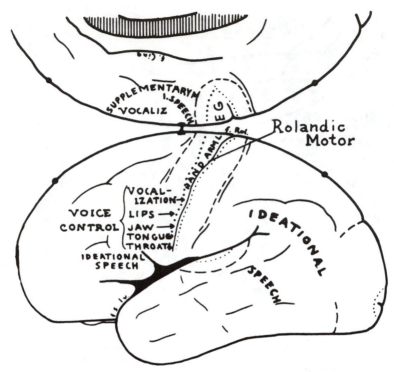

**Figure 2.2. Speech mechanisms in the dominant hemisphere. Three
areas are devoted to the ideational elaboration of speech; two areas
devoted to vocalization. The principal area devoted to motor control of
articulation or voice control, is located in lower precentral gyrus.
Evidence for these localizations is summarized from the analysis of
cortical stimulation and cortical excision. (Reprinted by permission of
Princeton University Press and the authors. Source: W. Penfield and L.
Roberts. *Speech and Brain Mechanisms*. Princeton: Princeton University
Press, 1959.)**

governing the upper face movement and the lip movement on the
precentral Rolandic gyrus (Figure 2.2). It was subsequently shown
that vocalization could be produced in the supplementary motor area
of either cerebral hemisphere (Penfield & Rasmussen, 1950). A gentle
electric current in one of these specific cortical areas causes a patient
who is lying fully conscious on the operating table to utter a long
drawn–out vowel sound, which he is completely unable to stop until
he runs out of breath. Then, after he has taken a breath, he continues as helplessly as before.

One of the major differences between the cortical motor responses of people and animals is manifested in human voice control. The cortical area that governs control of the voice, including articulatory movements and vocalization areas, does not permanently interfere with speaking.

The areas of the cortex that are utilized in the ideational elaboration of speech have been determined by applying a gentle electric current to the relevant areas of the cortex of the dominant hemisphere in conscious human beings. The interfering current causes the patient to become aphasic until the electrode is withdrawn.

Three areas have been outlined (see Figure 2.1):

1. A large area in the posterior temporal and posterior-inferior parietal regions (Wernicke's area)

2. A small area in the posterior part of the third frontal convolution, anterior to the motor voice-control area (Broca's area)

3. A part of the supplementary motor area within the mid-sagittal fissure and just anterior to the Rolandic motor foot area (the supplementary speech area).

All three of these cortical areas, which are organized to function in one hemisphere only, play roles in the ideational speech mechanism under normal conditions. The primary function of these areas of the cortex is the "memory" of words.

In addition, part of the temporal cortex (chiefly on the superior and lateral surfaces of both lobes, and probably extending a little way into the parietal lobe) and parts of the hippocampal gyrus assume the function of interpreting experiences; hence they are known as the interpretive cortex. Referring to these areas, Penfield and Perot (1963) concluded the following:

> There is within the adult human brain a remarkable record of the stream of each individual's awareness. It is as though the electrode cuts in, at random, on the record of that stream. The patient sees and hears what he saw and heard in some earlier strip of time and he feels the same accompanying emotions. The stream of consciousness flows for him again, exactly as before, stopping instantly on removal of the electrode. He is aware of those things to which he paid attention in this earlier period, even twenty years ago. He is not aware of the things that were ignored. The experience evidently moves forward at the original pace. This was demonstrated by the fact that when, for example,

the music of an orchestra, or song or piano, is heard and the patient is asked to hum in accompaniment, the tempor of his hum-
ming is what one would expect. He is still aware of being in the
operating room but he can describe this other run of consciousness at the same time.

The patient recognizes the experience as having been his
own, although usually he could not have recalled it if he had
tried. The complete record of his auditory and visual experience
is not subject to conscious recall, but it is evidently used in the
subconscious brain–transaction that results in perception. By
means of it, a man in normal life compares each succeeding experience with his own past experience. He knows at once whether
it is familiar or not. If it is familiar, he interprets the present
stream of consciousness in the light of the past.

There is, apparently, no overlap of the boundaries that separate the
speech cortex, which endows one with memory of words, and the interpretive cortex, which gives one access to the memory of past similar experiences and thus enables one to understand the present
(Penfield, 1965).

CONCLUDING OBSERVATIONS

Not all prelinguistic communications systems—such as the use of
pheromones—have a very direct bearing on language, but to the extent that they have played a part in our own evolutionary development, they have probably influenced various behavior patterns on
which natural selection has acted to produce a creature capable of
developing language. If Bickerton is correct, some extremely old
patterns, antedating the development of mammals, may have had an
influence on the nature of the earliest forms of language. It is perhaps too soon even to speak of "missing links" in this type of quest.
For example, Bickerton hypothesizes a direct relationship between the
neurologically–based semantic distinctions that were first established
in the course of the development of mammals and the kinds of distinctions that will be marked first in the course of human language
development. It may be possible to test this after a fashion by seeing
if such old distinctions (once they have been properly described) are
among the easiest to learn by the apes who are currently being taught
to communicate by manual or other symbols based on language. But
for the moment there is even heated controversy over whether it is
language that the apes in question are employing.

There is another controversy over the development of the

so–called speech organs—the extent to which even our most immediate ancestor, Neanderthal Person, could have had speech as we
understand it today. But of course controversy makes the scientific
world go round, as it were, and tends to stimulate more research. We
can take comfort in the sense that where once there was only pure
speculation over the development of language, today there is speculation tied to an increasingly vast body of research.

Another source of comfort is that the outline of the neurophysiological basis of speech seems to be well-established. The three speech
areas have been clearly mapped and their function in word–recall has
been described. Although the location may be different from person
to person, their presence is certain. Penfield has demonstrated the
existence of an interpretive cortex, which complements the function
of the speech centers. It has the function of presenting a background of experience against which the individual can compare and
interpret his present situation. Connecting pathways integrate these
speech mechanisms, linking them to each other, to other areas of the
cortex, and to the thalamus. It is the thalamus (plus the hypothala-
mus and limbic system) that functions as the integration center for
all bodily functions.

The neurophysiological aspects of speech are still far from completely understood, however. Not only are we learning more about
the functions of the right cerebral hemisphere, but it is probably still
true that, as van der Berg (1961) noted:

> The present data show a certain degree of specialization in the
> tremendous number of neurons and associated interconnecting
> structures. A large number of "centers" seems to be imbedded in
> a vast network of multipurpose neurons. The topography be-
> comes gradually better known and with it a rough outline of the
> channels interconnecting the "centers," but we are yet far away
> from the point where it would be possible to build an electrical
> analog. (p. 65)

REFERENCES

Berlin, B., & Kay, P. *Basic color terms: Their universality and evolution*. Chicago:
     University of Chicago Press, 1969.
Bickerton, D. *Roots of language*. Ann Arbor: Karoma Publications, 1981.
Brock, S., & Krieger, P. *The basis of clinical neurology*. Baltimore, Md.: Wil-
     liams & Wilkins Co., 1963.
Campbell, B. *Human evolution* (2nd ed.). Chicago: Aldine Publishing Co.,
     1974.

Carlisle, R.C. & Siegel, M.I., Some problems in the interpretation of Neanderthal speech capabilities: a reply to Lieberman. *American Anthropologist*, 1974, *76*, 319–322.

Cleveland, J. Signs of more talking chimps. Gannett News Service. In *The Sunday Star-Bulletin & Advertiser*, Honolulu, Hawaii, October 19, 1980, p. C-6.

Esch, H. The evolution of bee language. *Scientific American*, April, 1967. *216* (4), 96-104. (Note also the exchange of letters between Wenner, Johnson, Wells, and Esch in *Scientific American 217* (2), 6-7.)

Falk, D. Comparative anatomy of the larynx in man and the chimpanzee: Implications for language in Neanderthal. *American Journal of Physical Anthropology*, 1975, *43*, 123-132.

Frisch, K. von. *The dancing bees*. New York: Harcourt, Brace & World, Inc., 1955.

Frisch, K. von. Honeybees: Do they use direction and distance information provided by their dancers? *Science*, 1967, *158*, 1072-1076.

Gardner, R.A. & Gardner, B.T. Teaching sign language to a chimpanzee. *Science*, 1969, *165*, 664-672.

Gardner, B.T., & Gardner, R.A. Two-way communication with an infant chimpanzee. In A. Schrier & F. Strollnitz (Eds.) *Behavior of Non-human Primates* (Vol. 4, Chap. 3). New York: Academic Press, Inc., 1971.

Gardner, B.T., & Gardner, R.A. Comparing the early utterances of child and chimpanzee. In A. Pick (Ed.), *Minnesota Symposium on Child Psychology* (Vol. 8). Minneapolis: University of Minnesota Press, 1974.

Gardner, B.T., & Gardner, R.A., Evidence for sentence constituents in the early utterances of child and chimpanzee. *Journal of Experimental Psychology*, 1975, *General 104*, 244-267.

Gardner, R.A., & Gardner, B.T. 1983. Early signs of reference in children and chimpanzees. Mimeo.

Gardner, R.A., & Gardner, B.T. *n.d.* Comment on Terrace, prepared for *NYU Educational Quarterly*.

Hall, E.T. *The hidden dimension*. Garden City, N.Y.: Doubleday & Company, Inc., 1966.

Hayes, C. *The ape in our house*. New York: Harper & Row, 1951.

Head, H. *Aphasia and kindred disorders of speech*. London: Cambridge University Press, 1926.

Herman, L.M. Cognitive characteristics of dolphins. In L. M. Herman (Ed.), *Cetacean behavior: Mechanisms and functions*, NY: John Wiley & Sons, 1980.

Herman, L.M., & Tavolga, W.N. The communication systems of Cetaceans. In L. M. Herman (Ed.), *Cetacean Behavior: Mechanisms and functions*, NY: John Wiley & Sons, 1980.

Hockett, C.R. The origin of speech. *Scientific American*, 1960, *203*, 89-96.

Hockett, C.R., & Ascher, R. The human revolution. *Current Anthropology*, 1964, *5*, 135-168.

Johanson, D., & Edey, M. *Lucy: The beginning of mankind*. New York: Simon & Schuster, 1981.

Kellogg, W.N. Communication and language in the home-raised chimpanzee. *Science*, 1968, *162*, 423-427.

Kroeber, A.L. *Anthropology*. New York: Harcourt, Brace & World, Inc., 1948.

Lamendella, J. 1976. Relations between the Ontogeny and Phylogeny of language: A neo-recapitulationist view. In S.R. Harnad, *Origins and evolution of language and speech*, H.D. Steklis, & J. Lancaster (Eds.). New York: Annals of the New York Academy of Science (Vol. 280), 396-412.

Lenneberg, E.H. Understanding language without ability to speak: a case report. *Journal of Abnormal and Social Psychology*, 1962, *65*, 419-425.

Lieberman, P. On the evolution of language: A unified view. Paper presented at the IXth International Congress of Anthropological and Ethnological Sciences, September 2, 1973.

Lieberman, P. *On the origins of language: An introduction to the evolution of human speech*. New York: Macmillan, 1975.

Lieberman, P., E.S. Crelin, & D.H. Klatt. Phonetic ability and related anatomy of the newborn and adult human, Neanderthal Man, and the chimpanzee. *American Anthropologist*, 1972, *74*, 287-307.

Lilly, J.C. *Man and dolphin*. Garden City, New York: Doubleday & Company, Inc., 1961.

Lilly, J.C. *The mind of the dolphin*. Garden City, New York: Doubleday & Company, Inc., 1967.

Miller, G.A. *Language and speech*. San Francisco: W.H. Freeman & Co., 1981.

Mowat, F. *Never cry wolf*. Boston, Mass.: Little, Brown & Company, 1963.

Miller, G.A., & Lenneberg, E. (Eds.). *Psychology and biology of language and thought: Essays in honor of Eric Lenneberg*. New York: Academic Press, 1978.

Patterson, F.G. Ape language. *Science*, 1981, *211*, 86-87.

Penfield, W. Conditioning the uncommitted cortex for language learning. *Brain*, 1965, *88*, 787-798.

Penfield, W., & Jasper, H.H. *Epilepsy and the functional anatomy of the brain*. Boston, Mass.: Little, Brown & Company, 1954.

Penfield, W. & P. Perot. The brain's record of auditory and visual experience: A final summary and discussion. *Brain*, 1963, *86*, 695-696.

Penfield, W. & T. Rasmussen. *The cerebral cortex of man*. New York: The Macmillan Company, 1950.

Penfield, W. & Roberts, L. *Speech and brain-mechanisms*. Princeton, N.J.: Princeton University Press, 1959.

Premack, A.J., & Premack, D. Teaching language to an ape. *Scientific American*, 1972, *227*, 92-99.

Rumbaugh, D.M. (Ed.). *Language learning by a chimpanzee*. New York: Academic Press, 1977.

Terrace, H.S. *Nim*. New York: Washington Square Press, 1979.

Terrace, H.S., Petitto, L.A., Sanders, R.J., & Bever, T.G. Can an ape create a sentence? *Science*, 1979, *206*, 891-902.

Terrace, H.S., Petitto, L.A., Sanders, R.J., & Bever, T.G. Ape language. *Science*, 1981, *211*, 87-88.

Van den Berg, J.W. Physiological basis of language. *Logos*, 1961, *4*, 56-66.

Washburn, S.L., & Moore, R. *Ape into man*. Boston: Little, Brown & Company, 1974.

Wenner, A.M., & Johnson, D.I. Honeybees: Do they use direction and distance information provided by their dances? *Science*, 1967, *158*, 1076-1077.

Wilson, E.O. Pheromones. Reprinted from *Scientific American*, *157*, May 1963.

Chapter 3

THE ORIGIN AND DIVERSITY OF LANGUAGES

When Roger Brown produced his justifiably popular study *Words and Things* (1958), he commented that theories on the origin of language had hardly changed since Plato's time. The speculations had rarely led to scientific inquiry, with the result that we are not offered theories so much as "a choice of myths" [p. 135]. We still lack a "satisfactory" origin myth, to use Brown's phrasing, but as we saw in the previous chapter, speculation has been leading to some intriguing research. Now we shall look at some essentially linguistic approaches to the problem—even when they have failed to provide us with an original language, they have helped greatly in our understanding of how languages have become so diverse.

COMPARATIVE LINGUISTICS

An early approach to the question of an original language was through comparative linguistics, in which related languages are compared to determine older, parental forms. Ultimately, it was hoped, successive reconstructions would reveal an "original" language. The *comparative method* failed in this respect, but examining the correspondences of sounds in groups of related languages enables us to reconstruct plausible protoforms. The protoforms of closely related languages can then be compared to similar reconstructions of less closely related groups to provide the basis on which to posit yet older forms. In this way it has been possible to describe proto-Indo-European, an enormously widespread superfamily that includes most of the European languages and some in India and places between the two areas. Lehmann (1973) lists a dozen major subgroups of the superfamily. One of these is the Italic subgroup, including the Romance languages, which we may use to give a simple illustration of the sound correspondences (examples from Lehmann, 1973, p. 4).

The word for "dear" in French is *cher*, Italian *caro*, Spanish *caro*, and Portuguese *caro*. The *c* has a [k] sound, while the French *ch* has an "sh" sound [š]. Assuming that we can rule out the possibility of *caro* as a loan-word in any of these languages, it seems apparent that *caro* is the form the word had before Italian, Spanish, and Portuguese diverged enough to gain separate identities. The French case is less obvious, but if we find a number of regular correspondences we assume that the relationship is there, but that a change has taken place in the language that is different. In the present case we see that the French [š] corresponds to [k] in the other languages in a regular way. Thus French *champ* "field" corresponds to *campo* in each of the other three languages; and French *chez* "house" corresponds to *casa* in the other three as well as in Latin.

In other cases the correspondences are not all that tidy. French *chandelle* "candle" is *candela* in Italian and Spanish, but *candeia* in Portuguese (Latin *candēla*). That is, while the correspondence of [š] and [k] may be regular, there are other sounds that show a divergence in some languages, as illustrated by the loss of *l* in the Portuguese for "candle." But where there is sufficient material to work with, each of these problems can usually be explained in terms of phonological change.

To give another example from a different part of the world, we may note that among the Polynesian languages *t* regularly corresponds to *k* in Hawaiian (examples from Meinecke, 1968). The divergence of the *k* from the general *t* suggests that the change took place some time after the Hawaiians had become physically separated from other Polynesian speakers. The idea is further supported by evidence from the sheltered speech community on the privately owned island of Niihau in the Hawaiian group. There the *k* sound alternates freely with the *t*. To monolingual speakers of English this sounds a bit strange, but if one pronounces a *k* a little more forward and the *t* a little more to the back than English speakers do, the sounds become much more similar than we ordinarily think of them. We can see a similar shift from an older [k] sound, as reflected in the popular spelling of Pe*k*ing for the Chinese capital, to the modern spelling with a *j*, indicating a sound which is articulated with the tongue shifted toward the front of the mouth, approximately to the place where the [š] is made for the French *ch* sound. The difference in spacing for the Hawaiian *k* versus Polynesian *t* is only slightly greater than for the shift in Mandarin Chinese from the *k* to *j* or the French *ch* from Romance *c*. Thus this type of change in the place of articulation is not at all unusual.

The backing tendency of the Hawaiians that eventually resulted in a *k* instead of the original *t* illustrated a kind of "drift" (Sapir, 1921) and presumably helps account for a great deal of the gradual divergence of speech in groups that become physically separated from the parent community. Of course drift is also taking place in the parent community, but not necessarily in the same direction as in the speech of groups that have left the parent community.

To illustrate a little more broadly the way closely related languages can be compared to arrive at a protolanguage, we may note that Hawaiian *lani* "sky" corresponds to Tahitian *ra?i*. The vowels remain the same, but the Hawaiian -*n*- here corresponds to the Tahitian glottal stop [?] (the sound, or catch in the throat that separates the syllables in our "oh-oh!"). The Hawaiian *l*- equates to the Tahitian *r*-:

Hawaiian	lani	"sky"	lima	"hand, five"
Tahitian	ra?i		rima	

A wider comparison among the Polynesian languages reveals that the *r* versus *l* problem is rather like the previously discussed *k* versus *t* problem, in that the two sounds do not contrast in a way that results in different meanings. The *?* versus *n* question is only slightly more involved. The Hawaiian *n* that corresponds to the Tahitian *?* elsewhere corresponds to ŋ, the sound that we popularly describe as *ng*, as in "sing." So we hypothesize that the proto-Polynesian form— the form from which the Tahitian, Hawaiian, and other Polynesian variants are derived—is **laŋi*; the asterisk indicates a theoretical form In Fiji the word actually has the form *laŋi*, but further west, among more distantly related languages such as Tagalog (in the Philippines), Javanese, and Indonesian, we find the form *laŋit*. It appears, then, that before the eastern group of Austronesian languages (formerly called Malayo-Polynesian languages), including Hawaiian,

Tahitian, and other Polynesian languages, became effectively separated from the western group (Tagalog, etc.) the word had the form *laŋit,* and we hypothesize that this is the proto-Austronesian form of the word (**laŋit*). Evidently the final *-t* disappeared in the course of the general eastward migration of the Polynesians; as the Polynesians subsequently went their several ways the word underwent other changes in form, ultimately yielding the Hawaiian *lani* and the Tahitian *raʔi.* (Meinecke, 1968)

Of course the wider the comparisons the more likely we are to encounter problems that require yet more comparisons. Thus if we look for correspondences in the words for "mouth, beak," we find again the same relationships for the *n,* ʔ, and ŋ:

Hawaiian	*nuku*
Tahitian	*ʔutu*
Tongan	*ŋutu*

where the usual *k* in Hawaiian corresponds to general *t,* and the proto-Polynesian form is **ŋutu.* But the Fijian form is *ŋusu.* The *-s-* thus departs from the other Polynesian forms, but is in accord with the forms found in the western group of Austronesian languages.

In this way Hawaiian is compared with other Polynesian languages; the Polynesian languages are compared with other groups of Austronesian languages, and reconstructions are posited as proto-forms of the "original" language. Before returning to the question of how close the approach gets us to that "satisfactory" origin myth, we must consider briefly one other method of arriving at older forms of a language.

INTERNAL RECONSTRUCTION

In some cases, of course, there are no obviously related other languages available for comparison. In such cases it is still possible to engage in a measure of reconstruction through the method of *internal reconstruction*. This method depends upon information available in the patterns of a single language at a single point in time. Thus today we distinguish the words "sin" and "sing" on the basis of the difference in how the final sounds are articulated. The first is pronounced [sin], with the tongue touching the gum ridge above the teeth; the second is pronounced [siŋ], with the back of the tongue rising to divert the flow of air from the lungs through the nasal passages. Thus the two sounds are called "nasals." We also have a bila-bial nasal, [m], in which the air is diverted by the lips. There are many pairs of words (minimal pairs) where [m] and [n] contrast: *night/might*, *seen/seem*, *nit/mitt*, *din/dim*, and so forth. But there are few such pairs involving the velar nasal [ŋ], and these usually occur only at the end of a word. Further, the [ŋ] does not occur at the beginning of a word, the way the other two do, and in general tends to occur mainly be-fore [k] or [g]. Even in other positions, as in the words "length" or "strength" [leŋθ] and [streŋθ] respectively, many speakers change the [ŋ] to [n].

In other words, there is something different about the [ŋ], lead-ing us to suspect that it was not a distinctive sound in Pre-Modern English. In fact, internal reconstruction suggests that previously the [ŋ] occurred only before the [k] and [g]; which are articulated at the same place in the mouth. Notice that we use the [ŋ] pronunciation in words like "bank" and "brink." Similarly; in the past the [ŋ] before [g] was pronounced [ŋ], and then it seems that the final [g] was dropped. Thus we should hypothesize a Pre-Modern English form of "sing" to be *[siŋg]. And written records of Old English indicate that the [g] existed then. And the modern spelling "sing" suggests the same, even though the final [g] is no longer pronounced (Julia S. Falk, 1978, pp. 285-286).

While the comparative method and the method of internal re-construction are very helpful in ascertaining older forms of the lan-guages under investigation, they only tell us that at some time in the past the language had such-and-such characteristics. In some cases we can relate changes to other events that provide a better link to time. That is, for example, the Hawaiian *k* developed, it seems, after the Hawaiians separated from the other Polynesians; and other changes took place within the Polynesian group as a whole at some time sub-sequent to their separation from other speakers of Austronesian lan-guages. But this still does not by itself provide an absolute chronology. One effort to achieve an absolute chronology using quantitative methods in comparing related languages is *glottochronology*.

GLOTTOCHRONOLOGY

The statistical treatment of words (lexicostatistics) as a means of demonstrating the relative closeness of related languages dates from 1928 when the Polish anthropologist Jan Czekanowski published a study of European languages in which he used quantitative methods he had previously used with success in physical anthropology and ethnography (see the review by Kroeber & Chrétien, 1937).

A special application of lexicostatistics to determine in absolute terms the time which had elapsed since two related languages had diverged from a single speech variety was proposed shortly after World War II by Morris Swadesh (1951). Swadesh assumed that the common lexicon shared by the speakers of a language at the time they split into two groups would diminish at a constant rate. That is, after a certain period of time they would only have a certain percentage of those words still in common. Thus if one could determine that constant rate of loss, then it would be possible to calculate the time that had elapsed since the groups became separate from each other.

Unfortunately, retention rates for the basic words used for the measure are not constant from language to language, and may well not be constant over time for a particular language. Another problem is that the lists of 100 or 200 words used for comparison are not equally basic for all cultures. For these reasons glottochronology is not taken very seriously by many linguists, but Lehmann (1973) suggests that within similar culture areas glottochronology can provide useful information about related languages.

With all the questions about the reliability of glottochronology, if we give it the benefit of all the doubt, what can we say about the origin of language? George Grace (1959) applied the technique to determine the separation of the relevant Melanesian and Polynesian languages and arrived at a date between only 3400 to 3800 years ago, and comparative studies have nowhere provided a sound basis from which to derive dates of more than 6000 to 8000 years ago (Trager, 1972, p. 175). Since the oldest reconstructed protolanguages seem to be just as complex grammatically and extremely rich in vocabulary, a few thousand years is clearly far too short a period if we would determine the time and form of any original language.

A final note on these approaches is in order. In a work published posthumously, Swadesh (1971) used many of the concepts and findings of comparative studies to define the most basic and universal features that presumably would characterize an original language. One approach was to look for general trends over a period of 2,000 years or more, using historical and reconstructed materials. Thus he noted that internal inflections (as the alternation of vowels in "man" and "men") have been lost or reduced; there are fewer inflective categories of this sort today; the average size of morphemes (minimal meaningful units) is greater today; and there has been a trend away from a uniform length or morphemes of the sort found in the classic languages. To illustrate, ancient Semitic relied on roots of two or three consonants; modern Arabic, Amharic, and Hebrew still have such roots, but they now add both shorter and longer forms in loan words. (Swadesh, 1971, p. 76)

Swadesh felt that there were many structural similarities among the languages for which we have the oldest evidence, and proposed a common origin for several language families that are usually considered to be quite unrelated. Ural–Altaic (including Tungusic, Mongolian, and Turkic), for instance, agrees with Indo–European in emphasizing the use of suffixes, the use of syntactic and adverbial cases, the placement of modifier before modified in compounds, and the distinction of singular, dual, and plural by means of suffixes. Similarly, common features can be described for Indo–European and Semitic. In short, Swadesh found that "evidence is favorable to the notion of the common origin of Indo–European, Semitic, and Ural–Altaic in some remote period" [p. 126].

Even though Swadesh died before he could put his argument in final form, he provided far more food for thought than we can even hint at here. To say the least, the possibility of such ancient relationships seems less improbable than before Swadesh turned his attention to the possibility.

THE DIVERSITY OF LANGUAGES

Whenever, wherever, and however language originated—whether it was a single development or whether it developed independently in more than one human population—the result is an incredible array of speech varieties today. It is not really possible to give an exact figure for the number of languages now in use throughout the world, in part because it is very difficult even to decide when two speech varieties constitute different languages. Sometimes we say that if two speech varieties are mutually intelligible they are varieties, or dialects, of the same language, but if they are not mutually intelligible then they constitute different languages. But people differ in their receptivity to similar varieties. Some of us, say native speakers of a general type of American English, will admit to an essential understanding of most varieties of English, even if some in England or Australia take a bit of getting used to. On the other hand, some English speakers from the mainland profess not to understand the local variety of English in Hawaii and are perfectly willing to deny that variety the status of "English."

On the other hand, as Trager (1972) and many others have noted, in Scandinavia speakers of "Swedish," "Danish," and "Norwegian" talk to each other without great difficulty. In this case, which is matched by dozens of others around the world, the names of the languages reflect political rather than linguistic facts. There are several major varieties of Chinese, some of which, according to Chao (1947), are as different from each other as are English and German. Yet we refer popularly just to "Chinese." In brief, the specification of a particular language often depends on social and political considerations as well as on linguistic factors. If, however, one must provide a number, Trager's (1972) estimate of 2,500 to 5,000 languages is probably representative of most educated guesses.

THE ORIGIN OF DIVERSITY

Languages are in a constant state of change, and when the speakers of a language disperse and form separate speech communities, the changes continue but in somewhat different directions for each, depending on "drift" (Sapir, 1921) and contact with speakers of different languages. Eventually the cumulative changes may obscure the common origin of the varieties.

Not only may varieties of the same language come to differ radically from each other, but a given language may show radical differences at different points in time. Thus Hsieh (1975) cites Fries (1940) to show the change in frequencies of verb-object order and object-verb order over a 500-year span for English. Around A.D. 1000 the verb preceded the object 47.5 percent of the time (as in "bit the fig") and followed it 52.2 percent of the time (as in "[someone] the fig bit"). By 1300 the verb preceded nearly 60 percent of the time and followed just over 40 percent of the time, and by 1500 the verb–object order, with which we are so comfortable today, was well established, occurring 98.13 percent of the time, while the verb followed the object only 1.87 pecent of the time. (Hsieh was arguing for the use of historically validated rules to achieve a better rationalization of contemporary descriptive rules.)

Elsewhere Hsieh (1974) argues that languages change through a chain of seven types of word order governed by an object-verb principle and a verb-object principle, with each arrangement having implications for the placement of objects before verbs, modifiers before nouns, and qualifiers after verbs under the OV principle, while contrary dispositions are found under the VO principle. While there is a growing literature on such concerns (see Hsieh 1977a, 1977b, 1979), one point in mentioning them here is to make it easier to see that comparisons for the purpose of establishing genetic relationships among languages must depend on demonstrating a common core vocabulary rather than on similarities in grammar.

LANGUAGE TYPES

Most contemporary discussions of language types seem to arise in connection with language universals and the predictability of syntactic features depending on whether a language is of the SVO (subject-verb-object), VSO, or SOV type. In the nineteenth century languages were often classified as analytic or synthetic, depending on whether grammatical categories were expressed by single words or were incorporated within words as inflections. Greenberg (1968) illustrates the difference with the English sentence *I shall go* and the Latin equivalent *ībō*. The English is analytic, with the first person singular subject (I), the future (signalled by "shall") and the concrete verbal meaning (go) expressed by individual words; in the synthetic example the root *ī* (to go) and the future first person singular inflection *(bō)* are contained in the same word (p. 128).

Later, some American Indian languages were observed to carry the synthetic principle even further, so the term *polysynthetic* was coined to describe this type. We can illustrate this with a sentence from Ainu, once spoken on Hokkaidô, Sakhalin, and the southern Kurile Islands (all in or near the northern part of Japan):

> usa-oruspe-a-e-yay-ko-tuyma-si-ram-suy-pa, "Regarding various rumors, we thought them over at some length." (Chiri, 1942, p. 80)

In this example, rather extreme even for the style found in the oral epics where it is most common, *usa-* is "various," *-oruspe-* "rumors," and the *-a-* marks the first person. The *-e-* designates the topic; *-yay-* "oneself," *-ko-* "toward," so *-yay-ko-* is "by or of one's own self "; *-tuyma-* "distant"; *-si-* reflexive, *-ram-* "heart," *-suy-pa-* (from *suy-e* "to shake") "to shake several times"; the sequence *si-ram-suy-pa* is literally "to shake one's heart several times," or "to consider hesitatingly." Some of the components can stand by themselves (*usa, oruspe, tuyma, ram*), but in the foregoing case they are all incorporated into a one-word sentence. A hint of the flavor is included in our compound words, such as "bookcase," where both "book" and "case" may stand as independent words. A little closer might be a less common device sometimes used in English, such as "It was one of those everyone's-gotta-do-his-own-thing sessions," where the hyphens incorporate separate elements into a single constituent.

In developing language typologies, nearly any criterion can be used: whether or not a language is tonal, for example. Sapir (1921) reviewed the major typologies and noted that few, if any, languages fall into any of the types cleanly and completely. Thus Chinese is essentially analytic, in that most words can potentially serve as nouns, verbs, or adjectives, and English is similar in that we have such words as "hit," which serve the same functions: the play is a hit; Mac hit Jane; a hit play. But English is synthetic in having such internal changes as sing-sang-sung or man-men. A synthetic language can express grammatical differences by prefixing, infixing, suffixing, and similar devices.

The Altaic languages and Japanese, among others, are agglutinating languages, in which grammatical particles are strung onto a root. To give the sense of this we may take an extreme example from literary Japanese (Chamberlain, 1924): *kirashimerarubekarazaredomo* "though [one] should not have been caused to cut," which is formed by stringing particles onto the root *kir-* "cut," in approximately the reverse order of the English gloss. That is, the English has the "though" first, which corresponds to the -*domo* of the Japanese, and so forth.

Nineteenth-century concern with typology was linked to evolutionary thought, but we have now accepted the notion that we cannot place known languages in any sort of evolutionary sequence. As mentioned earlier, there seem to be permutations of the SOV sequence, but these are not dealt with in terms of evolution. And, of course, genetic classifications are of continuing interest because we would like to account for the historic relationships of all languages and the people who speak them.

MAJOR LANGUAGE GROUPINGS

Since there are several thousand languages in the world today, we shall only comment on some of the major groups and on a few of the more important or interesting individual tongues. For a brief survey based on more comprehensive studies, see Hickerson (1980).

Where the approximate number of speakers of a language (in millions) is given, the source is *The World Almanac* for 1980.

With close to two billion speakers, Indo-European is the greatest of the language phyla and it covers the greatest geographical expanse. There are four major language families within Indo-European: Romance, Balto-Slavic, Germanic, and Indo-Iranian.

The Romance languages include Romanian (23), Portuguese (141), Spanish (238), Catalan, French (100), and Italian (61).

The Balto-Slavic family includes Lithuanian, Latvian, Russian (259), Czech, Polish (37), Bulgarian, Greek, Albanian, and Armenian.

The Germanic family includes Norwegian, Swedish, Danish, Dutch (20), German (120) and English (380).

Finally, the Indo-Iranian family includes Persian (27), Hindi (230), Bengali (140) and Punjabi (61).

The second largest phylum in terms of speakers is Sino-Tibetan, with perhaps more than a billion speakers. The largest family in the group is Chinese, including Mandarin (690, the language with the greatest number of native speakers in the world), Cantonese (50), Wu (44), Min (40), and Hakka (22).

The second family of the Sino-Tibetan phylum is Tibeto-Burman, including Tibetan and several languages of Burma and the Malay Peninsula. Not everyone accepts the affiliation of the third family, Tai. Tai includes Thai (35), Lao, Miao, Shan and several others.

The Uralic or Finno-Ugric family and the Altaic family are sometimes grouped together under the label of Ural-Altaic, though the justification for this needs stronger support than is presently available. At any rate, the Uralic group includes Hungarian (Magyar), Finnish, Lapp and several smaller groups extending into central Siberia. The Altaic family includes Turkic (42), Mongol, and Tungus-Manchu. In recent years the addition of Korean (57) to this family has gained considerable acceptance, and there is increasing evidence for linking Japanese (115) to the Altaic family.

Dravidian is a large family found mainly in southern India and includes Telegu (56), Tamil (56), Kannada (30), Malayalam (28), and several others spoken in Pakistan.

An Afroasiatic Phylum includes five families in Africa and western Asia. The largest family in the group is Semitic, which includes Hebrew, Aramaic, Arabic (142), and Amharic. The second family is Egyptian (Hamitic), but that exists now only as the liturgical language of Coptic Christians. The third family, Berber, is spoken by scattered groups in northern Africa. The fourth is Cushitic, in eastern Africa, and includes Somali, Galla (or Oromo) and Beja. Finally, the Chad family is found around Lake Chad in west-central Africa, the main language being Hausa (20).

The Niger-Congo superfamily dominates most of sub-Saharan Africa and includes some 300 languages. A West Atlantic family includes Wolof, Fula (or Fulani) and several others in Senegal, Guinea, and Gambia. A Mande family includes Mande, Kpelle, Malinke, and others along the Ivory Coast. A third family is Gur in Nigeria and neighboring countries; it includes about 50 languages, Tallensi and Nupe being the most familiar to most of us. Kwa is a fourth family, found around Liberia and Nigeria, icluding several large groups, such as Akan, Kru, Ewe, Yoruba, and Ibo. Another family includes a scattered group of languages east of Lake Chad. Finally, a sixth family, Benue-Congo, includes several languages in Nigeria, such as Efik, Tiv, and the very widespread Bantu languages. The latter include Ganda (or Luganda), Kongo, Kikuyu, Ruanda and Zulu, each with several million speakers, and Swahili (27), which is well known as a trade language.

The Khoisan family is found mainly in the arid regions of South Africa and includes Bushman and Hottentot.

One of the most widespread families in the world is Austronesian, stretching from Hawaii and Easter Island at one extreme to Madagascar off the east coast of Africa at the other, and includes some 500 languages. There is a highly diverse Western Division that includes Malay and Indonesian (106), Javanese (47), and Tagalog (23) and Ilocano in the Philippines, as well as the non-Chinese aboriginal languages of Taiwan and various languages of the hill people of Vietnam and Kampuchea. Malagasy is found on Madagascar and several other related languages are found in western Micronesia and New Guinea.

The Eastern Division has a Melanesian branch extending to Fiji, New Caledonia, New Hebrides, parts of the Solomons and coastal areas of northern and eastern New Guinea. A Micronesian branch includes Gilbertese, Ponapean, and most of the languages of Micronesia. A Polynesian branch includes Maori in New Zealand, Hawaiian, Marquesan, Tongan, Samoan, and others.

The Australian Phylum includes some 200 aboriginal languages of Australia, mostly spoken by relatively small groups.

The Papuan Phylum includes several hundred languages in New Guinea and various islands in eastern Indonesia, most notably Timor and Alor, and is found on New Britain, New Ireland, and some of the Solomon Islands.

The aboriginal languages of North America must to a large extent be spoken of in the past tense and for this reason will be largely ignored here. Algonkian languages were spoken over much of the eastern and northern parts of North America, extending west as far as the northern Great Plains; the related Muskogean family covered much of the southeastern quarter of the continent.

The Aztec-Tanoan languages were (and in some cases are) spoken from the Great Basin to northern and central Mexico. Macro-Siouan languages were spoken in Eastern Canada, New York, the Carolinas, and widely over the plains.

Hokan languages were found mainly in different parts of California, but the group included several languages in Mexico as well as Jicaque in Honduras.

The Penutian Phylum was represented in languages from the coast of British Columbia, down into Oregon and as far south as central California. It has been suggested recently that the large Mayan family should be linked to Penutian and there is a possibility that Uru-Chipaya in Bolivia may also belong to the Penutian Phylum.

The Na-Dene Phylum includes languages of western Canada, several in northern California and Oregon, and in Arizona, New Mexico, and neighboring parts of the southwest (Navaho is probably the most familiar of these languages for most of us). Other Na-Dene groups are found along the coast of Alaska and British Columbia.

Oto-Manguean is a phylum found essentially in mountainous part of central America.

Eskimo-Aleut consists of an Aleut branch in southern Alaska and the Aleutian Islands and an Eskimo branch that extends from Point Barrow in Alaska to eastern Greenland, as well as a small group in Siberia.

The Wakashan family was found mainly in the American northwest, but may be related to Coeur d'Alene and Flathead in the plateau area as well as several small groups around Puget Sound and on the Pacific coast of Washington, Oregon, and British Columbia.

As we move south of the American border we encounter an increasing number of Indian languages that are still in use. A Macro-Chibchan Phylum includes several families in Columbia, one in Panama, another in Nicaragua, and languages of the related Waican family is spoken by the Yanomamö and others along the border of Venezuela and Brazil. Less certainly affiliated languages may be found again in Venezuela, as well as in Ecuador and Peru.

Macro-Ge, including the Ge family in central Brazil, is joined with Macro-Carib and Macro-Panoan into a Super-Phylum. Macro-Carib includes the large Carib family and several smaller families in northeast Brazil, Venezuela, and the Guyanas as well as in more scattered areas in southeastern Brazil and in the Lesser Antilles.

Macro-Panoan consists of languages scattered along the border of Brazil and its western neighbors. Other families in the Ge-Pano-Carib group include Huarpe in Argentina, Nambicuara in south central Brazil, and Bororo in the Matto Grosso of Brazil and eastern Bolivia.

The largest of the South American macro-phyla is the Andean-Equatorial group, extensively distributed in the tropical forests and highland areas. It includes the Arawakan family, with more than a hundred languages—found mostly in Venezuela, the Guyanas, Brazil, and the West Indies. There is a Tupi-Guarani family, mostly along the Amazon Basin in central Brazil and in a large section of eastern Brazil and Paraguay, where Guarani is the official language. The Quechumaran family includes Quechuan, the language of the Incas, in Peru, Bolivia, and Argentina; Aymara is found mostly in Bolivia. Another family in the Andean-Equatorial Super-Phylum is Jivaro, including Jivaro and other languages in northern Peru and Ecuador. Tucanoa is another family found among small groups in northwestern Brazil and Colombia. Finally, Chon is a diversified group including some of the southernmost languages of the continent: Ona, Yaghan, and several others.

As indicated above, this has been a very sketchy survey with hundreds of languages being slighted. The object has been mainly to indicate, without being too tiresome, that there is a mind-boggling diversity of languages in the world today. There are in addition many languages whose affiliation is a mystery. It is customary to mention Basque in northern Spain, along the border area with France, and Ainu, in northern Japan. Ainu is virtually extinct as a practical medium of communication, but the Basque are alive and protesting politically, in part, at least, in their own language.

REFERENCES

Brown, R. *Words and things*. New York: The Free Press, 1958.

Chamberlain, B.H. *A simplified grammar of the Japanese language*. Chicago: University of Chicago Press, 1924.

Chao, Y.R. *Cantonese primer*. Cambridge, Mass.: Harvard University Press, 1947.

Chiri, M. Ainugohŏ kenkyŭ—Karafuto hŏgen o chŭshin to shite. *Karafuto-chŏ Hakubutsukan Kôkoku*, 1942, *4*, 51-172.

Falk, J. *Linguistics and language*. (2nd ed.). New York: John Wiley & Sons, 1978.

Fries, C. On the development of the structural use of word-order in Modern English. *Language*, 1940, *16*, 199-204.

Grace, G. The position of the Polynesian languages within the Austronesian (Malayo-Polynesian) language family. *International Journal of American Linguistics*, 1959, *Memoire 16*.

Greenberg, J.J. *Anthropological linguistics*. New York: Random House, Inc., 1968.

Hickerson, N.P. *Linguistic Anthropology*. New York: Holt, Rinehart & Winston, 1980.

Hsieh, H.I. The SOV cycle: Toward a hypothesis of word order change, 1974. Mimeo.

Hsieh, H.I. Historical perspectives on language description, 1975. Mimeo.

Hsieh, H.I. Noun-modifier order as a consequence of VSO order. *Lingua*, 1977a, *42*, 91-109.

Hsieh, H.I. Synchronic syntax in historical perspective. *Lingua*, 1977b, *43*, 41-54.

Hsieh, H.I. Logical, syntactic, and morphological notions of subject. *Lingua*, 1979, *48*, 329-353.

Kroeber, A.L., & Chrétien, C.D., Quantitative classification of Indo-European languages. *Language*, 1937, *13*, 83-103.

Lehmann, W.P. *Historical linguistics*. (2nd ed.). New York: Holt, Rinehart & Winston, Inc., 1973.

Meinecke, F.K. Linguistic unity and diversity: Polynesian, a case study. Paper presented at the University of Indiana, March 29, 1968.

Sapir, E. *Language*. New York: Harcourt, Brace & World, Inc., 1921.

Swadesh, M. Diffusional cumulation and archaic residue as historical explanations. *Southwestern Journal of Anthropology*, 1951, *7*, 1-21.

Swadesh, M. *The origin and diversification of language*. Chicago and New York: Aldine-Atherton, 1971.

The world almanac and book of facts. New York: Newspaper Enterprise Association, Inc., 1980.

Trager, G.L. *Language and languages*. San Francisco, Calif.: Chandler Publishing Co., 1972.

Chapter 4

NONVERBAL COMMUNICATION

Communication between humans can take a multitude of forms, implicit as well as explicit, and frequently unconscious and unintended. When we nudge or nod, smile or scowl, fidget, flush, or yawn, we communicate nonverbally. When we interact socially, the very way we handle time and space serves to communicate, sometimes more tellingly than the verbal accompaniment. There are culturally defined conversational distances and durations, violations of which tell the other party that the relationship has been redefined, at least temporarily. A former companion who ignores our outstretched hand and cuts short our greeting tells us that he or she no longer considers the relationship to be close.

Most students of nonverbal behavior seem agreed that the nonverbal part of communication is much more potent than the verbal part. Thus if *what* one says is contradicted by *the way one says it*, it is usually the case that people will place a higher valuation on the nonverbal part. Birdwhistell (1970) says that at least 65 percent of social information is conveyed nonverbally, while Mehrabian (1972) claims that only seven percent of feelings is conveyed by the words we use.

Contradictions between verbal and nonverbal aspects of communication have been credited with the development of schizophrenia (double-bind theory). Sometimes we can deny the serious intent of a statement or action—the effort may be attempted in court (Goffman, 1971, p. 111), but in everyday life if we are, for instance, insulted and the nonverbal message suggested a serious intent, then later efforts to deny the seriousness of the insult may not be persuasive. If we may rely on television depictions, at least, individuals on the stand may be required to "answer 'yes' or 'no,' " so that the nonseriousness of the statement or action (presumably conveyed nonverbally at the time) is not allowed to become part of the official record. And as Goffman (1969) has noted, one is not permitted to make nonserious statements about a bomb on a commerical flight: "apparently any kind of bomb tease in an airplane is an indictable offence" (p. 125).

Sometimes "nonverbal communication" is limited to such behavior as facial expressions, hand and arm gestures, and postures; for some it includes the acoustic, paralinguistic phenomena that accompany language, such as speech rhythms and other factors that communicate emotional states (Mehrabian, 1972). For most purposes we may say that the nonverbal aspect includes everything but the words of an utterance.

We may further distinguish between aspects of communication that seem arbitrary, learned, specific to a particular culture or social group from those that appear to have a genetic basis. One of the classic studies of the latter variety was Charles Darwin's *Expression of the Emotions in Man and Animals* (1872). It is important to recognize the universal, genetically based features to gain the perspective necessary to recognize features that are culture-specific, while a knowledge of the latter, learned features serves as a check on overgeneralizing from a particular case.

SEMIOTICS

We can consider the universals of nonverbal communication at two levels. The most basic involves features or patterns found generally throughout the animal kingdom; or we can look more specifically at patterns universal within our own species. Students of semiotics seem the most likely to uncover the patterns found widely throughout the animal kingdom, since the term now seems to designate the communicative aspects of ethology.

The term "semiotics" has a long history in philosophy, where it refers to the study of sign systems in general, including communication through the secretion of pheromones, bird calls, the dances of the honeybees, and so forth, as well as language. Some follow Charles Sanders Peirce (1931) in dividing a semiotic system into three components: *syntactics*, the relationships among signs (as the relationships among the green, yellow, and red lights of a traffic light system); *semantics*, the relationship between signs and the outside world (as the red light with the meaning of "stop," the yellow for "caution," and the green for "go"); and *pragmatics*, the relationships between signs and behavior (as when a driver stops on a red signal) (see Morris, 1946). Two European linguists, Saussure and Hjelmslev, have been discussed in terms of semiotics by Lehmann (1976).

More recently, semiotics has been broadly defined as "patterned communications in all modalities," as proposed by the late Margaret Mead toward the end of a conference on paralinguistics and kinesics in the early 1960s (Sebeok, Hayes, & M. C. Bateson, 1964). One effect of the conference was again to encourage concern with the commonunciations of species other than our own.

If the signals of the decomposition products to living ants, as discussed earlier, are very tangible items of communication, then at the other end of the scale one of the most general and subtle aspects of communication is the general understanding of the situation. This is rarely touched on in discussions of semiotics, perhaps because it is too difficult to spell out. An increasing number of language teachers, however, are concerning themselves with "communicative competence," which goes beyond the relatively concrete facts of grammar.

Perhaps the best statement on the general understanding of the situation is that offered by Mead. She noted that she was not particularly adept at foreign languages, but somehow the people she worked with credited her with much greater facility in their language than the competent linguists with whom she was working in the field. She explained it this way: "I am a very poor speaker of any language, but *I always know whose pig is dead* (emphasis added), and, when I work in a native society I know what people are talking about and I treat it seriously and I respect them, and this in itself established a great deal more rapport, very often, than the correct accent" (Sebeok, Hayes, & Bateson, 1964: 189).

KINESICS

Much of our nonverbal communication consists of learned features overlaid on a base that is unlearned. Thus, all normal humans are programmed for walking and the only "learning" developmental—acquiring the muscular coordination and balance for biped-al locomotion. Yet there are many different ways of walking. Some differences in male-female walking is attributable to differences in anatomy, but there are in addition stylistic differences (which are likely to be exaggerated by female impersonators).

Among American males, some ethnic groups develop distinctive styles of walking. Cooke (1972) has studied several aspects of non-verbal communication among Chicago blacks. These include several styles of walking, most of which have a rhythmic aspect. Those as-piring to middle-class status are said to drop the rhythmical styles and "walk like a robot," the way whites are seen to do. There is a basic soul walk, a cool walk (apparently a variant of the pimp walk), and so forth, with the differences among them being largely defined by the positioning or movements of the arms and hands. Among the women there is a style called "shaking it up," with back-and-forth hip-swing-ing movements and forward-backward motion of the shoulders that creates movement in the breast area.

Some of the walks and stances are intended to communicate suggestive messages to members of the opposite sex; some, particu-larly among males, may be intended as part of a *macho* display, per-haps enticing females and warning away other males.

Cooke also deals with hand contact (giving skin), another way of symbolizing solidarity. His concern was mainly to analyze the units of each pattern, applying the methodology of kinesics.

The term kinesics was introduced by Ray Birdwhistell (1955) to refer to the "systematic study of how one communicates through body movements and gestures" (p. 10). His lifelong study grew out of his realization that Kutenai speakers (British Columbia) moved differ-ently when speaking Kutenai and when speaking English. Eventually he became convinced that there was a systematic relationship be-tween audible and visible communicative behavior: these were inter-dependent systems (Birdwhistell, 1970).

Birdwhistell (1962, 1963) believes that no body movement or expression lacks meaning in the context in which it appears, and since these are patterned they are subject to systematic analysis. His early studies revealed that kinesic activity was patterned within the hier-archical structure of the communicative system and its parts. In most varieties of American English, for example, changes in pitch over the units of a sentence have a functional relationship with these syntactic elements. Thus the units of the sentence are marked by a terminal pitch contour: a rise in pitch denotes a type of question ("Are you going?"); a fall denotes completion ("I'm going"); and constant pitch denotes that the speaker is continuing ("I'm going, but I'll be late."). Birdwhistell found that movements of the head, eyes, and hands accompanied these changes of pitch throughout the syntactic unit. For instance, the eyelids as markers lowered at the completion of the syntactic unit, widened at the question, and remained half open at the points of continuation. More specifically, raising the eyelids at the end of a statement constituted a postural cue intended to elicit a response. Similarly, upward and downward movements corresponding to the pitch changes characterized hand and head movements.

Scheflen (1964), studying postural-kinesic markers in 18 psychotherapeutic sessions, found kinesic activity to be a reliable indicator of at least three aspects of the communication situation: to

1. demarcate the beginnings and endings of structural units of the communication system;
2. denote how individual communicants are related to each other;
3. mark steps in the program of the interaction (p. 316).

Conventional Human Gestures

Gestures such as waving and shaking hands in greeting all seem quite natural to us as Americans, yet they may not seem natural in some other cultures. The gesture is only a significant means of communication when both parties attach the same meaning to it. Similarly, the expression of emotions and the circumstances that arouse particular emotions vary culturally. A vivid example is presented by LaBarre (1947):

> The sticking out of the tongue among Europeans (often at the same time "making a face") is an insulting, almost obscene act of provocative challenge and mocking contempt for the adversary, so undignified as to be used only by children. In Bengali statues of the dread black mother goddess, Kali, the tongue is protruded to signify great raging and anger and shock; but the Chinese of the Sung dynasty protruded the tongue playfully to pretend to mock terror, as to make "fun of," the ridiculous and unfeared anger of another person. Modern Chinese in South China at least, protrude the tongue for a moment and then retract it to express embarrassment at a faux pas.
> Kissing, as is well known, is in the Orient an act of private love-play and arouses only disgust when indulged in publicly.

We might add that some Japanese also stick out the tongue to signify embarrassment. Finally, the following example from Seward (1969) shows disparate interpretations of a gesture by individuals unfamiliar with Japanese culture. Seward notes that the beckoning gesture involves extending the right arm straight out, bending down the wrist and fluttering the fingers:

> One day in Hakone, I was watching a Japanese girl-guide whose American tourist-charges had become separated from her by a considerable distance and saw her use this gesture to try to gather her flock of about 20 elderly, bewildered-looking souls about her. The diverse effects were amusing. Some thought that they had been abandoned by their girl-guide and began to mill about like worried sheep. Others appeared to think that this was the signal for a drink and started to straggle back toward the bar of the hotel. Still others apparently interpreted it to mean that they were now on their own and began to disperse through the town. (p. 42)

On the other hand, the right gesture often makes important points for the alien. Much too long after an American submarine sank a Japanese freighter in 1981, Ambassador Mike Mansfield called on the Japanese foreign minister to offer an apology on behalf of the U.S. government. He greeted the foreign minister with a deep bow, which may have startled the American naval attache, but the bow appeared on the front pages of newspapers all over the country the next day. One Japanese journalist is quoted as commenting that Mansfield "is a rare diplomat in that he understands the Japanese mentality very well" (*Newsweek*, September 14, 1981, p. 54).

PROXEMICS AND PERSONAL SPACE

E. T. Hall (1963b), an anthropologist, introduced the term *proxemics* to refer to "the study of how man unconsciously structures microspace—the distance between men in the conduct of daily transactions, the organization of space in his houses and buildings and ultimately the layout of his towns" (p. 1003). The term *personal space*, on the other hand, originated with a social psychologist named Sommer (1959). It refers primarily to "the meaning of space to the individual in terms of the effects of crowding, territoriality, and architectural design, and so on, and is only peripherally concerned with intercultural variations" (Weitz, 1974, p. 199).

The Hidden Dimension

Hall pointed out that one's use of physical space differs from culture to culture, and in intercultural situations misunderstandings and alienation can occur. One of Hall's original and pioneering insights was his notion that how people employ space in various settings is largely affected by factors that lie outside of awareness. He identified four zones within which most spatial behavior can be observed: intimate distance, personal distance, social distance, and public distance (Hall, 1966).

These zones represent the different areas in which we move—areas that increase as intimacy decreases. Intimate distance extends from actual contact to about 18 inches for most Americans. Unavoidable intrusions into this space, as in a crowded elevator, usually results in tensing and efforts to avoid actual contact with a stranger. If contact occurs, according to Fast (1970), efforts to withdraw or tensing of muscles in the contact area serve as an apology and assurance to the victim that the intruder will "let nothing intimate come of this" (p. 21).

Personal distance extends from about 18 inches to about 4 feet. This is about the range of normal conversational spacing. Social distance extends from about 4 feet, as in the case of a housewife and a repairman, for example, to about 10 feet, for somewhat more formal social or business transactions. Public distance may be about 12 to 25 feet for informal gatherings, as with a teacher and a room full of students, more than 25 feet—often the case for politicians, where distance also serves as a security or safety factor.

In times of crisis the spatial boundaries may temporarily dissolve, as Fast (1970) has remarked.

> During the Great Northeast Power Failure everybody reached out to everybody else, to help, to comfort, to encourage, and for a few warm, long hours the city was a vital place.
>
> Then the lights went on and we fell back into our rigid zones of privacy (p. 34).

Cultural and Ethnic Factors

Hall (1963a) feels that Americans overseas frequently experience difficulties in interacting with people in host countries because of cultural differences in the handling of distance and personal space.

In a culture where normal conversational distance falls within what the American feels is intimate distance, he or she will feel uncomfortable and tend to back off. The other party is felt to be pushy, while the American is perceived as cold, aloof, withdrawn, and uninterested.

Arabs, Hall notes (1963b), experience alienation when Americans move outside the olfactory zone (which is too intimate for them); and Americans seem to have a suspiciously low level of the voice and direct the breath away from the face; there is also reduced visual contact when dealing with Americans. Americans were disturbed by the Arab look, touch, voice level, the warm moisture of his breath, and by the penetrating stare of his eyes. In American culture, such behavior is felt to be permissible only on a nonpublic basis with a person of the opposite sex.

In a different cultural setting, a Chinese was alienated during an interview by being seated on the opposite side of a desk and being faced directly because this was defined as being on trial (Hall, 1963b, pp. 1005-1006).

Elsewhere Hall (1966) reports that Latin Americans and the French share the Arab tolerance for closer interaction than Americans. (See also Watson & Graves, 1966). Subsequent investigations involving Swedish, Scottish, Greek, Southern Italian and Central and South American subjects (Little, 1968; Shuter, 1976) have demonstrated that consistent differences can be observed in social schemas which reflect the use of interpersonal differences.

Researchers have also looked at racial and ethnic differences among black, white, and Hispanic people in natural and experimental settings (Aiello & Jones, 1971; Baxter, 1970; Jones, 1971; Leibman, 1970; Tolor, 1968; Thayer & Alba, 1972), though differences in approach and observational techniques make it difficult to compare the studies and derive valid generalizations. It does seem, however, that Hispanics are more comfortable with a closer interpersonal distance than whites or blacks.

VISUAL BEHAVIOR

Heron (1970) has stated that eye contact constitutes the most "fundamental primary mode of interpersonal encounter. . . . For it is mainly here, throughout the wide ranges of social encounter, that people actually *meet*" (p. 244). The efficacy of the visual encounter has been illustrated by Exline (1974) who relays the story of how Sophia

Loren was advised to perform a striptease for the film *Yesterday, To-day, and Tomorrow*. To do a convincing job, she was told, she must pick out someone in the audience and gaze directly into his eyes. Miss Loren vouches for the advice; she had been very uncomfortable with the stripping assignment, but

> Now I can be positive of one thing, if I was able to do suc-cessfully the scene it was because I picked one person and per-formed only for him, looking straight into his eyes. My audience in the film is composed of one lonely spectator, Marcello Mas-troianni! (*Life*, April 10, 1964)

An impressive amount of research has already been published on visual behavior in nonverbal communication. Cranach (1971), for example, has described the roles played by gaze as part of a "hier-archically ordered" sequence of orienting behavior which signals readiness to communicate. Cary (1974) has observed visual signals by females to males in experimental and natural (barroom) settings. Having noted that a second look by females was the determinant of whether conversation recurred in the experimental setting, he noted the same sequence in the bar: "Inexperienced males can occasionally be seen to pick the most physically appealing females; the more ex-perienced males seem to know better and try to join the females who look to them" (p. 8).

Gaze avoidance has also received a good deal of attention from investigators. In addition to its apparent significance as a signal of unwillingness to communicate, gaze-aversion may indicate emotional arousal (Exline, Gray, & Schuette, 1965; Jurich & Jurich, 1974; Kleck, 1968; Knapp, Hart, & Dennis, 1974).

Visual behavior is an important source of feedback in the regu-lation of speech, which is regarded as central to the processes of so-cial interaction. Mutual looking, as Goffman (1964) has pointed out, is fundamental to the initiation and maintenance of speech.

Pupil Dilation

After Hess (Hess and Holt, 1960) presented slides of male and female pinups to male and female subjects and found that males' pupils showed a greater dilation to female pinup than to male pic-tures and vice versa for female subjects, he concluded that pupil di-lation was a reliable index of positive emotional arousal and pupil constriction was an index of emotional aversion. This prompted the advertising industry to expend large sums of money in pupillometry, but after more than 20 years and many additional studies, Hess's conclusions have been found to be overly simple and of dubious validity. Tryon (1975) identified no fewer than 26 variables that may influence pupil size. The sensitivity of the pupil to confounding stimuli makes it difficult to support Hess's notions about the meaning of dilation and constriction in relation to emotional arousal.

FACIAL EXPRESSIONS

Charles Darwin (1872) discussed the possibility that expression of the emotions might be similar among different species—in some cases it seemed very likely that the same muscles were involved. He assumed that expressive behaviors have survival value and thus are subject to the processes of natural selection in much the same manner as are physical structures and attributes.

If the expression of emotions is similar among different species, then it is all the more likely that the facial expression of the emotions are universal within a species. In particular, we might expect the facial expression of emotion to be universal within our own species, rather than either racially or culturally determined. On the other hand, Birdwhistell (1963) has argued that facial expressions are culture bound, and he rejects the notion of universal symbols of emotional state. LaBarre (1947, 1962) seems also to reject the universal thesis, though Graber (1981) feels that LaBarre's position is not so much opposed to universality as it is complementary to it.

Perhaps the most plausible view of the nature-nurture problem is the one formulated by Paul Ekman, who is basically in Darwin's universalist camp, but who understands that cultural learning also plays an important part in the way emotions are expressed. His "neurocultural theory" (recently summarized in Ekman, 1980) proposes that "facial expressions are the product of both evolution and culture, and are thus both universal in some respects and specific to each culture in others. . . . it is the appearance of the face for each emotion—produced by particular, different actions of the facial muscles—which is the product of evolution. When someone feels an emotion and is not trying to disguise it, his or her face appears the same no matter who that person is or where he or she comes from. It was this which Darwin had noted and, indeed, explained." [p. 7]

But there are cultural influences on facial expression. For one thing, culture teaches us how to feel about events. Something that amuses an American may generate fear in someone from a different culture, for example. That is, the meaning of an event may vary from one culture to another, so that the emotional response will also vary. A second way culture influences the expression of the emotions is through what Ekman and his associates call *display rules*. Culture teaches us which feelings we may (or must) show to whom, and when. To illustrate, Japanese college students in Japan and American college students in the United States were shown pleasant and unpleasant films. Part of the time the students were alone, without any social constraints on the expression of emotions. In this condition the facial expressions were virtually the same for both the Japanese and the American students. Where others were present, the cultural-display rules were in effect and tended to mask the facial expressions of the Japanese. That is, the "Japanese looked much more polite and constrained, showing less negative feeling than did the Americans" (Ekman, 1980, p. 8). Of course precautions have to be taken to insure that the films are suitably defined as "pleasant" or "unpleasant" for the cultures in question.

Ekman suggests that a third way in which culture influences facial expression is by teaching its members what to do after they have expressed a particular emotion. That is, a given facial expression may be predictive of different behavior in different cultures. It is not clear that this aspect of the problem has been systematically studied, however.

PARALANGUAGE

Special vocabularies have been developed by different groups who deal with acoustic phenomena. Musicians speak of intonation, timbre, and tempo; acousticians talk of noise, decibels, and frequencies; linguists speak of pitch, stress, and intonation; and voice therapists describe hoarseness, registers, and melody (Barbara, 1958). Trager (1965) described the acoustic phenomena that accompany language as *paralanguage*. Paralanguage is divided into *voice set* as background for, and *voice qualities* and *vocalizations* as accompaniments of, language proper.

Voice set involves the physiological and physical peculiarities which result in the patterns that identify individuals as members of a societal group, persons of a certain age, sex, state of health, body build, and so forth. Whether we whisper or shout, sound infirm or vigorous, and use a high-pitched or a low-pitched voice are matters of voice set, and have communicative significance. Voice quality can be analyzed into variations in pitch range and control, vocal lip control, control of the glottis, and control of rhythm, articulation, resonance, and tempor, but more simply it is what enables a grown woman to sound like a little girl and a grown man to whine (Trager, 1972). Vocalizations are activities such as laughing and crying, clearing the throat, and in general all of the nontalking noises we make in our social interaction.

According to Trager, different languages are accompanied by different paralanguage systems. Paralanguage, like language, is a cultural system, and is therefore learned and arbitrarily symbolic. Trager suggests that paralanguage is more simply structured than language, but is careful to point out that we should not conjecture that it existed prior to language. As a learned, cultural system, Trager maintains, paralanguage came into being with the invention of language. At the same time, some paralanguage phenomena may have been converted into language. Thus if one goes "Sh!" this is paralanguage, but if that becomes "hush," it has been converted into an item of language.

Paralanguage and Personality

Early voice research focused mainly on stable personal characteristics which were presumed to be identifiable from voice. The age, sex, and physical characteristics of a speaker were found to be assessable with varying degrees of accuracy. It has been suggested that the influence of preconceived thoughts or vocal stereotypes, had a considerable effect upon such judgments. Stereotypes were even more clearly evident in the judgment of attitudes and interests from the voice. For example, ratings of occupations were consistently found to have higher agreement among judges than with the speaker's actual vocation.

Personality traits have also been examined from the voice. Subjective voice judgments were typically compared to clinical observations or to the speaker's scores on psychometric tests. Yet these early comparisons often incorporated psychological tests which have subsequently been considered to be of questionable validity (e.g., the Bernreuter Inventory). Further, judgments of personality traits were also confounded by stereotypical expectancies. One aspect of these voice stereotypes was identified in terms of the effective and efficient use of speech.

Clinical observations have emphasized that emotional qualities in speech reflected the character of the speaker. For example, effective speech has been considered indicative of effective personality (Sanford, 1942). Markel and his associates have contributed significantly in this area by the identification of speech elements which correspond to personality factors. These speech elements (speech rate and intensity) were, therefore, suggested to underlie vocal stereotypes (Markel, 1969a, 1969b; Markel, Phillis, Varga, & Howard, 1972a; Markel, Prebor, & Brandt, 1972b).

Paralanguage and Emotions

More recent examinations of the voice have eliminated the influence of stereotypes and controlled for semantic (verbal) aspects of speech by focusing on non-content (nonverbal) elements of voice. Pauses and speech intrusions (e.g., laughs and sighs), for example, have been considered important signs of anxiety (Dibner, 1956; Kramer, 1963).

Methods which have been found effective in studying actual emotional experiences from voice have either ignored or electronically controlled for semantic effects. In particular, advances in electronic instrumentation have overshadowed observational techniques by offering methods to both control content and analyze speech elements. Acoustical filtration has been employed for 3 decades to eliminate semantic effects in speech (Kramer, 1963; Starkweather, 1961). Advanced applications of technology have monitored the vocal spectrum for objectively identifiable signs of anxiety (Kuroda, Okamura, & Utsuki, 1976; Williams & Stevens, 1972). Similarly, standardized instrumentation has been developed to evaluate state anxiety from specific voice parameters (Fuller, 1972). Still, no evaluative voice method has proven consistently effective in measuring emotion in the voice. It appears that such a breakthrough will be as dependent on theoretical achievements, to define and explain the complex interaction of emotion in the voice, as it will on technological advances.

SOUND SYMBOLISM

Wolfgang Köhler (1947) credits the German poet Morgenstern with the observation that "All seagulls look as though their names were Emma" (*Die Möwen sehen alle aus, als ob sie Emma hiessen*). The name flows as smoothly as the bird, but we *hear* the name and *see* the bird. Evidently we are somehow able to enjoy some part of the same subjective experience through different sensory modalities. The point can be made even more clearly if we ask subjects to match Köhler's (1947) nonsense words *maluma* and *takete* to the shapes given in Figure 4.1 (Köhler, 1947, p. 225). Again, nearly everyone reveals in his match a feeling that the smoothly convoluted figure best fits the sound series that is uninterrupted by stoppages in the flow of breath.

In speaking of language, the term "symbolism" ordinarily refers to the arbitrary relationship that obtains between a sound sequence or word and its referent. That is, the object that this word describes may be represented by virtually any sound sequence, so long as the parties in communication understand that the connection exists. We say "book," but the Japanese say *hon*, the French *livre*, and so on. The type of symbolism we are discussing now is what Sapir (1929) called "a more fundamental, a psychologically primary sort of symbolism"; this he defined as expressive symbolism. This kind of symbolism certainly operates within specific languages, and possibly even universally.

Giving an English example of this phenomenon in which the affective component of meaning exceeds the referential component, Markel (1961) argued that there is a common affective connotation in many /gl-/ words: glad, glance, glass, gleam, glimpse, glitter, globe, glove, and glow. In the same vein, but somewhat earlier, Bolinger (1950) analyzed both the initial sounds and the residues in the following two series: glitter, glow, glare, and flitter, flow, flare. Thus the /gl/ indicates phenomena of light, /fl/ phenomena of movement, /itr/ intermittent, /ow/ steady, and /r/ intense. Similar examples are to be found in German, where initial /gr-/ seems to indicate the connotation "sinister, eerie": *grasslich, grauen, grausig, Greuel, greulich, gruselig.*

Needless to say, phonetic, or sound, symbolism is not peculiar to Indo-European languages. Samuel Martin (1964) suggests that Korean may be the champion, since it has more than a thousand lexemes that do not occur simply as isolated items: each is a whole set of words, with systematic variations in shape that correspond to subtle but structured differences in connotation. And Arabic has extensive, complex networks of connotative relationships, connected by means of the sound symbolism implicit in root radicals. To take but a single illustration, many words that contain *ghayn* (no close English approximation of this letter is possible) as the first radical connote "concealment, darkness, obscurity." Thus we have *ghaaba* (to set, as the sun), *ghaara* (to seep into the ground), *ghabasa* (to become dark), *ghabana* (to hoodwink, gyp), *ghataa* (to cover, conceal), *ghatasa* (to immerse, submerge), *ghamma* (to cloud over), *ghilaaf* (covering, book jacket), and so on, for many more words. The early nineteenth-century French grammarian Antoine Fabre d'Olivet made a similar study of Hebrew, another Semitic language (Whorf, 1956).

The hazards of this line of inquiry are clear: semantic continuity may be governed only by the imagination of the investigator. Benjamin Lee Whorf, for example, saw "dispersal" in a set of words with Maya roots that included "sand," "white," "weave cloth," "much," and "dislocate." This was a bit much, even for the generally sympathetic Sapir (Carroll, 1956, p. 24). Whorf (1956) was on intuitively stronger ground when he suggested that the reason we will pronounce hypothetical new words such as "thog," "thag," "thig," and "thuzzle" with the unvoiced value of the *th* found in "thin" and "threw" is that the voiced value of *th* occurs initially only in the cryptotype of demonstrative particles such as *the*, *this*, *that*, *than*, *those*, and so forth.

Empirical Studies of Sound Symbolism

The first published empirical study of sound symbolism was that of Edward Sapir (1929), who felt that some phonetic symbolism must be universal rather than language-specific. He had noted, for example, that "teeny" is smaller than "tiny;" this corresponds to the different sizes of the oral cavity when the vowels of each are pronounced. Sapir conducted a number of analytical experiments to test the symbolic magnitude of different consonants and vowels. In his first experiment he presented subjects with pairs of consonant-vowel-consonant (CVC) nonsense syllables and asked them to rate the syllables on a scale of relative magnitude. For example, subjects were told that "mal" and "mil" both meant "table," and were asked which word designated the larger table. More than 75 per cent of the subjects consistently selected "mal" as larger than "mil," which again parallels the difference in the size of the oral cavity. Somewhat later, Newman (1933) followed up Sapir's work and found that the symbolic magnitude judgments were due to three mechanical factors: (1) the kinesthetic factor of the articulatory position of the tongue (front-back), (2) the acoustic factor of the characteristic frequency (high-low), and (3) the kinesthetic factor of the oral cavity size (small-large). In a second, similar experiment, Newman found similarities between a large-small and a dark-bright scale, but whereas the large-small scale was patterned on all three factors used in the first experiment plus vowel quantity, the brightness scale was patterned exclusively on the basis of articulation and frequency.

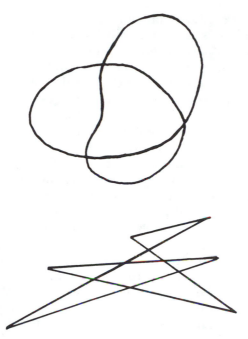

Figure 4.1. Stimulus Figures to Accompany Takete and Maluma.
(Reprinted by permission from W. Köhler, *Gestalt Psychology*, New York:
Liveright, 1947, p. 225.)

Davis (1961) has used jagged and curved drawings matched with
the nonsense words *uloomu* and *takete*, modified from Köhler (1947;
cf. Figure 4.1), in a crosscultural study. African children who spoke
only a Bantu language (Kitongwe) and children speaking only English matched *takete* to the angular drawing and *uloomu* to the curved
drawing with significantly more than chance frequency, leading Davis
to the conclusion that universal phonetic symbolism provided the
proper cues for "correct" matching in both groups.

Not all investigators have reached the same conclusion, however. Taylor and Taylor (1962), for example, conducted a series of
crosscultural experiments that supported the notion of phonetic
symbolism within a single language, but cast considerable doubt on
the theory of universal phonetic symbolism. In a later article, Taylor
(1963) hypothesized that a major variable of phonetic symbolism must
be the language habits of the speakers of a given language. These
habits force them to associate a specific sound or sound sequence with
a generalized meaning. For example, English speakers habitually associate an initial *g* with bigness, simply because many words that con-

note bigness in English begin with *g*. For the same reason, Taylor argued, an initial *d* is associated with bigness in Japanese (from *debu* "fat," *dekkai* "huge," *daikibo* "on a grand scale," and so forth). Taylor claimed that this hypothesis explained not only why speakers associate certain sounds with certain meanings, but also why the associations differ for speakers of different languages.

Taylor, in turn, has been repudiated by Weiss (1964a), who charged that Taylor's criticisms of earlier research in phonetic symbolism were the result of bias and selective reporting. Further, Weiss stated that the language habits theory begs the question of why certain unrelated words that share a connotation in a given language also share structural components, and it fails to explain why only initial consonants are associated with meanings. Weiss felt that a theory of phonetic symbolism should rely on sound and semantic hierarchies, rather than using isomorphic relations between single sounds and single meanings. Such a theory, of course, happens to have been proposed by Weiss (1963, 1964a, 1964b, 1966). Much of the post-Sapir work, however, has become complex enough that Vetter and Tennant (1967) have suggested that future experiments in phonetic symbolism must impose stricter controls upon the stimuli used in order to eliminate extraneous variables.

Word-Matching Studies

A somewhat different approach to the question of sound symbolism involves matching words in different languages. For example, Brown, Black, and Horowitz (1955) presented 21 pairs of antonyms of sensory continua to 86 American subjects. The pairs were presented audiovisually in three languages (Hindi, Czech, and Chinese), and the subjects were asked to match an English meaning to each stimulus word. In nearly all cases the matching was correctly made at well above a chance level, in some cases 90 percent or better. In order to explain this correct guessing, the experimenters accepted the theory of a "physiognomic language," composed of universal, unlearned intersensory connections—a sort of universal synesthesia. They postulated that the origin of speech could have been in the arbitrary association of sounds and meanings, but that it then progressed toward phonetic symbolism, so that a given speech form survived only if it were "representational." Brown *et al.* (1955) concluded, perhaps whimsically, that in the evolution of languages, "speech forms have been selected for symbolism and that we are moving toward a golden millennium of physiognomic speech" [p. 393].

Maltzmann, Morisett, and Brooks (1956) found that English-Japanese and English-Croatian pairs were matched well above chance levels but that Japanese-Croatian pairs were not. It seemed that (for English speakers, at least) for sound symbolism to be effective, English had to be involved. But Brackbill and Little (1957) found good matching for Japanese-Chinese and Japanese-Hebrew pairs, while Chinese-Hebrew pairs were matched well below chance levels. Clearly universal phonetic symbolism cannot apply to all words of all languages, but the positive findings suggest that there may be interesting possibilities for further research in connection with language typologies.

Subsequently, Brown and Nuttall (1959) suggested that universal phonetic symbolism is sensitive to the form of presentation (auditory, visual, etc.) because only the English-foreign condition allows subjects to determine the appropriate semantic contrast. They then reformulated Brown's original phonetic symbolism theory into one that requires a referent continuum:

> Antonyms naming opposite ends of sensible referent continua (in languages with which the subject is unfamiliar) contrast with one another on appropriate phonetic dimensions often enough to make possible better than chance matches with the equivalent terms in the subject's native language. This condition, if it exists, need not be explained by a myth about the origin of speech in physiognomic representation. It is possible that in the history of languages, antonyms evolve toward phonetic contrasts appropriate to this semantic contrast and that pairs so contrasting sound "right" to native speakers and so have a superior prospect for survival. [p. 445]

In a direct test of the Brown-Nuttall hypothesis, Weiss (1963) used English-Hindi and English-Chinese word pairs that included both antonyms and pairs on different semantic dimensions. He found that correct guessing did not depend on the kinds of contrast represented by antonyms, but it seemed that the presence of an English word in a test pair provides a category of experiences that the subjects use to find the appropriate meaning of a sound sequence. Weiss concluded that "to the extent that sound-sense relations congruent with the subject's experiences have found their way into all natural languages, correct guessing is likely to occur" [p. 106]. Weiss (1966) then had 318 subjects match the Japanese equivalent of one of a pair of English stimulus words in 28 word sets. The words were not antonyms, but were sensation-related. The rate of correct guessing was again significantly high, supporting his earlier findings and leading him to postulate the following sequence of events to account for phonetic symbolism: (1) experiences are assimilated as categories, some of which are bipolar ("large-small") and others of which are not ("hoarse, vibrating"); (2) many experiences are accompanied by more or less characteristic sets of sounds; (3) consistent pairings of the sounds and experiences are learned, and are associated with the above categories; (4) conversely, the experiences and categories are hierarchically associated with the sounds; (5) when the subject is presented with an unmeaningful sound sequence, he attributes these learned associations to it; (6) the sounds associated with categories of meaning are incorporated into words that denote those categories; (7) some categories of meaning are shared by different language groups; and (8) some sounds associated with those categories are associated universally. Step 6 explains the phenomenon of phonetic symbolism, while steps 7 and 8 explain universal phonetic symbolism.

SUMMARY

Nonverbal communication is a very broad topic that is subject to different disciplinary approaches, though there is some overlap and ultimately an adequate framework may be developed to deal with the subject in its entirety.

One of the broadest approaches is that of semiotics, the study of patterned communication in all modalities. When applied to nonhuman species in particular, it is sometimes called zoösemiotics. One of its goals is to determine very general features of communication, including those applicable to all species, including our own. Somewhat more specifically, among humans, one problem is to ascertain features of nonverbal communication that are universal and which are culture-specific.

Human nonverbal behavior may be divided into five categories: kinesics, proxemics, visual behavior, facial expression, and paralanguage. Kinesics refers to the study of communication through body movements and gestures; proxemics refers to the study of the way we organize space, including personal space; visual behavior refers to looking behavior, including eye contact or its absence as well as pupil dilation; studies of facial expression have been particularly embroiled in a nature-nurture controversy. One influential theory holds that there are universals based on the movement of facial musculature elicited by a particular emotion, while expressions specific to a particular culture are governed by culturally learned display rules. Finally, paralanguage refers to the acoustic phenomena that accompany language, including voice sets that constitute the background for speech and voice qualities and vocalizations that accompany spoken language.

Sound symbolism is not usually discussed in connection with nonverbal communication, though it is of peripheral relevance at least, and may be a consideration in the origin of language as well as being of interest for the problem of how we respond to different language sounds. The phenomenon of universal phonetic symbolism has been seriously challenged by the crosscultural study of Taylor and Taylor (1962), but the existence of language-specific phonetic symbolism has received wide empirical support. The next step in the study of sound symbolism would seem to be the systematic examination of the patterns of connotative meaning of the sounds in a large sample of natural languages.

REFERENCES

Aiello, J.R., & Jones, S.E. Field study of the proxemic behavior of young school children in three subcultural groups. *Journal of Personality and Social Psychology*, 1971, *19*, 351-356.

Barbara, D.A. (Ed.). *Your speech reveals your personality.* Springfield, Ill.: Charles C. Thomas, Publisher, 1958.

Baxter, J.C. Interpersonal spacing in natural settings. *Sociometry*, 1970, *33*, 444–456.

Birdwhistell, R.L. Background to kinesics. *ETC Review of General Semantics*, 1955, *13*, 10-15.

Birdwhistell, R.L. An approach to communication. *Family Process*, 1962, *1*, 192-201.

Birdwhistell, R.L. Kinesic level of the investigation of emotions. In P. Knapp (Ed.), *Expression of the emotions of man*. New York: International Universities Press, Inc., 1963.

Birdwhistell, R.L. *Kinesics and context*. Philadelphia, Pa.: University of Pennsylvania Press, 1970.

Bolinger, D.L. Rime, assonance, and morpheme analysis. *Word*, 1950, *6*, 117-136.

Brackbill, Y., & Little, K.B. Factors determining the guessing of meanings of foreign words. *Journal of Abnormal and Social Psychology*, 1957, *54*, 312-318.

Brown, R., Black, A.H., & Horowitz, A.E. Phonetic symbolism in natural languages. *Journal of Abnormal and Social Psychology,* 1955, *50,* 388-393.

Brown, R. & R. Nuttall. Method in phonetic symbolism experiments. *Journal of Abnormal and Social Psychology,* 1959, *59,* 441-445.

Carroll, J.B. (Ed.). *Language, thought, and reality: Selected writings of Benjamin Lee Whorf.* (Introduction) Cambridge, Mass.: The M.I.T. Press, 1956.

Cary, M.S. Nonverbal openings to conversation. Paper presented at the Eastern Psychological Association Meeting, Phila., PA, 1974.

Cooke, B.G. Nonverbal communication among Afro-Americans: An initial classification. In T. Kochman (Ed.), *Rappin' and stylin' out.* Urbana, Ill.: University of Illinois Press, 1972.

Cranach, M.V. The role of orienting behavior in human interaction. In A.H. Esser (Ed.), *Behavior and environment: The use of space by animals and men.* New York: Plenum Press, 1971.

Darwin, C. *Expression of the emotions in man and animals.* London: Murray, 1872.

Davis, R. The fitness of names to drawings: A cross-cultural study in Tanganyika. *British Journal of Psychology,* 1961, *52,* 259–268.

Dibner, A.S. Cue-counting: A measure of anxiety. In Interviews. *Journal of Consulting Psychology,* 1956, *20,* 475–478.

Ekman, P. *The face of man: Expressions of universal emotions in a New Guinea village.* New York: Garland STPM Press, 1980.

Exline, R.V. Visual interaction: The glances of power and preference. In S. Weitz (Ed.), *Nonverbal Communication: Readings with Commentary.* New York: Oxford University Press, 1974.

Exline, R.V., Gray, D., & Schuette, D. Visual behavior in a dyad as affected by interview content and sex of respondent. *Journal of Personality and Social Psychology,* 1965, *1,* 201–209.

Fast, J. *Body language.* New York: M. Evans and Company, 1970.

Fuller, F.H. Detection of emotional stress by voice analysis. Final Report. Decision Control, Inc. Bethesda, Maryland, 1972.

Goffman, E. *Behavior in public places.* New York: The Free Press, 1964.

Goffman, E. *Strategic interaction.* Philadelphia, PA: University of Pennsylvania Press, 1969.

Goffman, E. *Relations in public.* New York: Harper and Row, 1971.

Graber, R.B. Review of Ekman (1980). *Studies in Visual Communication,* 1981, *7,* 83–85.

Hall, E.T. Proxemics—The study of man's spatial relations and boundaries. In I. Gaston (Ed.), *Man's image in medicine and anthropology.* New York: International Universities Press, 1963a.

Hall, E.T. A system for the notation of proxemic behavior. *American Anthropologist,* 1963b, *65,* 1003–1026.

Hall, E.T. *The hidden dimension*. Garden City, N.Y.: Doubleday and Company, Inc., 1966.

Heron, J. The phenomenology of social encounter: The gaze. *Philosophy and Phenomenological Research*, 1970, *31*, 243–264.

Hess, E.H., & Holt, J.M. Pupil size as related to interest value of visual stimuli. *Science*, 1960, *132*, 349–350.

Jones, S.E. A comparative proxemic analysis of dyadic interaction in selected subcultures of New York City. *Journal of Social Psychology*, 1971, *84*, 35–44.

Jurich, A.P., & Jurich, J.A. Correlations among nonverbal expressions of anxiety. *Psychological Reports*, 1974, *34*, 199–204.

Kleck, R.E. Physical stigmata and nonverbal cues emitted in face-to-face interaction. *Human Relations*, 1968, *21*, 19–28.

Knapp, M.L., Hart, R.P., & Dennis, H.S. The rhetoric of duplicity: An exploration of deception as a communication construct. *Human Communications Research*, 1974, *1*, 15–29.

Köhler, W. *Gestalt psychology*. New York: Liveright Publishing Corp., 1947.

Kramer, E. Judgment of personal characteristics and emotions from nonverbal properties of speech. *Psychology Bulletin*, 1963, *60*, 408–420.

Kuroda, I., Fujiwara, O., Okamura, N., & Utsuki, N. Method for determining pilot stress through analysis of voice communication. *Aviation, Space, and Environmental Medicine*, 1976, *47*, 528–533.

LaBarre, W. The cultural basis of emotions and gestures. *Journal of Personality*, 1947, *16*, 49–68.

LaBarre, W. *Paralanguage, kinesics, and cultural anthropology*. Report for the Interdisciplinary Conference on Paralanguage and Kinesics. Bloomington, Ind.: Indiana University Research Center in Anthropology, Folklore, and Linguistics, 1962.

Lehmann, W. *Descriptive Linguistics*. New York: Random House, 1976.

Leibman, M. The effects of sex and race norms on personal space. *Environment and Behavior*, 1970, *2*, 208–246.

Little, K.B. Cultural variation in social schemata. *J. of Personality and Social Psychology*, 1968, *10*, 1–7.

Maltzmann, I., Morrisett, L. & Brooks, L.O. An investigation of phonetic symbolism. *Journal of Abnormal and Social Psychology*, 1956, *53*, 249–251.

Markel, N.N. Connotative meanings of several initial consonant clusters in English. *Georgetown University Monograph Series on Language and Linguistics*, 1961, *14*, 81–87.

Markel, N.N. Orientation. In N.N. Markel (Ed.), *Psycholinguistics: An introduction to the study of speech and personality*. Homewood, Ill.: Dorsey Press, 1969a.

Markel, N.N. Relationship between voice-quality profiles and MMPI profiles in psychiatric patients. *Journal of Abnormal Psychology*, 1969b, *74*, 61–66.

Markel, N.N., Phillis, J.A., Varga, R., & Howard, K. Personality traits associated with voice types. *Journal of Psycholinguistic Research*, 1972, *1*, 249–255.

Markel, N.N., Prebor, L.D., & Brandt, J.F. Biosocial factors in dyadic communication: Sex and speaking intensity. *Journal of Personality and Social Psychology*, 1972, *23*, 11–13.

Martin, S.E. Speech levels in Japan and Korea. In D. Hymes (Ed.), *Language in culture and society*. New York: Harper & Row, 1964.

Mehrabian, A.S. *Nonverbal communication*. Chicago: Aldine-Atherton, 1972.

Morris, C. *Signs, language, and behavior*. New York: Prentice-Hall, 1946.

Newman, S.S. Further experiments in phonetic symbolism. *American Journal of Psychology*, 1933, *45*, 53–75.

Newsweek. September 14, 1981, p. 54.

Peirce, C.S. *Collected papers* (8 Vols.) C. Hartshorne, P. Weiss, & A.W. Burks (Eds.). Cambridge, Mass.: Harvard University Press, 1931–1958.

Sanford, F. Speech as a personality trait. *Psychological Bulletin*, 1942, *39*, 811–845.

Sapir, E. A study in phonetic symbolism. *Journal of Experimental Psychology*, 1929, *12*, 225–239.

Scheflen, A.E. The significance of posture in communication systems. *Psychiatry*, 1964, *27*, 316–331.

Sebeok, T.A., Hayes, A.S. & Bateson, M.C. (Eds.). *Approaches to semiotics*. The Hague: Mouton & Company, 1964.

Seward, J. *Japanese in action*. New York: Weatherhill, 1969.

Shuter, P. Proxemics and tactility in Latin America. *Journal of Communication*, 1976, *26*, 46–52.

Sommer, R. Studies in personal space. *Sociometry*, 1959, *22*, 247–260.

Starkweather, J. Vocal communication of personality and human feelings. *Journal of Communication*, 1961, *11*, 63–72.

Taylor, I.K. Phonetic symbolism re-examined. *Psychological Bulletin*, 1963, *60*, 200–209.

Taylor, I.K. & M.M. Taylor. Phonetic symbolism in four unrelated languages. *Canadian Journal of Psychology*, 1962, *16*, 344–356.

Thayer, S. & Alba, L. A field experiment on the effect of political and cultural factors on the use of personal space. *Journal of Social Psychology*, 1972, *88*, 267–272.

Tolor, A. Psychological distance in disturbed and normal children. *Psychological Reports*, 1968, *23*, 695–701.

Trager, G.L. Paralanguage: A first approximation. In D. Hymes (Ed.), *Language in culture and society*. New York: 1965.

Trager, G.L. *Language and languages*. San Francisco: Chandler, 1972.

Tryon, W.W. Pupillometry: A survey of sources of variation. *Psychophysiology*, 1975, *19*, 90–93.

Vetter, H.J., & Tennant, J.A. Oral-gesture cues in sound symbolism. *Perceptual and Motor Skills*, 1967, *24*, 54.

Watson, O.M., & Graves, T.D. Quantitative research in proxemic behavior. *American Anthropologist*, 1966, *68*, 971–985.

Weiss, J.H. Role of "meaningfulness" versus meaning dimensions in guessing and meanings of foreign words. *Journal of Abnormal and Social Psychology*, 1963, *66*, 541–546.

Weiss, J.H. Phonetic symbolism re-examined. *Psychological Bulletin*, 1964a, *61*, 454–458.

Weiss, J.H. The role of stimulus meaningfulness in the phonetic symbolism response. *Journal of General Psychology*, 1964b, *70*, 255–263.

Weiss, J.H. A study of the ability of English speakers to guess the meanings of non-antonym foreign words. *Journal of General Psychology*, 1966, *74*, 97–106.

Weitz, S. (Ed.). *Nonverbal communication: Readings with commentary*. New York: Oxford University Press, 1974.

Whorf, B.L. A linguistic consideration of thinking in primitive communities. In J.B. Carroll (Ed.), *Language, thought, and reality: Selected writings of Benjamin Lee Whorf*, pp. 65–86. Cambridge, Mass.: The M.I.T. Press, 1956.

Williams, C. & K. Stevens. On determining the emotional state of pilots during flight: An exploratory study. *Aerospace Medicine*, 1972, *10*, 1369–1372.

Chapter 5

THE THEORY OF LANGUAGE:
SOUNDS

While most of us are startled to realize that *ghoti* can be pronounced "fish" (if we use the phonetic values of enou*gh*, w*o*men, and na*ti*on), we all acknowledge that our system of orthography is extremely cumbersome. We have at least a vague understanding that the problem lies in the fact that the same letters can stand for different sounds in English. Thus, *I* has the same phonetic value as *eye*, but in mach*i*ne it has the value of c*lea*n, and as we have seen, in f*i*sh it has the value of w*o*men. It is little comfort to know that there are complicated historical reasons for our spelling, and we are inclined to feel that the letters we use should be employed with consistent values.

A script that attempts to reflect pronunciation in fine detail is *phonetic*. We might suppose that a phonetic script is an ideal kind of writing system, and for some purposes it would be extremely useful. Actually, however, a strictly phonetic script is neither feasible nor desirable for most purposes. A phonetic version of our speech would contain many distinctions that would confuse rather than foster our understanding, so a simpler and more economical *phonemic* script is far more practical for our everyday communication. Phonetics and phonemics together constitute *phonology*.

PHONETICS

Phonetics is concerned with the sounds of language in general rather than with the sounds of a particular language. The ways the stream of air from or to the lungs can be modified to form the sounds of language is far beyond the imagination of most of us who have had experience with only one language. The air may vary in the force with which it is expelled from the lungs; at the vocal chords it may be completely blocked, simply subjected to vibrations, or allowed to pass freely through the throat, which serves as a resonating chamber, to the nose or mouth. At the back of the mouth the air may be partly or completely diverted to pass through the nasal passages. If it passes through the mouth it is subject to potential blockages of varying degrees by the lips at the front and by the tongue, which can approach or contact the teeth and/or the roof of the mouth in various ways. And many of these possibilities hold also if, instead of ejecting air from the lungs, sounds are made in the opposite direction, through the inspiration of air.

The study of how we make the various sounds of language is called *articulatory phonetics*, while the study of the physical properties of the sounds we make is called *acoustic phonetics*. Sometimes *auditory phonetics* is used to distinguish the study of the effect of sounds on the hearer, including their impact on the ear and nerves that result in the perception of sound in the brain (Lehmann, 1976). For most purposes, however, it is sufficient to distinguish articulatory and acoustic phonetics.

Acoustic phonetics is primarily a development of the post-World War II era, though the first important work on the psychophysics of tone was produced by Helmholtz in 1863 and much of our technical advance is indebted to work in telephone engineering over the past century or more (Hirsh, 1966). The subject is still of considerable importance to telephone, or more generally, communications engineering, and has contributed to such things as the development of voice simulators. Of more immediate concern here, technological developments in the area of acoustic phonetics has permitted us to gain insights into the precise nature of the sounds we utter and hear. Sound spectrograms, or "voice prints," provide visible depictions of short segments of speech in terms of sound frequencies and duration. Since the "pictures" consist essentially of columns that vary in height, darkness, and thickness, some training is required for their interpretation, but they are now being used in courts to establish the identification of individuals recorded on tapes of telephone conversations (Fromkin & Rodman, 1978). As an illustration of a linguistic application of the technology, Falk (1978) cites the case of a youngster whose pronunciation of "tank" and "thank" appeared to be the same (that is, both sounded like "tank"), but the acoustic analysis showed that the "t" of "thank" was actually different from the "t" of "tank," so the child may have been trying to make the "th" sound that it had not yet mastered.

While acoustic phonetics is more important than this very brief mention implies, it is less central to our immediate objectives than articulatory phonetics, to which we shall devote considerably more attention. Hirsh (1966) has a concise review of acoustic phonetics and Ladefoged (1975) offers a comprehensive introduction to both acoustic and articulatory phonetics.

ARTICULATORY PHONETICS

While acoustic phonetics is primarily concerned with the physical nature of speech sounds, articulatory phonetics is essentially concerned with the way speech sounds are formed. Of course the techniques of acoustic phonetics have taught us much about how we achieve certain sound effects that we cannot understand simply by studying specific sounds in isolation. Much of our interpretation of *consonants* (sounds which depend on the complete or partial obstruction of air as it passes through the vocal apparatus) depends on the influence of the *vowels* (where there is no obstruction) that precede and follow them. And the vowels differ in frequencies, fundamental vocal tone harmonics reinforced by the resonating properties in the vocal tract (Hirsh, 1966), and so forth.

As a practical matter for the nonspecialist, however, a great deal can be accomplished by learning to become aware of the *place* and *manner* of articulation. The manner of articulation refers basically to the way the passage of air is obstructed. That is, in some cases the flow of air is completely blocked, as with our *p*, *t*, or *k*; in other cases it is merely slowed down, as with our *f* and *s*; while in yet other cases it is diverted, as with our *m* and *n*, in which the air is blocked in the mouth, but is permitted to take a detour through the nasal passages.

Charts showing an array of consonants are usually arranged to reflect the place of articulation, while there is less agreement on the arrangement for the manner of articulation. One other feature that is usually indicated is *voicing*, which refers to the vibration of the vocal cords. Voicing is what distinguishes an *s* from a *z*. If one takes a deep breath, makes an s-sound, then shifts to a z-sound and back several times the vibrations (in the area of the Adams apple) can be detected quite easily.

If we begin with sounds that are important for English, we have a row that starts with *stops* made by blocking the outflow of air at the two lips (thus they are *bilabial* stops): *p* (unvoiced) and *b* (voiced). Then we have a pair of stops in which the air is blocked by the front part of the tongue pressing against the gum ridge (alveolar ridge) above the teeth; *t* (unvoiced) and *d* (voiced); the *k* (unvoiced) and *g* (voiced) in which the back of the tongue presses up against the soft palate (velum) to block the outflow of air. Finally, there is the glottal stop, the sound that separates the two main segments of *oh-oh*! This is usually indicated by a question mark without the dot: ?. As the name implies, the glottal stop is formed by blocking the air down the throat at the glottis, more or less right at the vocal cords.

The possibilities for making different sounds by blocking the flow of air is bewildering. In some African languages, for example, there are double stops, in which, for example, there is simultaneous blockage with the lips and at the velum, which Smalley (1973) represents as ^kp and ^gb (voiceless and voiced, respectively). In most cases our *t* and *d* are made at the gum ridge, but in a careful pronunciation of "width," the tongue touches more forward, on the teeth. For some languages, this is the normal way to effect the blockages, Japanese, for instance, in which case the sounds are called dental stops. We describe our *k* and *g* as velar stops, but sometimes they are made a little more forward or a little more to the rear, which articulations may be "normal" in other languages.

In English our sounds usually depend on the passage of air from the lungs to the outside world, but the so-called "click" languages in Africa have stops that depend on a flow inward from the outside. We can make some of these sounds, such as lip-smacking (pursing the lips and kissing) or the "tsk-tsk" sound of reproval. The difference is that in the relevant African languages such sounds are incorporated with vowels and other consonants to form words: they function in the same way as our *p*, *t*, or *k* function.

Our unvoiced stops are aspirated at the beginning of a word: that is, the blockages are released with a puff of air, but this is not critical for our system (but the voicing is critical). In other systems the voicing is not critical, but the degree of aspiration is, while in yet other systems both the voicing and the aspiration are critical.

It is unusual to find an aspirated glottal stop, but Chao (1968) shares a surprise he once received:

> . . . I was watching some bargaining on a street market in Yunnan (where the dialect is a variety of Mandarin). I couldn't be sure whether they were quarrelling or coughing. Listening more closely to what they were saying, I began to realize that the cough was simply the dialectal cognate of standard Mandarin aspirated *k*, the unaspirated *k*, as I knew, being a glottal stop in that dialect. [p. 24]

After listing stops, it is common to list the *fricatives*, consonants that depend on the audible friction created by slowing down the flow of air at different points in the vocal tract. Again, there are possibilities not represented in the sounds that are important for English. In Japanese, for example, there is a bilabial fricative before the vowel *u*, but in English we get the friction by slowing the air by blowing it through the teeth when we bite lightly on the inside of the lower lip. We write our fricative with an *f* and when representing Japanese words we use the same spelling (as in Mt. Fuji), but the Japanese classify their fricative with their *h* sounds, which makes sense in their system. The voiced counterpart of our *f* is *v*.

Our next fricative pair consists of voiced and unvoiced sounds which we usually spell the same way, *th*. But the initial sound of "*th*ick" is unvoiced and is rendered with the symbol θ (theta) and the initial of "*th*is" is voiced and written with a barred d (đ). Our *s* and *z* are alveolar, which is to say they are made where we make *t* and *d*, but without the air getting completely blocked. Next is the initial sound of *sh*ould (š) and the ž (in a*z*ure), voiceless and voiced respectively, and made with the tongue raising in the middle toward the roof of the mouth, or palate, though the front of the tongue is still close to the *s/z* position. So we say they are alveolar-palatal fricatives. Finally, we have our *h*, which is made back at the glottis, at the vocal cords.

Again the potential variations in articulation are realized in different languages. In German we can find a palatal fricative (ç) in I*ch* (the value of which is approximated in the first part of our *h*uge) and a velar fricative (x), as in a*ch*. In addition to variations produced by articulating at different points, further variations may be achieved by differently shaping the tongue. For our θ and đ the tongue is flat where it slows the air at the teeth, but if the tongue is grooved, as with our *s* or *z*, but otherwise treated as the *θ* or *đ*, then another pair of fricatives is produced. And if the tongue makes firm contact at the teeth and the air is released via the sides of the tongue, yet another pair of fricatives is produced. Similar additional examples could be given on the basis of tongue shape at different points of articulation.

Another consonant category consists of *affricates*, which consist of a stop plus fricative articulated at the same spot. In English we are familiar with the combination *ts* (as in ca*ts*), which we treat as consisting of two sounds, though this need not be the case for all languages. In Japanese, for instance, the *ts* is a variant of *t* that occurs before *u*. In our own case we do recognize one pair of affricates that are considered to constitute single sounds: *t* plus *š*, which is frequently represented by *č* (the first and last sounds of *church*); and *d* plus *ž* (the first and last sounds of *judge*), often represented by *j*. In these instances, the *t* is actually articulated with the blade, or flat part of the tongue rather than with the tip, as we are likely to do in the pronunciation of *t*ip. The *d* is also articulated with the blade as part of the affricate *j*. But the possibilities for forming affricates is impressive—Smalley (1973), for example, lists 48 different affricates!

Nasals are sounds formed by blocking the outflow of air in the mouth but releasing it through the nasal passages. In American English the inventory is small: *m* (bilabial), *n* (alveolar), and *ŋ* (velar), but Smalley's (1973) inventory of 21 different nasals again suggests the great variety to be found, perhaps especially in languages of Africa.

A variety of methods are used for placing the different kinds of *l* and *r*. Sometimes they are handled as "liquids"; or the *l* may be called a "lateral," because the air is released to the sides of the tongue, while varieties of *r* are dealt with as "trills and flaps." We usually make our *l* with the tongue touching the alveolar ridge and releasing the air to the side just behind the point of articulation, but sometimes the air is released further back, as at the end of litt*l*e. For some languages the two kinds of *l* have to be distinguished. (Smalley, 1973, lists 17 kinds of *l*.) The general American *r* is rather different from "r" in most other languages, because it does not involve a flap (as in Standard Japanese or the English style in which ve*r*y is conveyed with the popular spelling of "veddy") or trill (as in most varieties of Spanish and the "macho" style of Japanese). Perhaps the best way to deal with the American *r* is to call it a "semivowel," along with *w* and *y*, following Carroll's (1964) solution (see Table 5-1, where it will be noted that *h* is also treated as a semivowel).

Table 5.1: English Phonemes and Some Words and Sentences Exemplifying Them

33 Segmental Phonemes

20 Consonants   *4 Semivowels*

Occurring as initial, medial, or final:		*As consonant*	*In diphthong*
/b/ as in *buy*	/s/ as in *so*		
/d/ as in *do*	/t/ as in *toe*	/h/ as in *hoe*	*bah* /bah/
/f/ as in *foe*	/v/ as in *vow*		
/g/ as in *go*	/z/ as in *zoo*	/r/ as in *roe*	*err* /ər/
/k/ as in *key*	/θ/ as in *thigh*		
/l/ as in *lie*	/ð/ as in *thy*	/w/ as in *woe*	*now* /naw/
/m/ as in *my*	/š/ as in *show*		
/n/ as in *no*	/č/ as in *chow*	/y/ as in *you*	*boy* /boy/
/p/ as in *pay*	/j/ as in *Joe*		

Occurring only as medial or final:

/ž/ as in *pleasure, rouge*
/ŋ/ as in *singer, thing*

9 Vowels

Simple vowel + consonant	*Followed by semivowels*				
	/-y/	*/-w/*	*/-h/*	*/-r/*	*/-yr/*
/i/ as in *pit*	*pea*	*	*	*	*pier*
/e/ as in *pet*	*pay*	*	*	*	*pare*
/æ/ as in *pat*	*	*	/æh/†	*	*
/ɨ/ as in *roses*	*	*	*	*	*
/ə/ as in *putt, but*	*	*	/əh/**	*purr*††	*
/a/ as in *pot*	*pie*	*now*	*pa*	*par*	*pyre*
/u/ as in *put, look*	*buoy*	*coo*	*boo!*	*poor*	*
/o/ as in *	*boy*	*low*	*oh!*	*pore*	*
/ɔ/ as in *	*	*	*law*	*war*	*

12 Suprasegmental Phonemes

4 Pitches: /¹/ (lowest), /²/, /³/, /⁴/ (highest).
4 Stresses: /´/ (primary), / / (secondary), / / (tertiary), / / (weak).
4 Junctures: /+/ (internal), / | / (level), / ‖ / (rising), /#/ (falling, terminal).

A Sample Transcription

He: /²dɪ̌jə + sîyðə + ³hwáythàws³ ‖ /
She: /²nów³ ‖ ²kə́zay + wəhntid + tə + vɪ̂zɨtðə + smiəsôwnɨyən +myùw³ziyəm² | ² ðə + lâybrəríy əv + ³káhngris³ | ²aen ðə + jéfərsən + mə³móhriyəl² ‖ ⁴óhl² | ²in + tûw + ⁴áwrz²#/
He: /²im⁴pahsibəl#/

He: Didja see the White House?

She: No, 'cause I wanted to visit the Smithsonian Museum, the Library of Congress,
and the Jefferson Memorial—(*excitedly*) all in two hours!
He: (*incredulously*) Impossible!

§After Carroll (1964, pp. 14–15). The phonemes are given as they occur in Carroll's Lower Connecticut Valley dialect.
*Does not occur as a monosyllable in Carroll's dialect, but may occur in other dialects of English.
†An interjection of frustration or disgust.
**The hesitation form.
††In Carroll's dialect, this is a single *r*-like vowel, but it fits best into the pattern if considered a diphthong with /ə/.

Needless to say by now, we have hardly exhausted the possibilities for dealing with "liquids," whether lateral, flapped, or trilled. We can summarize the consonants that are of particular relevance for English in the following chart:

Stops	Bila-bial	Labio-dental	Den-tal	Alveo-lar	Alveo-palatal	Pala-tal	Velar	Glottal
Voiceless	p			t			k	ʔ
Voiced	b			d			g	
Fricatives								
Voiceless		f	θ	s	š			h
Voiced		v	đ	z	ž			
Affricates								
Voiceless					č			
Voiced					j			
Nasals	m			n			η	
Laterals				l				
Semivowels	w			r		y		

VOWELS

Compared with the vowel system of Standard Japanese, which only distinguishes *a, i, u, e* and *o* (but with long and short varieties of each), ours seems relatively rich. But as in the case of the consonants, the possibilities seem endless. Vowels may be uttered with the lips pursed or rounded or they may be pronounced with the lips drawn back; vowels may be voiced or unvoiced (though we normally voice them); they may or may not be nasalized (pronounced with some air escaping through the nose, in the former case); they may vary in length; they may or may not be laryngealized:

When Americans (especially men) are tired, their voices usually drop from normal voicing to a quality called laryngealization. In this quality, the voice rumbles like a stick being drawn along a picket fence. In English, laryngealization may signal either weariness or boredom. In many other languages it is used to distinguish various vowels; it also functions as part of the basic sound system of the language. [Gudschinsky, 1967: 53]

In presenting the array of vowels it is customary to arrange them in accordance with how far forward and how high the tongue is when they are pronounced. Thus the first vowel in the chart is usually the one that is highest and most forward, for us the vowel of f*ee*t; nearly as far to the front and only slightly lower is the vowel of f*i*t. In the International Phonetic Alphabet, which many linguists rely on even for English, the two vowels are described by different symbols. Others, however, in dealing with English treat the higher vowel as the vowel of f*i*t plus a glide, which is represented by a *y*. And that is the system we shall use here, since it is so convenient for discussing English.

Nearly as far forward as the *i* but with the tongue down slightly we have the vowel of g*a*te [ey], again with a glide; without the glide we have the vowel of g*e*t [e], which is fractionally lower than [ey]. And still lower and a bit more retracted is the vowel of c*a*t [æ]. All of the foregoing are called front vowels. In American English there are three central vowels. The highest is at about the level of it [i]; it is often heard as the last vowel of church*e*s and is written with a barred *i* [ɨ]. A little lower than [ɨ] is one of the most common sounds of English, since it is so often found as the value of unstressed vowels, as the *a* of *a*bout, the *e* of ag*e*nt, and for many speakers the *i* of bas*i*s. It is designated by reversed *e* [ə] and is called a schwa. Some linguists find it convenient simply to use the schwa and ignore the [ɨ] that sometimes replaces it as the value of the unstressed vowel. Other linguists include [ʌ] as a mid-central value, particularly to indicate the vowel in stressed position, as b*u*t. The importance of these distinctions depends to a considerable extent on the goal of the person making them. For many purposes it is sufficient only to note the [ə] as *the* central vowel, though in that case it is necessary to treat the first vowel of f*a*ther [a] as if it were a back vowel. The confusion here is probably due more than anything else to minor dialect differences of the writers. Here we treat [a] as a central vowel because it is forward relative to the lowest of our back vowels, which is represented by an open *o* [ɔ] and is the vowel of c*au*ght or h*au*l in many pronunciations, though a large number of American speakers do not distinguish the pronunciation of "caught" and "cot" (both being in this case [kat]) or "haul" and "hall" (both being in this case [hal]).

The mid-back vowel for American English is [o], though it does not usually occur as a pure vowel for us, being followed in most cases by a glide [w] or [y], as in the vowel sounds of *boat* or *boy*, respectively. The next higher back vowel is [u] as in p*u*t, while the highest is [uw], as in b*oo*t.

We have already dealt with the effects of the [y] glide after [i] and [e]; it also occurs after [a], as in the pronunciation of "eye" [ay], as does [w], as in the pronunciation of "out" [awt].

A chart of the basic vowels for American English, omitting the diphthongs formed by the glides, then, is:

	Front	Central	Back
High	i	ɨ	u
Mid	e	ə	o
Low	æ	a	ɔ

THE PHONEMIC PRINCIPLE

For most purposes it is not the exact acoustical quality of speech sounds that must be graphically represented but rather certain ranges of sound that are significant for a specific language or speech variety. This is the essence of the phonemic principle. While the linguist or other specialist may have to be concerned with a very precise transcription of speech, for most of us, who only want to communicate with each other in writing, a script that tells us all we have to know and nothing that we need not know—a phonemic script, in other words—is most practical. This means that each letter we use will represent the same value each time it appears, but that value will not be a specific sound. Each time we write a *p*, we will want to designate a sound in which the two lips completely block the outflow of air momentarily while the vocal cords are *not* vibrating. The specific sound value of the *p*, however, will vary somewhat in accordance with its phonological environment. The most obvious variation in the case of the *p* is the presence or absence of a puff of air (aspiration) when the *p* is released. Thus at the beginning of a word the *p* is followed by aspiration, but after an *s* it is not. This difference can be appreciated by holding a lit match two or three inches in front of the mouth and pronouncing, in a normal speaking voice, the words "bin," "spin," and "pin." The match should continue to burn cheerfully through the first two and go out easily when subjected to the aspiration of the "pin."

Thus we can see from these and other examples that aspiration as such is not critical for the /p/ phoneme. But voicing is critical, since that is what distinguishes the /p/ and the /b/, and if we want to compare meaningful sequences that begin with each of these sounds but are otherwise the same, as "pin" and "bin," the difference matters. We say that we are dealing with two different words, or that the two sequences have different meanings.

A precise *phonetic* transcription would always indicate that the [b] is unaspirated in English and it would indicate when the [p] is and when it is not aspirated. But in our *phonemic* transcription we need not concern ourselves with that sort of variation because it does not influence meanings.

Because virtually all our phonemes show some phonetic variation because of the sounds that come before and after them, we can say that the phoneme is actually an abstraction, and that we do not speak or hear a phoneme but rather a specific representation of that phoneme. The actual variations that we speak or hear are called *allophones* of the particular phoneme in question. We can illustrate this further by considering the variations in the four words "cool," "school," "kill," and "skill." Here there are two vowel phonemes to contend with, /uw/ and /i/, and three consonant phonemes, /k/, /s/, and /l/. The /k/ varies not only with respect to aspiration, as in the case of the /p/ (and we might add /t/), but it varies with respect to the place of articulation. When the /k/ appears before the front vowel /i/, we have a tendency to anticipate the /i/ by forming the /k/ just a little bit more forward than when we anticipate the /k/ of "cool" /kuwl/, which is followed by the back vowel /uw/. With a little practice and a lot of concentration it is possible to isolate the two kinds of /k/, by "thinking" the variety in "cool," without actually pronouncing the rest of the word and comparing that with the other variety, again without actually pronouncing the rest of "kill."

At any rate, we can see that we have at least four allophones of the phoneme /k/: one which is fronted and aspirated (in "kill"), one which is fronted but unaspirated ("skill"), one which is backed and aspirated ("cool"), and one which is backed but unaspirated ("school").

Similarly, there are at least two allophones of /l/, since value after the front vowel (in "kill" and "skill") is a little different than its value after the back vowel ("cool" and "school").

It should be clear, then, that because of such variations, however subtle, a particular phoneme always appears in a particular manifestation that will contrast with the other allophones. Again, we do not hear or speak the phoneme, but rather a particular allophone, and we may consider the phoneme to constitute an abstraction of all of the allophones of the phoneme.

In trying to determine the phonemes of an alien tongue, the linguist must initially note down in the finest detail the range of sounds he hears (in phonetic transcription) because he (or she) cannot know ahead of time what features will be relevant for the language. Then, as patterns seem to emerge, it is possible to check for *minimal pairs*, sequences which are identical except for a single feature and differ in meaning. In English, for instance, "sing" and "zing" differ only in the feature of voice, and, indeed, the two sequences differ in meaning. We have found a *contrast within a frame*, in which the frame consists of silence before the sequence and [-iŋ] after the suspicious feature. So we say that the /s/ and the /z/ represent two different phonemes.

In such cases as the aspirated and unaspirated stops, we cannot find any minimal pairs, and we notice that the aspiration is completely predictable. The aspirated and unaspirated forms are in *complementary distribution*, and thus do not define different phonemes.

Vowel Length

Sometimes we will lengthen a vowel for emphasis: "He's one baaad dude!" but the meaning of the sequence does not alter in the way it would if a minimal pair were involved. There is in English a more regular occurrence of long vowels, though: before voiced sounds. Thus the vowel of "pot" is short, the vowel of "pod" is long, while at the end of a word the vowel is even longer, as in "pa." These varieties are in again in complementary distribution and do not define different phonemes. But in many languages, including Hawaiian and Japanese, vowel length is *distinctive*—that is, length is a distinctive feature of the phonemic system and must be indicated if confusion is to be avoided. Thus Japanese *kofun* is a "burial mound," but the morbid meaning is magically transformed to "(sexual) excitement" by extending the vowel /ko•fun/. Consonant length may also serve to define different meanings in many languages, again including Japanese. Thus *sato* is a "village," while *satto* is "suddenly."

Moving into Alien Phonemic Systems

When we learn another language we must learn to make the same kinds of distinction made by the native speakers of that language. To speak Korean intelligibly we must learn to distinguish degrees of aspiration, for instance; for Hawaiian we must distinguish long and short vowels and attend to glottal stops. If we are alert to the kinds of distinction that must be made it is usually possible for us to learn them. The other side of the coin, which may not be so critical, is to *not* hear the distinctions that may be important in our own languages. Thus if we are studying Korean, we should learn that the voicing we hear for one series of stops between vowels is irrelevant. That is, the lightly aspirated stops in initial position are typically voiced intervocally. Since this voicing is not relevant for Koreans, if they learn Japanese, they often voice the unvoiced stops between vowels. Japanese *otoko* "a male human" may become *odoko* or *odogo*. In Japanese the difference between an [l] and an [r], which in Japanese is usually a flap, similar to a short [r] in some varieties of Spanish, is irrelevant. So when Japanese are speaking English they are likely to have difficulty tuning in to the difference between the two sounds, a difference that has now become important. Of course Americans usually fail to tune in quickly to vowel and consonant length, which are critical in Japanese, or to differences in rounding vowels, such as [ü] or [ö] in German.

SUPRASEGMENTAL PHONEMES

Thus far we have been discussing only *segmental* phonemes, those which we represent by various letters: consonants, vowels, and semivowels. We describe phonemes as the *minimal significant units of sound* in a language, since they define meanings even though they lack meanings themselves. That is, neither a /p/ nor a /b/ has any meaning, it matters which one we use in a given instance. But there are other kinds of phoneme, some of which are indicated in our punctuation and some of which we do not mark in writing. For English, these *suprasegmental* phonemes, which are in a sense superimposed on the segmentals, include *stress, intonation,* and *juncture.* And, as in the case of the segmental phonemes, the suprasegmentals must be established through contrastive analysis, the discovery of minimal pairs.

Stress

For many of us the following constitute minimal pairs for the placing of stress, which refers to the relative loudness of different syllables (in other languages relative loudness is not relevant, though degrees of highness, or pitch, may serve the same function—Japanese, for example):

1. transport   /trǽnspɔrt/   /trænspɔ́rt/
2. import   /ǐmpɔ́rt/   /impɔ́rt/
3. transfer   /trǽnsfɨr/   /trænsfɨ́r/
4. increase   /ǐŋkriys/   /iŋkríys/

In all four cases the shifting of the primary stress from the first syllable to the second shifts the meaning from that of a noun to that of a verb. This is sufficient evidence to establish stress as phonemic in English. It is difficult to identify minimal pairs which will demonstrate that there are more than two degrees of phonemic stress in English, but most linguists feel there are at least three degrees, and many feel there are four degrees of stress in the pattern for English phrases. The subject is too complex for a detailed discussion here, but we may note that the syllable carrying the highest or primary stress in a word may lose it if the word occurs in a phrase. Thus stress cannot be dealt with only in terms of single words. The authoritative treatment of this and other aspects of sound patterning in English is by Chomsky and Halle (1968), *The Sound Pattern of English.*

Nucleus and Intonation

We have what we can think of as normal stress patterns in English. Paul Roberts (1967) says that in English, a kernel sentence is made up of a nucleus and an intonation. The nucleus is represented by a word or several words, while the intonation is a combination of stress (loudness) and pitch (the high or low quality that depends on the speed of vibrations with which sounds are uttered). Any kernel sentence has a syllable that carries the main stress. More often than not, this stress falls on or within the last word in the sentence:

I bought a new *book.*

This carries no special implications; it is simply a casual sentence, which does not suggest a particular context. But if we shift the stress pattern, we change the meaning: we are answering different questions.

I bought a new book

tells us who bought it.

I *bought* a new book

implies the question of how I acquired it.

I bought *a* new book

emphasizes the question of number.

I bought a *new* book

suggests that there was some doubt about whether the book was new or used.

And if the *book* is given greater than normal stress the doubt is removed from the question of what was acquired.

Joe Pierce (1966) insists that overstress is not phonemic, serving only to call attention to that segment of the utterance; the fact that overstress alters the meaning (in that the utterance thereby answers different questions) would seem to indicate that it is, indeed, phonemic.

Pierce also suggests that because stress and pitch are so closely related, there are two "intensity" phonemes, rather than stress or pitch. The first is a phonemic stress-pitch and the second is a sentence stress-pitch. We need not choose sides here, but the argument depends in part on the claim that stress does not show up on the sound spectrograph even if it is "heard." Whatever the final decision may be so far as English phonemes are concerned, it is difficult to accept the idea that stress is altogether illusory: American students of Japanese, for example, have to learn to avoid applying stress in Japanese, which relies on pitch accent. Americans must learn to make the right syllables higher in pitch without at the same time making those syllables louder.

We have already shown that stress is phonemic in English (because shifting the stress results in different meanings), but so too is intonation. If, for example, we ask "Where?" with a rising intonation, we are asking to have the statement repeated, as if we did not hear it clearly or cannot believe the answer. But if "Where?" has a falling intonation, it means we want more detailed information. Suppose A says "I'm going shopping," and B asks where with a falling intonation: the name of a specific store would be an appropriate answer. But if a rising intonation were used, then a repeat of "I'm going shopping" would be the appropriate answer.

While intonation contours are thus phonemic in English, our use of them is relatively limited. In Mandarin Chinese, where theoretically every syllable has a characteristic tone (though in practice it works a little like our nuclei—a polymorphemic string will usually have a single syllable that predominates) the problem is more complex. As Robins (1964) describes the phenomenon, "The pitch levels or the rising and falling pitches are properties of the words as lexical items; the substitution of a different word in a sentence may change the pitch sequence, if the two words concerned are different in tonal composition" [p. 112]. As an example, the sequence [ta] in Mandarin may represent four different words, depending on its tone: "to raise" (level tone), "to penetrate" (rising tone), "to hit" (rising-falling tone), or "great" (falling tone). The local dialect of Hong Kong is more complicated yet, having three tones in each of two registers (high and low).

Juncture

A moment ago we mentioned that not only stress and pitch, but also the intonation contour are phonemic in English. The intonation contour, however, is a combination of pitch and *juncture*, and at least one kind of juncture is phonemic and is not confounded by the question of pitch. This is the kind of pause that distinguishes "night rate" from "nitrate." The junctures are transitions that have a great deal to do with the rhythm of the language and its overall sound. Many speakers of Cantonese, for instance, have a distinctly choppy sound when they tackle English, partly because they introduce too many *open* (or internal) transitions of the sort that separates the "night" and the "rate" mentioned above. Some Spanish speakers, on the other hand, ignore certain open transition in English, or else shift them: instead of saying an + ashtray, they may produce a+ nashtray. We tend to think generally that the open transitions separate the words of an utterance (Sawyer & Silver, 1960), but this does not work out quite so neatly. In the sentence "Here it is," for example, the open transition /+/ divides the vowel and the consonant of "it." (See also the sample transcription in Table 5-1.)

We distinguish three other kinds of juncture in English. There is a rising juncture, represented by a double bar / ‖ / which usually comes at the end of a yes-no question ("Is he coming?"). One of the characteristics of many English speakers in Hawaii (and in some varieties in England) is that a falling juncture is used in this type of question. The falling, or terminal juncture, represented by a double cross /#/, marks the end of most of our sentences. Finally, there is a level juncture, marked by a single bar / | /, which is characteristically indicated by a comma when we write.

Variance Analysis

The foregoing discussion of phonemes that are based on contrastive analysis implies too tidy a system. It is true that we have had to note from time to time that pronunciations may vary from one dialect area to another, or that not all of us display exactly the same phonemic system. Some of us, for instance, distinguish the sounds of "caught" and "cot," while for others there is no /ɔ/, and both words are pronounced "cot" /kat/. Further, we all show some variation that depends on how informally we are speaking. Thus final [-ŋ] tends to disappear in favor of [-ŋ], a fact represented in our popular spelling convention where by "something" becomes "somethin' " or "walking" becomes "walkin'." Indeed, the actual pronunciation of "something" in rapid casual speech is likely to be [sə́mpm], where the [m] represents a syllabic consonant.

Most such variations can be accounted for on the basis of phonological processes that offer little in the way of mystery to the journeyman linguist. In other cases the variation is more troublesome. In New York City it is possible to establish /æ/ (as in "bad," "ask," and so forth in most American dialects) as a phoneme through contrastive analysis based on particularly careful speech, but in casual speech the values cover a range of sounds as high as in the NYC pronunciation of "beer" on the one hand and as low and central as the NYC pronunciation of "dock" or "doll," on the other hand. There is similar variation with other vowels, while the initial consonants of "thing" and "then" may have the usual fricative values, stop values, or affricate values; and preconsonantal and final /r/ may or may not be present. In all of these cases there are social class and ethnic group differences, but the main point is that for most speakers there is a variation in accordance with casual versus careful speech. It is the former, according to Labov (1966), which is closest to the speech pattern acquired in the formative, preadolescent years. This is the pattern that is particularly important for the linguistic structure of the speech community and the source of linguistic change. The sort of picture that develops from contrastive analysis emerges in later years and is less fundamental, in that it is superimposed and often imperfectly learned.

In effect, Labov proposed that we need a kind of calculus to deal with phonemic systems of casual speech wherever there is a wide range of stylistic and social variation. The calculus may not be in our future, in part because the notation is likely to be awkward, in part because the conventional phonemic representation serves well if augmented by such phonological comments as may be necessary in a given case, and in part because the phoneme as such excites much less interest than it once did. For many technical purposes a phonetic treatment, especially of the distinctive feature variety that developed from a concern with generative phonology, is considered adequate and appropriate by many linguists. But the emphasis on variation that Labov has so effectively called to our attention seems to have become fixed in the thinking of many linguists today. (Labov was not the only linguist concerned with variation a generation ago, of course, but he has been particularly influential. Other important figures are mentioned in the discussion of sociolinguistics.)

SYSTEMATIC PHONEMICS

The kind of phonemes established traditionally through contrastive analysis, as discussed above, are called *autonomous* phonemes, but in the view of generative phonologists, having autonomous phonemes simply adds unnecessarily to the description of language. Yet, as Lehmann (1976) notes, "dismissing an autonomous phonemic representation leads to exceedingly complex representations of phonology" (p. 217). At the moment, it looks as though one's objective should determine which approach to use. For our purpose, autonomous phonemes are quite convenient, no matter how faulty for other purposes. Since the approach of the generative phonologists, relying on systematic phonemics, is becoming increasingly popular for technical purposes, it is necessary to at least give some idea of what that approach is.

We have seen that a phonemic script ignores the predictable features of phonemes—more correctly, as we shall see, it ignores certain predictable features. Thus for English we need not specify that a /p/ is sometimes aspirated and sometimes it is not aspirated, because it always aspirated in initial position and never after a fricative. (Here we need not concern ourselves with other environments to develop a more elegant statement.) Our earlier discussion lacked any hint that the fricative, /s/, for example, needed the kind of qualification offered for the unvoiced stops that may follow them. Yet the /s/ of "sea" is different from the /s/ of "ski," and the predictable features of the /p/ actually include more than aspiration.

To back up for a moment, generative phonology has its point of departure in *The Sound Pattern of English*, by Noam Chomsky and Morris Halle (1967), where our significant speech sounds are analysed in terms of distinctive features that include a much greater inventory than we dealt with earlier. The objective is to mark every feature that must be marked to identify accurately each phoneme but to exclude all of the predictable features.

To borrow an example from Falk (1978), a full description of the [p] of "pea" would involve sixteen features, ten of which are unnecessary or redundant. Thus we need not indicate that it is [- round] (i.e., unrounded), [- back], [- low], and so forth, but there are six features that must be specified if the [p] is to be unmistakably identified and not mistaken for some other sound segment such as [t], [m], or [s]. With the specification of six features, however, the [p] is distinguished from every other segment in English. These may be listed in square brackets as follows:

$$\begin{bmatrix} - \text{ vocalic} \\ + \text{ consonantal} \\ + \text{ abrupt release} \\ - \text{ voice} \\ + \text{ anterior} \\ - \text{ coronal} \end{bmatrix}$$

If we know that the sound in question is not vocalic but that it is consonantal, it cannot be a vowel, liquid, or glide. The specification of abrupt release eliminates the fricatives and affricates, while the lack of voice indicates that the segment is neither a nasal nor a voiced stop. To indicate that the segment is a front (anterior) sound rules out the possibility of a [k], while the minus coronal eliminates [t], in which the blade of the tongue is elevated above its pre-speech position.

In the previously mentioned case of "sea" and "ski," again drawing on Falk (1978, which is recommended for a more detailed yet clear discussion), the same phonetic sound [s] occurs in both words, but the two examples of /s/ differ at the phonemic level. The difference is not indicated in traditional phonemics, but is clear in the systematic phonemics. Thus in order for the sequence "sea" to be distinguished from all other similar sequences, such as "tea," "me," "lea," and so forth, six features must be specified:

$$
\begin{bmatrix}
- \text{ vocalic} \\
+ \text{ consonantal} \\
- \text{ voice} \\
+ \text{ strident} \\
+ \text{ anterior} \\
+ \text{ coronal}
\end{bmatrix}
$$

The fact that it is minus vocalic eliminates the vowels, the [l] and the [r]; there is an obstruction of the air stream in the oral cavity (plus consonantal); the sound is unvoiced; to say that it is plus strident means there is audible friction; again, it is a front sound (plus anterior); and it is coronal, since the blade is elevated above the pre-speech position.

But for the initial sound of "ski," we need only specify that it is [− vocalic] because in English if there is an initial sequence of two consonants and the second is [− continuant], the first has to be [s]. In English we simply do not have such initial consonant clusters as [mp], [bd] and so forth.

A final note about generative phonology serves as a convenient transition to the next chapter, which is concerned with the sequencing of significant sounds, traditionally called morphology and syntax.

Some generative phonologists reject the phonemic level altogether, feeling it to be too close to the phonetic ground, insufficiently abstract. Schane (1973), for example, concedes that in many cases the systematic phonemic representations will equate to autonomous or taxonomic phonemic representations, but notes that, for example, some occurrence of the [s] sound in "electricity" are derived from [k], as in "electric." The traditional approach to phonemics, Schane feels, cannot deal with this sort of problem. (There are, however, ways of dealing with such problems more generally, usually in terms of alternate realizations of more abstract events—that is, in terms of allomorphs, which we shall take up in the next chapter.)

Another aspect of generative phonology is its concern with "naturalness." This is a probabilistic approach, in which some features of phonology are more predictable than others because they are more widely found among the languages of the world. Thus among the languages that only distinguish three vowels, the combination of [i], [a] and [u] is more "natural" than the combination of (for example) [i], [o] and [œ] (which is about the same as [o] except that the lips are rounded), because the former is more likely to occur than the latter (Schane, 1973).

REFERENCES

Carroll, J.B. *Language and thought*. Englewood Cliffs, N.J.: Prentice-Hall, Inc., 1964.

Chao, Y.R. *Language and symbolic systems*. London: Cambridge University Press, 1968.

Chomsky, N., & Halle, M. *The sound pattern of English*. New York: Harper and Row, 1968.

Falk, J. *Linguistics and language: A survey of basic concepts and implications*. (2nd ed.) New York: John Wiley & Sons, 1978.

Fromkin, V., & Rodman, R. *An introduction to language*. (2nd ed.) New York: Holt, Rinehart & Winston, 1978.

Gudschinsky, S.C. *How to learn an unwritten language*. New York: Holt, Rinehart & Winston, 1967.

Hirsh, I.J. Audition in relation to perception of speech. In E.C. Carterette (Ed.), *Brain Function*. (Vol. III) *Speech, language, and communication*, 93-116. Berkeley, CA: University of California Press, 1966.

Labov, W. *The social stratification of English in New York City*. Washington, D.C.: Center for Applied Linguistics, 1966.

Ladefoged, P. *A course in phonetics*. New York: Harcourt Brace Jovanovich, 1975.

Lehmann, W.P. *Descriptive linguistics*. (2nd ed.). New York: Random House, 1976.

Pierce, J. The supra-segmental phonemes of English. *Linguistics*, 1966, *21*, 54-70.

Roberts, P. *Modern grammar*. New York: Harcourt Brace & World, 1967.

Robins, R.B. *General linguistics: An introductory survey*. London: Longmans, Green & Co., 1964.

Schane, S.A. *Generative phonology*. Englewood Cliffs, N.J.: Prentice-Hall, Inc., 1973.

Smalley, W.A. *Manual of articulatory phonetics*. (Rev. ed.) South Pasadena, CA: William Carey Library, 1973.

Chapter 6

THE THEORY OF LANGUAGE:
SEQUENCES

While the traditional concept of the phoneme seems no longer to serve the interests of some linguists, historically the development of the concept was an important breakthrough in linguistic analysis. In some ways, perhaps, the development was too successful: the differences between phonemes could be demonstrated fairly neatly and the same methodological approach could be applied to the smallest meaningful segments, *morphemes*, and longer stretches could be built up from morphemes.

But the striking success attained with phonemes tended to focus attention on that relatively low level of analysis to the virtual exclusion of other aspects of language, in particular syntax and semantics. This limitation was enhanced by the very useful work of missionaries, who were primarily concerned to translate the Christian bible into languages that hitherto had been without a script. Since the targets of this enterprise already knew their languages, the main job of the missionary-linguist was to identify and label phonemes. For various reasons, then, phonemes were the first order of business, and all too often the researcher ran out of gas, as it were, before reaching the syntactic level. As Bolinger (1968) put it:

> What had started as a combination of practical necessity and historical accident was thus elevated to a theoretical precept: "Do not

attempt to deal with syntax before morphology, nor with morphology before phonology; to do so is to *mix levels*." Since the units of each lower level were the components of the units at the next higher one, it was impossible to move up until the proper foundation had been laid. [pp. 193-194]

We have probably implied that the identification of phonemes and morphemes is much simpler than it really is, but once the actual complexity of the task is appreciated, it is also easier to appreciate why so few attempts were made to deal seriously with syntax. And we should not be deceived into underestimating the task by anecdotes such as that offered by Chao (1968) about Edward Sapir, "who on our first meeting learned in little more than an hour not only the main phonemics of my native dialect Changchow, Kiangsu, but also what to say and when, and what expressive intonation to use" [p. vi]. Very likely Sapir, a leading linguist of his day, knew exactly what questions to ask, while Chao was able to respond immediately and knowledgeably. This is rather a different situation from that of an inexperienced linguist, uncertain of what he can expect, who is dealing with individuals who would not understand economical questions.

MORPHEMES

If we examine a corpus, or body, of material—a novel, for example—we will notice that it contains recurring partial similarities. The smallest units that occur in this way are of course letters and punctuation marks, but having established that these are simply derived from phonemes, we may consider larger segments. We may see, for example, strings such as "word," "words," "wordy," or "wood," "woods," "woody," and so forth. These six strings have four components: "word" and "wood," which may appear as independent units, and –s and –y, which appear only at the end of a string, so far as we can tell from these examples. We would have to modify the general statement as new evidence came into the picture, as the –sy in "the park has a *woodsy* feeling about it even though there are few trees in it." We can say, though, that both are *suffixes*, added on to independent units, and that if both occur, then the –y will follow the –s: sud*sy*, to give another example (though the singular no longer occurs).

Unlike the phoneme, which is the smallest *significant* unit of sound in a language but does not of itself have any meaning, the morpheme does have meaning. The minimal meaningful units that can stand alone are often called "free" morphemes, while those that consist of prefixes, infixes or suffixes, or are otherwise dependent on free morphemes, are called "bound" morphemes. Thus "wood" and "word" are free morphemes; the –s (meaning "plural") and the –y (meaning "like") are bound morphemes. The "sud–" was once a free morpheme, but no longer occurs alone, so we may say that it also has become a bound morpheme. Of course nouns are not the only free morphemes: the sentence "You may want to burn this book" consists only of free morphemes (leaving aside the question of tense markers, which are also morphemes).

Allomorphs

Just as a phoneme represents various allophones, many morphemes have allomorphic variants. In the case of the plural, for instance, we may note that typically there is an [s] sound after unvoiced consonants (excluding some fricatives). Thus we get [s] after the [t] in "cat," or after the fricative [f] in "cliff," but after the fricative [s] of "bus" or the [š] of "bush" we get [əz] or [ɨz]. The same central vowel(s) + [–z] also follows some affricates (which, it may be recalled, have fricatives as their second component). So "church" (which may be represented as /tšərtš/ or /čərč/, depending on the system of notation) has the plural form /čərčɨz/. Elsewhere the regular plural is just the [–z] sound, without the preceding vowel.

But this only accounts for the majority of noun plurals in English. There is also a zero allomorph of the plural, as in "sheep" or "deer," and there is another allomorph that depends upon an internal vowel change, as in "man–men" or "louse-lice." There are also a few nouns that form the plural with –en, as in "oxen," or –a, as in "datum–data," or –i, as "cactus-cacti."

The study of morphemics can seem formidable when we consider all the problems with nouns—singular versus plural, mass nouns (like "flour") versus count nouns (like "flower")—or morphemes that make nouns into other forms, such as adjectivals—book*ish*—or adverbials—moment*arily*—and so forth; other parts of speech add further complexities. Verbs are marked for tense in various ways (note the suffix to form the past of "walk," the vowel change for "wake," or the use of suppletion for "go"); verbs can function as nouns, as "*Running* is healthy" or as adjectives, as "The *running* man disappeared around the corner."

Some morphemic problems may not even come into focus until syntactic problems are tackled. In English, for example, we have many two-part verbs, but these are not obvious until we see how the parts can be juggled. The combination of "turn" plus "off" may either be a verb plus preposition (Turn off the road) or a two–part verb in which the "off" is a particle (Turn off the audience). In this case we can tell which is which by substituting "it" for the noun. Thus we can turn off the road, and may have to turn off it if we come to a detour. But we cannot turn the road off, though we can easily turn an audience off—we can turn it off with no difficulty at all, but there is no way we can turn off it. In other words, the permissible positions of "it" as well as the noun phrase distinguish the two kinds of verb.

SYNTAX

Until 1957 most linguistic analysis was focused on relatively low–order events such as phonemes and morphemes at the expense of syntax. Where the sentence was attacked the approach was rather like traditional parsing to determine its grammatical parts. The most popular method, perhaps, was called *immediate constituent analysis*, in which a sentence would first be divided into its two basic parts (which we may here identify in traditional terms as subject and predicate); then each half would be divided, and then each quarter, and so forth, until (at the level of the morpheme) all meaningful elements had been identified and explained in terms of the others. Even traditional parsing reveals a great deal about how the language works, of course, and with the greater sophistication of contemporary linguists who largely learned to avoid dealing with parts of speech in semantic terms—"a noun is a person, place or thing," for example—and relied on function to deal with such concepts, much progress was made during the second quarter of this century.

Still, it seemed as though a point of diminishing returns had been reached and there were problems that immediate constituent analysis seemed flatly incapable of dealing with: notably, ambiguous sentences and passive constructions. Langacker (1968) offers the example of "Steve or Sam and Bob will come" (p. 99). The immediate constituents are (1) Steve or Sam and Bob (2) will come. But we cannot know how to subdivide the first part of this to see which parts belong together in contrast to the other parts. If Bob is coming for sure, then Steve and Sam will consitute a unit. (Bob will come; either Steve or Sam will also come.) But it may be that Sam and Bob will come, but if they do not, then Steve will come. Immediate constituent analysis does not tell us how to group the three males. Another sentence, "Visiting relatives can be a nuisance," has become famous because Chomsky liked to use it as an example of an ambiguous sentence. In this case we do not know whether the speaker finds it troublesome to visit his/her relatives or is irked when they come to visit him/her.

We must assume that the speaker has one possibility or the other in mind—as, to paraphrase, "I hate to go to visit my relatives (but I do not mind if they come to visit me)." Of course we may in speaking have a double meaning in mind, and comedians rely on them often for humorous effect when the audience finally realizes it has been had.

The other main problem with immediate constituent analysis, passives, will be touched on a little later.

From Meaning to Utterance

We do not simply open our mouths and speak "from left to right" in a linear fashion. As in the examples given above, we have something in mind.

It is very difficult to trace the processes that lead to spontaneous utterances (that is, speech that has not been deliberately and carefully constructed). We know that there are a lot of decisions that have to be made—whether to speak or not, which language to use (if we have a choice), and the general level of formality; probably most of these are controlled by a general psychological set. Next, there is probably a concept of some sort that must be programmed into an utterance, and this is where the question of grammar enters consideration. Again there are decisions to be made: whether to make a statement or pose a question; whether to use an affirmative or negative construction, or even a negative–interrogative construction; whether to make the utterance active or passive, and so forth.

Case Grammar

Some sense of the possibilities for converting a concept into an utterance are well displayed by what Charles Fillmore (1968) has called "cage grammar," which depends on meaning-relations. Thus there are various possible descriptions for any given event. If "John opened the door with the key," for instance, the subject position is occupied by the actor or *agent* (John); if "the key opened the door," the subject slot is filled by the *instrument* by which the action was performed (the key); and if "the door opened," the subject slot is filled by the *goal* of the action (the door). As Crystal (1971, p. 237) puts it, "the function of the underlying meanings in relation to the verb does not change from sentence to sentence, despite the surface differences; and it is this fundamental, semantic identity which is the important thing to recognize about these sentences, and the central fact which a system of grammatical analysis should explain."

It is likely that the interpretative process will prove easier to demonstrate than the production process. Lakoff and Thompson (1975), for example, have discussed the idea of a "recognition grammar," which is to some extent indebted to natural recognition grammars for use with computers. While the speaker begins with a concept that must be encoded into linguistic form, the decoding process involves hypotheses about grammatical relations of elements in the surface utterance. But these hypotheses may have to be revised as more information is received—a problem that the speaker does not have. Consider, for example, the sentence

The aardvark was given a bagel by Irving.

Lakoff and Thompson (1975) suggest that in processing this sentence "we first hypothesize that the noun phrase *the aardvark* is the underlying subject. After encountering a verb in participle form with the auxiliary *be*, however, we change that hypothesis and consider it to be the direct object. Finally, on encountering another noun phrase, *a bagel*, we reconsider once more and decide that *the aardvark* is really the indirect object, and that *a bagel* is the direct object.

"Hopefully even this rough description demonstrates the possibility of a relationship between this sort of processing grammar and relational grammar rules; we have first said 'subject goes to object', and then 'object goes to indirect object', which are inverse analogues of the relational grammar rules of passive and dative respectively." (p. 297)

We have taken rather a long approach to the subject of deep and surface structure to indicate that there is a kind of *terra incognita* before we reach the more solid ground with which the linguist customarily works.

Before 1957 we may say that immediate constituent analysis and other approaches worked essentially with what is now popularly known as the *surface structure* of language. This is not exactly the same as the utterance we hear, since it is not concerned with the fine points of the precise realization of that structure. That is, the surface structure is a step removed from the actual verbal productions. *Morphophonemic* rules are required to convert strings of morphemes into strings of phonemes (as the term implies). Thus the plural morpheme will be in the surface structure, but the morphophonemic rules yield an /s/ sound in some cases, a /z/ sound in other cases, and no sound at all in words such as "sheep."

As we have seen, there are some problems that immediate constituent analysis could not handle. Then, in 1957 Noam Chomsky published his landmark *Syntactic Structures* in which he drew attention away from the surface forms of utterances to a more abstract level. At first he proposed that there are basic "kernel" sentences which are expanded and transformed through various rules that eventually generate the sentences that we hear and speak. Whatever the psychological reality of the kernel sentences, the new approach provided a more powerful descriptive model of language. The model was refined in another landmark publication, *Aspects of a Theory of Syntax* (Chomsky, 1965), with a distinction being drawn between deep and surface structure. Description in this system begins with the sentence (S), which is then rewritten as Noun Phrase plus Verb Phrase (NP VP); each of these is then rewritten in terms of more specific constituents. Thus, for example,

NP → (Det) N

means that the noun phrase consists of a determiner plus a noun; the arrow is read "is rewritten" and the parentheses indicate an optional feature. Thus a noun phrase must contain a noun, but may or may not contain a determiner, such as "the, a, an, some, etc." Rules of this sort are called *phrase structure rules* and can be represented through tree diagrams (as will be demonstrated later).

Application of the phrase structure rules yields the deep structure, but to get to the surface structure—the final arrangement of the major constituents of the sentence—it is necessary to apply *transformational rules*. In the sentence "He is big," a phrase structure rule tells us that the NP is rewritten "He," and another phrase structure rule tells us that VP is expanded to read "is big." If we would make the sentence into a question we need a transformational rule to bring the verb to the initial position: "Is he big?" The theory of language (grammar) promoted by Chomsky is currently known as transformational-generative grammar (TGG). Such grammars do not depend upon a fixed corpus; rather, they aim to design rules that will generate all of the grammatical utterances of a language while generating no nongrammatical utterances. The grammar deals with what is called *linguistic competence*, what one must know in order to produce and understand utterances. *Linguistic performances* are often flawed with false starts or other errors, but our underlying competence permits us to edit out the errors much of the time, so that if we are absorbed in the content of the discourse we may not even be aware of the miscues.

Typically, the transformationalist begins with the abstract concept of the sentence and applies successive phrase structure rules, as mentioned above. Over the years the exact notation and preference for ways of handling particular problems have changed and differences may be found among the presentations of different grammarians, but the following tree diagram will serve to show the grouping of constituents that results from the application of phrase structure rules for a fairly simple sentence:

NP	Det	N	A	slugger
S	AUX	can		
V	hit			
VP	NP	Det	the	
N	ball			
PP	Prep	over		
NP	Det	the	N	fence

Thus the notion of sentence (S) is expanded to consist of a noun phrase (NP), an auxiliary (AUX, which carries the tense marker), and a verb phrase (VP). The NP in turn is expanded to Determiner (Det) plus noun (N); the verb phrase is expanded to include a verb (V), noun phrase (NP) and a prepositional phrase (PP). The second noun phrase again consists of a determiner and a noun, while the prepositional phrase contains a preposition (Prep) and yet another noun phrase. Finally, the notation is converted to specific lexical choices.

In the example just given no transformations are needed to arrive at the surface structure. Akmajian, Demers, and Harnish (1979) provide a useful illustration of the Particle Movement Transformation to show the alternate ways two–part verbs can be handled. The transformation itself is informally stated in terms of a verb-particle construction:

> Given a verb–particle construction, the particle may be shifted away from the verb, and moved to the immediate right of the object noun phrase. [p. 158]

To illustrate the transformation concept, they use two related sentences. (1) Mary stood up her date, which is taken to be the base form, presumably because the verb and the particle occur contiguously. (2) Mary stood her date up, in which the particle has been moved away from the verb and to the right of the object noun phrase (her date).

The VP of the first may be diagrammed

VP

V   NP

Verb   Particle

stood   up   her date

After applying the transformation, the diagram becomes

VP

V   NP   Particle

stood   her date   up

Akmajian, Demers, and Harnish simplified their tree diagram to focus more clearly on the particle movement, but a detailed representation would have shown AUX as a constituent independent of the verb. Here it would consist only of the tense (past) and the V would have been represented in the form "stand." In the earlier tree diagram of "A slugger can hit the ball over the fence," the auxiliary is shown as an independent constituent, but it actually consists of the tense (present) plus the model (can); if it had been past, final form of the sentence would have been "A slugger could hit the ball over the fence."

As mentioned earlier, one of the major shortcomings of the older immediate constituent analysis was its inability to deal satisfactorily with passive constructions. Chomsky's (1957) solution was to posit an active counterpart for every passive and derive the passive from the active. Thus *the man past eat the food* would become *the food past be en eat by the man*. The passive transformation was characterized by the inclusion of *be + en* and *by*. A morphophonemic rule ensured that *past be* would be realized as "was," and an affix transformation shifted *en* to *eat*, yielding "eaten." The *en* is just the notation used to represent the past participle, and the final form of the participle is subject to a morphophonemic rule that depends on the particular verb to which the participle is finally attached. Thus the *en* takes the form *ed* in "The barn was painted by the farmer."

Perhaps the notation *past be en eat* for "was eaten" or *he past have en be ing go* for "He had been going" looks quite alien, but since the *be* and *ing* or the *have* and *en* belong together no matter what the verb (as "eat" versus "paint" in the passive example), it is very economical to keep them together until the last step in the generation of the surface structure.

SOME CURRENT CONCERNS

Chomsky's impact on contemporary linguistics has been monumental and continues, but even in the early 1960s there was interest in getting more into the semantic area than Chomsky had provided for. In 1963 Katz and Fodor offered a semantic component for transformational–generative grammar; this led to the development of interpretive semantics (discussed below). We have already noted Fillmore's case grammar (1968, with an elaboration in 1977), and the semantic nature of the processing grammar mentioned by Lakoff and Thompson (1975) should be apparent.

Efforts to deal with semantics accounts for much of the diversity in present linguistic theory. As early as 1968, for example, James McCawley doubted that in the quest to join semantic and phonological interpretations there was really a need to posit deep structure as a separate level. Chomsky (1972) argued strongly that deep structure should not be dropped or by-passed, but the question still has not been completely resolved. The term *interpretive semantics*—also known as the standard theory, then the extended standard theory, and more recently the revised extended standard theory—described the conceptual framework by which semantic rules provide for the meaning of the sentence by relying on its structure and lexical composition for interpretation (Falk, 1978). Thus the arrangement of components defines the meaning in "Joe bit the dog" versus "The dog bit Joe," but the standard theory holds that semantic interpretation takes place at the deep structure level. Problems with this led to the extended standard theory, which tries to establish semantic interpretation rules to apply to both deep and surface structures. And the revised extended standard theory posits semantic interpretation at the surface structure level.

Generative semantics, which would account for meaning directly rather than through syntactic structure, enjoyed a brief efflorescence in the early 1970s but has faded, perhaps because it was weak in relating semantic deep structures to syntactic structures, while interpretive semantics does not "provide a sufficiently formal account of the rules of semantic interpretation and the principles by means of which the theory incorporates information about presupposition, elocutionary force, and semantic relations." [Falk, 1978, p. 269]

Relational Grammar

One of the many present approaches to syntax, "most of which have not been shown to be superior to, or even distinct from, the others" within the broad framework of transformational generative grammar (Moravcsik, 1980, p. 1) is relational grammar (RG). But while "the direction of current syntactic research is unarguably toward nonabstract syntax, direct generation of surface strings, and interpretive semantics," RG is exceptional in being "more abstract than any of its predecessors or contemporaries" (Stockwell, 1980, p. 380). One reason for this more abstract tendency on the part of RG may be the effort of its proponents to take into consideration a wider variety of languages. In a recent technical presentation, one of the founders of RG, David M. Perlmutter (1980), offers examples from English, Russian, Italian, Indonesian, German, Swahili, and cites several others, including Georgian, Japanese, Kannada, Udi, Tzotzil, and Southern Tiwa. Relational grammar itself is based on the idea that a sentence consists of a verb and one or more noun phrases that bear some relation to it. That is, subject, direct object, and other relations are taken as basic to the description of language. A hierarchical relationship is seen to obtain among *terms* (subject, direct object, indirect object, which are ranked in the order given) which take precedence over *nonterms* that indicate other relations, such as means, location, and the like. Crane, Yeager, and Whitman illustrate the point with the passive sentence "The ball was hit by John," where the

NP *the ball* is "promoted along the relational hierarchy from direct object to subject. This aspect of the passive transformation is assumed to hold for all languages, but the grammar of each particular language must include other idiosyncratic details." [1981, p. 148]

We may say that today there is a relatively greater concern with trying to develop theoretical statements that will serve as universals, applicable to all languages. The goal seems to have been clear enough during the development of transformational-generative grammar under Chomsky's direct leadership, but most of the actual discussion was in terms of English and therefore limiting.

For most of us who need to have a practical knowledge of linguistics, as against being primarily concerned with the theory of grammar, it is likely that some modification of transformational–generative grammar will suffice for the immediate future at least—until one of the schools emerges with not only a good following among the theoreticians but with a presentation that will appeal to the marginal linguists who want to apply the theory to language for purposes that are not primarily linguistic. That is, a theory that can be readily used by psychologists concerned with first–language learning, or sociologists who are concerned with social relationships, or others seeking practical applications.

For the remainder of the chapter we shall deal with some areas that are providing a common vocabulary to the language area and some broader concerns of communication.

Pragmatics

In philosophy pragmatics has been described as one aspect of semiotics, or the theory of signs, along with syntactics and semantics, following Charles Sanders Peirce (Lehmann, 1976). Syntactics concerns the relationships among signs, as the green, yellow, and red of traffic light systems; semantics concerns the relationships between signs and outside events, as the fact that the red light denotes "stop," while pragmatics concerns the relationship between signs and behavior, as when driver stops on a red signal. These meanings are general enough to include the more specialized concerns of most language theorists, but perhaps the philosophical influence of greatest current importance concerns pragmatics, where the context of an utterance indicates meaning beyond its formal structure. Thus "Would you mind closing the door?" may in some contexts constitute, in effect, an imperative meaning even though it is structurally quite different from "Close the door!" Such considerations are important for understanding "speech acts" (Searle, 1969; see also Austin, 1962). Several useful concepts have emerged under these influences. One is that of *illocutionary force*, which refers to a speaker's intention, and not to the tightly defined linguistic meaning of the utterance. Different sorts of illocutionary verbs can be identified. Thus *verdictives* would include "acquit," "convict," "estimate," and "characterize," where a verdict is rendered; *exercitives* indicate decisions, such as "nominate," or "recommend"; *commissives* commit the speaker to a course of action, as "agree" or "promise" (Lehmann, 1976), and others could be identified as well. It is not obvious, however, that such labels define mutually exclusive categories. Further, many constitute *performatives*, verbs which actually constitute part of the action: "I promise to mend my ways," for instance, is a sentence, but it is also the act of promising. Similarly, "I now pronounce you man and wife," if spoken under the proper circumstances by someone with the proper authority, constitues part of the legal act of joining a couple in wedlock.

CONVERSATIONAL ANALYSIS

After the great steps had been taken in the development of transformational-generative grammar, marked in the main by the appearance of Chomsky's *Aspects of the Theory of Syntax* in 1965, one line of intensified inquiry was in the direction of phonology, particularly as inspired by the generative phonology based in Chomsky and Halle's *The Sound Pattern of English* in 1962; another line focused more on the semantic aspects of language; and yet another line that has been drawing increasing attention is *discourse analysis*. The heading above, "Conversational Analysis," represents a concession to John Hinds (1975), who argues that any kind of discourse can be considered a specific type of conversation. It seems worth making the concession because "conversation" implies a grander scope than the kinds of study which are usually described as discourse analysis at present. That is, the concern with discourse goes beyond the traditional concern with the sentence, and it is likely that the trend will continue as more and more is learned about relatively short discourses.

Presuppositions

One of the relatively simple demonstrations of the way utterances in normal discourse depend on events outside given sentences is in the information and understandings shared with the listener. Compare "I found a book" with "I found the book." The second sentence implies that the listener knows which particular book is at issue; the first sentence, if it initiates a conversation, is likely to elicit a raised eyebrow from an acquaintance and perhaps startled withdrawal from a stranger. The acquaintance can expect the speaker to fill in the context, while the stranger may suspect he has been approached by an eccentric—that would be an odd way to strike up a conversation. Even if the speaker suspects the stranger of having dropped the book (note that it is now *the* book because we have provided the context for it), it would be more in line with our customary practice to make a more indirect approach: "Excuse me, but did you drop this book?"

Thus presuppositions may be based on the relatively immediate linguistic context, as when we validate the use of "she" by establishing its referent in "Now, I have this cousin Mary, and is she ever a beauty!" By the time "she" appears we know that we are talking about Cousin Mary. Or the presuppositions may be based on broader considerations, such as customary behavior, as in the curious case of the questionable book above.

Falk (1978) offers some of the presuppositions of even a very simple-looking sentence: "Alan's wife works for the state of Michigan." (pp. 267–268) The presuppositions include

1. A person named Alan exists.
2. The listener knows Alan.
3. Alan is an adult male.
4. Alan is married.
5. Alan's wife is alive.
6. There is a state named Michigan.
7. Michigan has employees.

Dialogues

Even in the speech of an individual, one sentence depends on preceding sentences and sets up sentences to follow. Where this is not the case the speech is disjointed or even incoherent, possibly implying pathology. In a dialogue the speech of one party is linked to that of the other, in sequences of turn–taking.

Since adult dialogues can become quite involved, both semantically and syntactically, we may draw profitably from a brief paper by Ervin–Tripp (1975) on adult–child dialogues during the course of the child's third year. There are two aspects to the study: one is the development of the child's ability to deal with dialogues in the course of the year and the other is the accommodation made by the adult to facilitate that development.

At first the youngster's dialogue is most likely to concern the ongoing activity rather than to earlier talk. This means there may be only a relatively loose semantic relation between one utterance and the next, but gradually more talk-turns are likely to be semantically relevant to the previous turn and a transcript is more understandable without the support of a videotape.

In the course of the year tying devices appear in the child's dialogues, including pronouns, ellipsis, and conjunctions. Ervin–Tripp (1975, pp. 1-2) notes the pronoun switching, contrastive stress and ellipsis which removes all of the predicate except the subject and the auxiliary—the very parts so often missing in the earliest speech.

Adult: I'll give Liz the blue one.

Child: No you won't. *I* will.

Such uniquely tying devices as *and*, *but*, and *too* are absent at first; then *and* appears, first to join nouns (usually in direct objects); then whole predicates; then clauses, and finally to join contrasted items, as "Blue for Liz and green for Joe."

At first the youngster used *and* only with her own turn, then extended it back to her own earlier turn, and finally used it to link her turn to the partner's turn. The result of such developments is that the dialogue sounds integrated.

On the other side, the older partner (not necessarily an adult) must make accommodations to the child. This is done at four levels. One is through the selection of the *speech acts* that seem suitable to the age of the child, the objects at hand, and the situation. These speech acts include various kinds of directive—to do something, to name something, or questions to elicit an identification to indicate a location. The task is more involved than it might seem at first blush. For example, if too young a child is asked what someone is doing (perhaps in a picture), the youngster will not be able to respond very appropriately because she will not yet be able to deal with verb questions. In other words, simple speech acts may yet be syntactically too complex for the child.

A second accommodation for the older partners is to simplify semantically. In particular, they are more likely to talk about the present rather than the past and about what is present rather than what is absent. Temporal and causal questions are not posed to the youngest children. Thus at first the questions are likely to be those that can be answered by simple naming (about 40 percent of the time in Ervin-Tripp's material), but toward the end of the year these questions had fallen off sharply (to about 8 percent), in favor of the more difficult questions posed with *why, which,* and *when,* and questions about the past also increased.

Third, it seems likely that there is control over the difficulty of the vocabulary, based on the relative frequency of the words in normal conversation. And the fourth kind of accommodation is in the degree of politeness used in addressing the child. In the study being reported the older partner was usually one of the adult investigators, who would tend at first to use the embedding forms normal for the polite posing of questions and directives ("Where do you suppose this goes?") even though this made the syntax more complex for the child. But as the adult became more sensitive to the capabilities of the child such forms decreased.

Ervin–Tripp suggests that speakers seem to have little direct control over syntax, but the syntax tends to be simplified as a result of choices in speech acts, meanings, politeness, and vocabulary.

Hinds (1975) deals with characteristics of normal conversations, which include

> a speaker and hearer(s) who interact linguistically; topics of conversation; and linguistic events. Often these linguistic events are full sentences, but they may also be truncated versions of sentences. Most important, however, is the fact that sentences have certain specifiable relationships to one another. Topics of conversation control which elements may be deleted, pronominalized, definitized, or thematized. The speaker and hearer(s) interact liguistically in a limited number of ways: they participate in question-answer paradigm; command–obey relationships; statement–comment relationships; etc. [p. 25]

Hinds (1975) offers a diagrammatic description of some short conversations showing relationships that begin with a paragraph topic, or topic of conversation, move to a story line that shows changes in performative verbs, then to an event line that shows the sequencing of sentences and then down to the familiar type of tree diagram that describes the sentences themselves. What is particularly interesting, though, is that he provides for the specification of social desiderata. That is, for Japanese one constraint may depend on whether the parties to the interaction identify as members of the same in–group, calling for familiar forms, or are to be socially defined in a way that calls for the use of polite forms. He then provides for a new participant that may require a shift from familiar to polite forms, and he could have provided for asymmetrical patterns as well, where one speaker is obliged to use polite forms while the other has the option of using the familiar forms.

REFERENCES

Akmajian, A., Demers, R.A. & Harnish, R.M. 1979. *Linguistics: An introduction to language and communication*. Cambridge, Mass.: M.I.T. Press.

Austin, J.L. *How to do things with words*. J.O. Urmson, Ed. New York: Oxford University Press, 1962.

Bolinger, D. *Aspects of language*. New York: Harcourt Brace & World, Inc., 1968.

Chao, Y.R. *Language and symbolic systems*. London: Cambridge University Press, 1968.

Chomsky, N. *Syntactic structures*. The Hague: Mouton & Company, 1957.

Chomsky, N. *Aspects of the theory of syntax*. Cambridge, Mass.: The M.I.T. Press, 1965.

Chomsky, N. *Studies on semantics in generative grammar*. The Hague: Mouton & Co., 1972.

Chomsky, N., & Halle, M. *The sound pattern of English*. New York: Harper & Row, 1968.

Crane, L.B., Yeager, E., & Whitman, R.L. *An introduction to linguistics*. Boston, Mass.: Little, Brown & Co., 1981.

Crystal, D. *Linguistics*. Baltimore, Md.: Penguin Books, Inc., 1971.

Ervin–Tripp, S.M. Adult-child dialogues from two to three. Paper presented to the 74th Annual Meeting of the American Anthropological Association, San Francisco, CA, 2-6 December 1975.

Falk, J.S. *Linguistics and language: A survey of basic concepts and implications*. (2nd ed.) New York: John Wiley & Sons, 1978.

Fillmore, C.J. The case for case. In E. Bach & R.T. Harms (Eds.), *Universals in Linguistic Theory*. New York: Holt, Rinehart & Winston, Inc., 1968.

Fillmore, C.J. The case for case reopened. In P. Cole & J. Sadock (Eds.), *Syntax and semantics, 8: Grammatical relations*. New York: Academic Press, 1977.

Hinds, J. Aspects of conversational analysis. *Linguistics*, 1975, *149*, 25-40.

Katz, J. J., & Fodor, J. The structure of a semantic theory. *Language*, 1963, *39*, 170–210.

Lakoff, G., & Thompson, H. Introducing cognitive grammar. In C. Cogen, H. Thompson, G. Thurgood, K. Whistler, J. Wright (Eds.), *Proceedings of the First Annual Meeting of the Berkeley Linguistic Society*, February 15-17, 1975. Berkeley, CA: Berkeley Linguistic Society. 1975.

Langacker, R.W. *Language and its structure*. New York: Harcourt Brace & World, Inc., 1968.

Lehmann, W. *Descriptive linguistics*. (2nd ed.). New York: Random House, 1976.

McCawley, J. The role of semantics in a grammar. In E. Bach & R.T. Harms (Eds.), *Universals in linguistic theory*. New York: Holt, Rinehart & Winston, Inc., 1968.

Moravcsik, E.A. Introduction: On syntactic approaches. In E.A. Moravcsik & J.R. Wirth (Eds.), *Syntax and semantics, 13, Current approaches to syntax*, New York: Academic Press, 1980.

Perlmutter, D.M. Relational grammar. In E.A. Moravcsik & J.R. Wirth (Eds.), *Syntax and semantics 13: Current approaches to syntax*. New York: Academic Press, 1980.

Searle, J.R. *Speech acts*. Cambridge: University Press, 1969.

Chapter 7

THE ONTOGENESIS OF LANGUAGE

No one enters the world with demonstrable linguistic competence in any language, but the remarkable speed with which normal children the world over attain the ability to understand and produce utterances in a given language argues a large innate capacity for language acquisition. Theory and research on the nature of this process and how it is accomplished have been dominated by three viewpoints, which we might designate the behavioral, linguistic, and cognitive perspectives. Their respective contributions have helped make developmental psycholinguistics one of the more lively and controversial topic areas during the past decade and a half.

As Slobin (1971) has observed, "behavioristic psychology looked upon language, and the task of first language learning, as just another form of human behavior which could be reduced to the laws of conditioning" and thus were "governed by variables such as frequency, recency, contiguity, and reinforcement" (p. 40). Perhaps the most elaborate presentation of this view was made by Skinner (1957) and the most detailed rejection of it is by Chomksy (1959). Salzinger (1979) points out that Skinner's book left his followers, the operant conditioners, with no clear directions for further work because it presented no data, merely some interesting examples; and linguists, who might have been interested in some of the things Skinner had to say, "were turned off by Chomsky's scathing review . . . which came to be more widely read than Skinner's book and became a general rallying point of all those who had opposed the behavioral point of view" (p. 112). Salzinger's own *ecolinguistic* approach recognizes the importance of the environmental context or habitat in the study of language acquisition and questions the validity of generalizations about first language learning based on artificially constrained samples, whether they involve laboratory studies of "verbal behavior" using nonsense syllables or "computer simulations."

The basic problem that linguists faced in attempting to formulate a comprehensive account of language development, as Chomsky viewed it, was to conceive of a mechanism by which a grammar could be inferred from a finite set of utterances. Chomsky called such a mechanism a *language acquisition device* (LAD). The properties of such a device as pictured below in Figure 1 have been described by Paivio and Begg (1981) as follows:

Figure 7.1.   Language Acquisition Device
Source: Paivio, A., and Begg, I. 1981. *Psychology of Language.*
Englewood Cliffs, New Jersey: Prentice-Hall. p. 236. Reproduced by
permission of the authors and publisher.

1. It has a rational or *innate* basis as opposed to an empirical one. That is, it is a theory of children's inborn capacities.
2. It is essentially syntactic in that it is not dependent on semantic input, although such input could have a motivating influence and speed up acquisition.
3. It deals with syntactic *universals*—features common to all languages.
4. These syntactic universals can be described in part by Chomsky's theory of grammar, particularly the *grammatical relations* characteristic of the *deep structure* of sentences. These include the subject and predicate of the sentence, the modifier and head (noun) of the noun phrase, and the main verb and object of the verb phrase. Note that these are relational concepts. That is, they refer to the function of a unit in a higher-level unit. The subject, for example, is meaningful only in relation to the sentence–it is the subject *of* the sentence. (This relational view is explicit in

Chomsky's definitions of these concepts: the subject is that NP immediately dominated by S; the predicate is the VP directly dominated by S; and the object is the NP dominated by the predicate VP.)

5. The internal structure of LAD does not contain information required to produce appropriate linguistic transformations and surface structures directly. These vary from language to language and are presumably learned. LAD may contain universal transformational *types* (permutation, deletion, addition—perhaps a half dozen in all), but the child learning a language must discover the transformations of the particular language.

6. LAD reflects at least in part a *specific linguistic capacity*, as compared to a *universal cognitive ability*. The former was described by McNeill in terms of *strong linguistic universals*, which reflect a specific linguistic ability, and *weak linguistic universals*, which are the reflections in language of a universal cognitive ability (general intellectual ability).

7. Finally, the range of LAD's hypotheses about possible grammars is extremely limited (p. 236).

Cognitive approaches to linguistic acquisition emphasize the importance of sensorimotor experience and semantic factors in language development and are heavily indebted to the pioneering conceptions of Jean Piaget. Piaget's views on language acquisition reflect the basic conviction that the development of linguistic competence must be understood as part of a more general pattern of intellectual development, which occurs in roughly the following sequence:

1. A *sensorimotor period* (from birth to about 2 years), in which the infant is dependent on his body for expression and communication. The child comes to know objects in his environment by acting upon them—touching, tasting, biting, etc. The responses a child makes to objects constitute their meaning for him. By the end of this period, the developing infant is learning to distinguish external from internal stimuli by separating self from nonself.

2. A *period of concrete operations* (from age 2 to about age 11), during which the developing child gains skill in manipulating symbolic representations of the environment. He masters elementary relationships of space, time, and causality and slowly acquires understanding of conservation of mass, weight, and volume.

3. A final stage (from approximately age 11 onward) which Piaget called *a period of formal operations*. The growing adolescent achieves understanding of the conservation of area, number, and duration, and he begins to reason by manipulating reality through his symbolic representations of it. He constructs his own values and ideals; he invents and evaluates hypotheses about his enlarging world; and he begins to meaningfully plan for his future (adapted from Wiggins et al, 1971, p. 534).

According to this schema, language is an extension of the representational level (Phase 2) after symbols have become socialized. Linguistic structures are built upon the general cognitive structures established during the first two years (Paivio & Begg, 1981).

The task of the cognitive theorist, as Bruner (1979) identifies it, is to account for "how the human infant learns to meet the requirements of social living as a member of a culture-using species" (p. 265). Bruner rejects the syntactically-based, nativistic approach which incorporates the LAD as the central concept. "Being a witness at the feast of language is not enough of an exposure to assure acquisition," says Bruner. "There must be contingent interaction" (p. 267). Specifically he wishes to emphasize that language acquisition is heavily dependent upon the nature of the child-parent interaction. As we shall see, the systematic investigation of this interaction has assumed a great deal of importance in the past several years.

Some of the controversy that characterized developmental psycholinguistics a decade ago has abated. There appears to be little support for Chomsky's LAD model, at least in the form in which it was originally proposed, and even David McNeill (1979) has moved a considerable distance from his early enthusiastic support for the LAD to a position which reflects the influence of Piaget and other cognitive theorists. This is not to say that the issues raised by Chomsky have been resolved. But there seems to be greater hospitality toward a conceptualization of first language acquisition which assigns appropriate weight to innate predispostions toward the processing of the complex stimuli without denying the crucial importance of learning. Given that normal youngsters have a genetic predispostion for language-learning in general, they have no such predispostion for learning a specific language. They will in a matter of 3 or 4 years gain a mastery of the language appropriate to their cultural and linguistic environment. The essential independence of race, language, and culture has long been established in anthropology (Boas, 1949;

Kroeber, 1948; Linton, 1936; Sapir, 1921) A black younster raised in Paris will grow up speaking Parisian French; a Navaho Indian child raised in Peking will grow up speaking Mandarin Chinese; a Muscovite child raised in the appropriate part of Africa will grow up speaking perfect Swahili.

The fact remains, however, that the child must *learn* his or her language, and how this is accomplished is one of the most interesting questions in psycholinguistics. Rather than reviewing those arguments that seem inadequate in modern perspective, we shall simply outline some of the methodological and theoretical approaches that are employed by most researchers today.

First of all, the sound system of the child and the set of rules he or she uses to form sentences are described in their own terms; that is, they are described independently of the model presented by the adult community. A second aspect of the modern approach is that attention is devoted to the successive steps through which the child passes on the way toward mastery of the system employed by the surrounding adults (Ervin & Miller, 1963).

PRELINGUISTIC COMMUNICATION

Language acquisition does not occur in isolation, as if the child were learning to speak by listening to a tape recorder; it normally takes place, as Peter and Jill de Villiers (1979) have pointed out, "in the context of a rich interaction between the child and his parents. Several facets of this interaction seem to be important facilitators of language acquisition, and some of them may even be necessary for the acquisition of normal speech" (p. 98).

Children and parents communicate with one another in various ways long before the children have achieved even a rudimentary command of language. Vocalization, gestures, and the utilization or exploitation of contextual features are among the means by which communicative acts are carried out. As Bruner (1979) observes, "there is enough that is universal about such prelexicogrammatical communication to suggest that a part of it is innate, and easily triggered" (p. 267). Through interaction with the mother (= caretaker), these primitive procedures are successively replaced by less primitive ones until eventually they are replaced by standard linguistic procedures. Although we are lacking a comprehensive and fully detailed account of this process, we have amassed enough information to allow us to draw a rough sketch of its main features.

During the first year, the child and mother develop transactional procedures which establish a fund of shared knowledge and expectations. The child begins to use gestures, directs the gaze in order to draw attention to objects, and learns to interpret corresponding adult gestures. Through games and familiar situations, the child acquires an understanding of when a response is required and when it is not.

While parent-child interactions are establishing in the child the precursors of reference and conversational capabilities, the child is also learning about the world: "about actions, agents, instruments; about possession, location, belongingness; about natural categories, entities, and their attributes" (Bruner, 1979, p. 268). Upon these universal cognitive structures, semantic distinctions will be founded.

In summary, prelinguistic development of world knowledge and mastery of communicative competence set the stage for linguistic acquisition. It is during this stage that the first developments take place in the infant's, and later the child's, vocalization patterns. We shall try to highlight some of the major events which characterize this earliest period of developmental phonology and indicate their significance for later stages in the developmental sequence.

PRELINGUISTIC VOCALIZATION

Eisenson, Auer, and Irwin (1963) have suggested that there are five stages of prelinguistic vocalization: undifferentiated crying, differentiated crying, babbling, lallation, and echolalia. The vocalizations of deaf and hearing children are indistinguishable in the first three months, and it is only after the age of six months that there is a decrease in the range of sounds uttered by the deaf (Lenneberg, 1964). For the normal infant, babbling begins by the third or fourth month of life, but it is only at about six months of age that the vocalizations become typically differentiated into vocalic and consonantal components (Lenneberg, 1967).

Babbling is normal infant behavior, but it does not lead to normal language development in the case of the profoundly deaf, and it is' not critical for the later development of linguistic competence. At least one youngster who was incapable of speech articulation because of a congenital neurological defect was able to demonstrate normal comprehension of speech (Lenneberg, 1962). The period that features *lallation*, the child's imitation of his own accidentally produced sounds, begins at around six months of age, while *echolalia*, the imitation of sounds produced by others, begins around the ninth or tenth month (Eisenson et al., 1963). There is little reason to doubt that these exercises provide the infant with helpful practice in learning to control his vocalizations, but there is little evidence to suggest that the rehearsals are systematically related to the production of sounds that will eventually constitute the youngster's phonemic system.

There is no direct progression from a stage in which all sounds are random to the stage at which all sounds and sound sequences match those of the model; hence it should not be assumed that linguistically relevant behavior does not occur during the months prior to the production of unmistakable words. Weir (1966) and Eleanor Maccoby of Stanford sampled the vocalizations of infants between six and eight months of age in households in which the primary languages were Mandarin Chinese, Syrian Arabic, and American English respectively. They were usually able to identify the Chinese infant by its distinct pitch patterns, but were unable to distinguish easily the two Arabic babies from the American one.

A subsequent, more extensive study along the same lines was undertaken by the same investigators, and some very preliminary observations were reported by Weir (1966). At approximately six months of age, very different patterns could be seen developing for a Chinese baby, an American baby, and a Russian baby. Weir (1966) notes:

> The utterances produced by the Chinese baby are usually monosyllabic and only vocalic, with much tonal variation over individual words. A neutral single vowel with various pitches is also typical of another six-month-old Chinese infant, as well as of a still different seven-month-old one. The Russian and American babies, at six and seven months, show little pitch variation over individual syllables; they usually have a CV (consonant-vowel) syllable, often reduplicated or repeated at intervals several times, with stress patterns occurring occasionally and intonation patterns usually over a number of syllables.

On the basis of this and other evidence cited in Weir (1966), it appears that the first unmistakable steps toward the acquisition of a specific language are taken around the sixth or seventh month, with the acquisition of tonal or intonation patterns that depend on particular linguistic environments for their distinctive characteristics.

While it is likely that the majority of students of language acquisition prefer to begin their studies at the period when the child has "at least two systematically contrasted meaningful words, a point usually reached by the end of the first year" (Ervin & Miller, 1963, p. 109; see also Slobin, 1971, p. 41, who favors beginning with the two-word sequence), it is apparent that a great deal of important preparatory activity has taken place before intelligible sounds are produced.

LINGUISTIC DEVELOPMENT

First Stage

There is no clear point at which we can say without fear of contradiction that true linguistic behavior has begun and that all previous behavior, however vocal, is nonlinguistic. Intonation patterns, which in English constitute one aspect of the phonemic system, show the influence of the linguistic environment around the sixth or seventh month. Yet it is the use of *symbols* that more than anything else distinguishes language from other forms of communication, and the most elementary manifestation of this process is naming, or labeling. This means using words, where there is no intrinsic association between a sound sequence and its referent. Thus there is reason to designate the use of unmistakable words as the first stage of linguistic behavior.

Second Stage

If one-word utterances mark the first stage of linguistic development, then the first sequencing of words, the use of two-word utterances, is a convenient marker for the second stage. Of course there is no clear differentiation between the one-, two-, and multiword stages, and after a period in which two- and three-word utterances are pretty typical, events move swiftly. Not only is there a sharp increase in the vocabulary, but the grammatical patterns used increase in number and complexity. By the age of four years the normal child has acquired the essential patterns of daily verbal interaction. There is no final stage, of course, since many adults continue to refine their use of the language and add to the range of utterances they can comprehend. After treating the development of the phonemic system, we shall consider the stages that are characterized by one-word utterances, two-word utterances, and multiword utterances, and (rather briefly) some of the problems that arise through the study of reading and writing.

PHONOLOGICAL DEVELOPMENT

As we have already seen, we cannot identify phonemes until we have at least two consistent sound sequences that can be established as differing in meaning. Since babbling sounds have no direct bearing on what will become the phonemic system of the youngster, many sounds are produced that are later dropped, and some of them will have to be acquired again later, because they are significant in the models they need not be considered here. Intonation is relevant and seems to appear early, but we lack sufficient evidence to relate it usefully to a general discussion of the phonemic system as it develops later, beyond Lenneberg's (1967) observation that the child reacts to whole patterns rather than to small segments. This appears to explain why babies of Chinese-speaking parents show a remarkably different intonation pattern from that shown by the babies of English-speaking parents, as early as about six months (Weir, 1966). The difference is generally of the sort that we might expect to see developing in a potential speaker of a tonal language, as against the pattern for a potential speaker of a nontonal language.

One of the interesting, yet vexing, problems in the study of early language acquisition is the description of a *collapsed phonemic system*. Thus a three-year-old boy in the process of abandoning Japanese and acquiring English had a single initial /d/ for English /d/ and /l/. He would accordingly, say *I dike you* where we would say "I like you." In the present case it was obvious that his performance and his competence differed, because he would not accept imitations of his system. That is, if adults tried to employ a /d/ where the adult model called for /l/ (*dove* for "love," for example), the child indicated by means of headshaking and other signs that the substitution was inappropriate.

In general, it seems that the younger the child is, the broader the sound categories will be that constitute his phonemic system. This can considerably obscure the identification of vocabulary items, and can even delay recognition that the one-word stage has been reached. Who but an experienced linguist, for example, would be able to recognize the following pattern reported by Morris Swadesh (in Ervin & Miller, 1963) for his son's phonemic system?

> Final and medial consonants of the adult's words were dropped
> by the child. The initial consonant was replaced by a nasal if a
> noninitial nasal was found in the adult's word; a labial was re-
> placed by the labial nasal /m/, and a nonlabial was replaced by
> /n/: *blanket* /me/, *green* /ni/, *candy* /ne/. Complicated substitutions of
> this type are not at all uncommon, but they are ordinarily not
> recognized by the parent. (p. 115)

The final mastery of the adult model phonemic system may take
considerable time. Templin's (1966) data suggest that most children
have mastered all the phonemes of English by the age of eight years;
any gross distortion of a phoneme or substitution of one phoneme
for another is considered to indicate a speech (articulatory) problem.

Distinctive Features

Phonemes can be described in terms of distinctive features, which
are identified through the use of minimal pairs (different words that
differ only in the feature under investigation). Jakobson (1941, cited
in Carroll, 1960) has suggested that the child may learn to produce
the distinctions required by the model in a definite developmental
sequence. The order of learning is said to reflect the prevalence of
the contrasting features in the various languages of the world. The
distinctive features that occur most rarely in the world's languages
tend to be the last mastered by the children who speak those languages. Thus the distinction between the initial sounds of *f*ree and
*th*ree is required in English, but in very few other languages, and it
appears to be one of the distinctions learned relatively late by English-speaking children. (We might expect the same pattern to develop in language-contact situations, including Creole languages. In
the Hawaiian Creole, for example, the fricatives in bro*th*er and
*th*rough are replaced by their corresponding stops: [bradə], [truw] (or
by the affricate [čruw]).

Once a contrast has been learned, it tends to permeate the whole
phonemic system. When Joan, a child described by Velton (1943, cited
in Ervin & Miller, 1963), learned to contrast *p* and *b*, she also learned
to contrast *t* and *d*. That is, when she learned to distinguish the *p* and
b, she was not simply sorting out two phonemes that had formerly
been one in her system; she was developing a more abstract distinction—voiced versus voiceless stops. In this way, a child could double
his repertoire of consonants with each pair of contrasting features
learned. According to Ervin and Miller (1963), "The theory presents
an economical process of learning since the number of contrasting

features is much smaller than the number of phonemes. Radical changes in the system come at once rather than through the gradual approximation of the adult phonemes one by one" (p. 112).

SYNTACTICAL DEVELOPMENT

For about half a year, between the ages of twelve and eighteen months, the vocalizations of the child typically consist of single words. There are phonological, syntactic, and semantic differences between these utterances and those of the model: this Lenneberg (1967) sees as evidence not only of maturational factors, but also of a difference in learning strategy. The child learns patterns and structure first, rather than constituent elements. Most adults who are learning or teaching a second language seem to begin with particular attention to the phonetic skills required, and take up the problems of syntax and semantics later. Krech and Crutchfield (1958) have reported studies of the relative effectiveness for adults of learning complex skills as a whole process, as against mastering specific processes that are constituents of the whole and subsequently trying to join them into a single process. Their evidence suggests that the former approach is more effective.

The one-word utterance seems to be a universal stage, and most students of child language clearly prefer to begin the study of their grammar with a consideration of utterances of two words or more. But Lenneberg (1967) seems to have a point well taken when he suggests that "if we assume that the child's first single word utterances are, in fact, very primitive, undifferentiated forms of sentences, and that these utterances actually incorporate the germs of a grammar, a number of phenomena may be explained" (p. 283).

If Lenneberg is correct, it would seem that more attention should be paid to this stage than has been customary. It is apparent that "daddy" will not represent the same expansion of deep structure every time it appears, for example, and a study of the pitch contours with which it is associated in different contextual circumstances should provide further clues to the grammar of the one-word utterance. Not only may the one-word utterance represent a kind of sentence that will vary with different presumed deep structures, but there may yet be some validity to the more prevalent assumption that they are mere labels. That is, some one-word utterance may be labels in which the grammatical question simply is not relevant. And to the extent that one-word utterances serve reference functions, they are important to our understanding of early concept formation (Vetter & Howell, 1971).

Evidence from Comparative Linguistics

Our lack of adequate comparative material from non-Indo-European languages obscures several questions. First, different languages codify experience in different ways, and that may have implications for the kinds of problem encountered in first-language learning. Any normal child can learn any language as a native tongue, but all languages may not be equally easy or difficult to learn. It would seem likely that a language with a relatively simple phonemic system, such as Spanish or Hawaiian, would pose fewer problems of articulation than a language with a more complex phonemic system, such as Korean or English. This in turn would imply that the performances of beginning speakers of languages with simple phonemic systems should be more readily interpreted by those attending them. That is, there would be less need to puzzle out collapsed phonemic systems, and this in turn would mean that certain kinds of communication should be simpler at the early stages. The Japanese term *mamma* "food" is a term spoken by and to children, and is learned very early, probably before the first birthday in most cases. It conforms essentially to the phonemic pattern of the model, is easy to articulate, and serves very effectively in adult-child communication. In English, on the contrary, there seems to be nothing that quite corresponds to this. At least, we are not aware of common examples of terms for "food," "milk," or "bottle," or of any linguistic term that would be functionally equivalent. Our experience is that the youngster tends to cry, and thus leaves it to the ingenuity of the parent to determine what the response should be.

Another problem that we need comparative material to resolve is the effect of different morphosyntactic structures on the problems of first-language learning. Word order is more critical in English than in Russian, which has a highly developed inflectional system, yet the Russian child typically relies on the subject-object-verb order until around the end of the second year, when subject-verb-object begins to predominate. At first both languages are unmarked for tense, gender, number, and so forth, but we might reasonably expect that the Russian child would first learn the morphological markers for subject, object, and verb, and then combine them in any order, since they are exposed to such a variety of word orders by their linguistic environment. Slobin (1966) says, however, word order is as inflexible for Russian children as it is for American children.

The extent to which different language structures condition different learning patterns remains an important problem area. Kluckhohn (cited by Casagrande, 1948) felt that Navaho children take longer to learn their extremely complicated language than English-speaking children, whose task appears easier, take to learn theirs. Even in English there is a great deal to be learned about one-word utterances, but what of languages in which even the simplest words consist of several morphemes? In English, "open" is a single morpheme, but in Japanese the simplest equivalents are marked for aspect or tense, and contain two morphemes: for example, *akeru* means "will open," *aketa* means "opened," and as a request (imperative) *akete* is common in the speech of the Japanese child. Whether or not one chooses to treat these as equivalent to our one- or two-word utterances, it may be that the sequencing of *morphemes* is a more important general consideration than the sequencing of *words*.

Sequencing

In English, at least, the sequencing of two words marks a new stage of development, which usually begins at around eighteen months of age. A two-word sequence is more than a mere joining of two independent entities. As Brown and Bellugi (1964) have indicated, single-word utterances carry primary stress and have a terminal intonation contour, but when two such words, for example "push" and "car," are put into a single construction, "push car," the "push" will carry a lesser stress and a lower pitch, and will lose its terminal contour, while the "car" will retain its primary stress and terminal contour, and will gain a higher pitch.

Form Classes

In addition to tactical rules such as this, which become evident at the two-word stage, there are also different *form classes*. There is an open class, which has a large membership, consisting of many of the words that had formerly comprised the one-word utterances (Slobin, 1971). Words of the other class are variously called *modifiers* (Brown & Bellugi, 1964; Brown & Berko, 1960; Brown & Fraser, 1964), *operators* (Ervin, 1963, 1964), or *pivot words* (Braine, 1963). This is a relatively closed class: it has few members, but each member gets a greater piece of the verbal action.

With some exceptions, a two-word sequence may be generated by taking any member of one class and placing it in sequence with any member of the other class. In some constructions the pivot word comes first: "a coat," "a Becky," "a celery," "more nut," "dirty knee" (Brown & Bellugi, 1964). In the other major construction the pivot word is in the second position: "boot on," "tape on," and so forth (Slobin, 1971). The former construction contains sequences that seem to correspond to the sequences in the adult model, but some in fact do not. We use the indefinite article "a" only to modify common count nouns in the singular, and we consider it inappropriate before proper nouns (*a Becky) or mass nouns (*a celery). Similarly we require the plural when "more" modifies a count noun, so that we would not consider "*more nut" to be grammatical for us. (Again the asterisk marks theatrical forms.)

In a manner somewhat analogous to the notion of a collapsed phonemic system, the child's form classes are collapsed, in that there is a class of words that must ultimately be divided into subclasses such as the definite article, indefinite articles, demonstrative adjectives, possessive pronouns, and so forth. It is reasonably clear that some of the surface structures reflected in the two-word utterances represent different deep structures. Slobin (1971), on the basis of examples provided in Bloom (1968), suggests that such nonpivot structures as "cup glass," "party hat," "Kathryn sock," "sweater chair," and "Kathryn ball" represent five different semantic relationships. Thus the first may show conjunction, "a cup *and* a glass"; the second attribution, the *kind* of hat in question, the third possession, *whose* sock; the fourth location, *where* the sweater is; and the fifth a subject-object relationship, *who* will throw *what*. Of course a very careful examination of the context in which the utterance occurs is necessary before the semantic relationships can be guessed with any confidence. As Slobin points out, the semantic relationships are usually clear in the adult speech, because the syntactic forms are fully developed. But the youngster is limited to very short utterances, which cannot make the relationships explicit: "An important aspect of grammatical development, therefore, is the ability to produce longer utterances in which subparts of the utterance bear grammatical relations to one another" (p. 47).

IMITATION AND EXPANSION

A word about imitation is in order, since it has played such an important part in the older theories of language acquisition, and of course it still has some intrinsic interest. We have already indicated that in matters of phonology the productions of the very young child bear little direct relationship to those of the adult model. Even from the brief examples of two-word utterances just given, it should also be obvious that the early grammar of the child is not immediately related to that of the model.

Imitations may be made by the parent, in which case the parent typically expands the child's utterance, as when one mother expanded her son's "There go one" into "There goes one" (Brown & Bellugi, 1964). In this study, the mothers were found to respond to the speech of their children with expansions about 30 percent of the time. In general, the expansions consist of the original word order plus whatever additions are necessary to transform the child's utterance into an appropriate and grammatically acceptable equivalent in the adult model. The imitations of adult speech by the child tend to be reduced; for example, he or she may convert "That's an old time train" to "old time train." In both cases the imitations tend to preserve the word order of the original, while the omissions and additions are likely to be of function words (the words that serve to show the relationships among the lexical or content words).

One point of particular interest in the matter of adult expansions of infant speech is concerned with the development of what Bernstein (1966) calls *restricted* versus *elaborated* codes. To oversimplify a bit, the elaborated codes are what we think of as the grammatically complex speech associated with the more advantaged parts of the speech community, and the restricted codes are more typical of the culturally deprived and working classes. Ward (1971) has given a useful description of mother-child interaction in a black Louisiana community. Telegraphic expressions such as "It a bus?" are virtually never expanded into a form typical of Standard English, such as "Is it a bus?" Instead of focusing on the speech form, the mother advances the dialogue and thereby ends it. Mama initiates the conversation, determines the topic and the direction it will take, and terminates it. So far as the adults are concerned, the children of this community are not suitable companions in a conversation.

Ward appears to feel that her material casts doubt on some of the theories that have been advanced, partly on the basis of the expansions that are typical of white middle-class mothers. But many of the features are missing in the adult vernacular. That is, many potential expansions would be appropriate for the middle-class white model, but would not be appropriate for the local vernacular.

A final word on imitation is in order. Labov (1972, pp. 304-305) has noted that most models and studies of language acquisition focus on the mother-child interaction and tend to exclude the influence of the peer group. We learn that a child has acquired a particular feature, but we do not know with whom he or she has been interacting in the interim. Perhaps the key point in Labov's argument is that the children of immigrants almost always speak as their age-mates speak rather than as their parents speak (so far as English is concerned, at any rate). Indeed, so long as very young children interact with their age-mates in any linguistic environment, it is probably impossible to keep them from speaking in the local vernacular, and the parents need never learn even the most elementary features of that language—as with many American parents abroad, for example.

CHARACTERISTICS OF CHILD LANGUAGE DEVELOPMENT

There are a number of interrelated processes that appear to typify child language development in general. These include analogical formations, overgeneralization, the expansion of telegraphic speech, increase in the length of utterances, and the increasing mastery of rules that relate syntactic units.

Analogical Formations and Overgeneralization

Analogic formations involve generalization of the sort that goes from "cat/cats" to "coat/coats," but overgeneralization can yield forms that are not found in the model, such as "foot/foots," or "hit/hitted" (by analogy with "pit/pitted"). The "incorrect" forms imply strongly that the child is demonstrating mastery of a rule: a rule for generating the plural in "foots" and a rule for generating the past tense in "hitted."

This problem was investigated in Jean Berko's (1958) imaginative study of the acquisition of English morphology. If a young child can supply the correct ending for the plural of an ordinary noun, it may be merely a demonstration that he or she has memorized the correct form. If, on the other hand, the child is able to give the correct plural ending /-z/ for a nonsense word (for example, gutches as the plural of gutch), this suggests that he or she has internalized a working system of plural allomorphs and conditional variants, and is able to generalize to new cases and select the right form.

Berko was also interested in the manner in which these morphological rules evolve. Is there a progression from simple, regular rules to more irregular and qualified rules that are adequate to describe English fully?

The experiment began with an examination of actual vocabulary.

This is a wug.

Now there is another one.

There are two of them.

There are two ———.

Figure 7.2.   Illustration of Berko's Method for Eliciting Inflections. (Reprinted by permission from R. Brown and C. Fraser. The acquisition of Syntax. In U. Belliyi and R. Brown (Eds.), *The Acquisition of Language.* **Monograph, Society for Research in Child Development 29, No. 1, 1964.)**

The 1,000 words most frequently found in a first-grader's vocabulary were selected from a standardized list. These were examined to see what features of English morphology were commonly represented in the vocabulary of a child of this age. On the basis of actual vocabulary samples, estimates were then made of the kind of morphological rules that children might be expected to have acquired, and from these items a list was constructed. In order to gather some idea of the notions that children form about compound words in their language, it was decided to ask them directly about a selection of such words.

Thus, from within the framework of a child's vocabulary, a test was devised to explore the ability to apply morphological rules to new words. Subjects were called upon to inflect, derive, compound, and analyze words.

Nonsense words were made up according to the rules for possible sound combinations in English. Pictures were then drawn on cards to represent these nonsense words. There were 27 of these pictures;

they were brightly colored, and depicted objects, cartoonlike animals, and men performing various actions. Several actual words were also included. The text, which omitted the desired form, was typed on each card. The following is an example of the card used to test for the use of the regular plural allomorph /-z/. Each child was brought to the experimenter, introduced, and told that he or she was going to look at some pictures. The experimenter would point to the picture and read the text. The child was asked to supply the missing item, and these responses were phonemically transcribed. After all the pictures had been shown, the child was asked why he or she thought the things denoted by the compound words in the list (such as newspaper, Thanksgiving, fireplace, airplane, and so on) were so named. The general form of these questions was, "Why do you think a blackboard is called a blackboard?" The child who answered, "Because it's a blackboard," was asked, "But why do you think it's called that?"

The answers given by the children were not always correct so far as the English language is concerned, but they were consistent and orderly answers. The evidence strongly supports the conclusion that children in this age group operate with clearly delimited morphological rules. The children did not treat new words according to idiosyncratic patterns. They did not model new words on patterns that appear infrequently. Where they provided inflexional endings, they did best with those forms that are the most regular and have the fewest variants. With morphenes that have several allomorphs, they could handle forms that called for the most common of those allomorphs long before they could deal with allomorphs that appear in a limited distribution range.

It frequently happens that a youngster will initially have the correct irregular plural or past forms, and will later drop these for the overgeneralized forms. Presumably the initial use of the irregular form implies the learning of specific words, as against the generation of forms on the basis of abstract rules. Essentially the same sort of overgeneralizing has also been reported for Russian children (Slobin, 1966).

Slobin has traced the order of development and subdivision of grammatical classes in Russian children learning their language, and showed the importance of semantic and conceptual aspects of the classes. His analysis suggests that in English, we might also expect to find that the grammatical devices which carry the greatest personal significance for the child are learned first, even though they may be relatively less important in the adult grammar as a whole. Brown and

Bellugi (1964), for example, noted that conversations in which the child is involved are highly contemporaneous, without references to events at other times and other places.

Bellugi (1966) has conducted an analysis of the development of questions, in which she sees three stages. First, a string of words may be turned into a question by a gradual rise in pitch; Slobin (1971, p. 45) notes that yes-no questions can be produced by pronouncing any two-word sentence with a rising intonation in English, German, Russian, Samoan, and Luo (in Kenya), but not in Finnish. And according to Melissa Bowerman (cited by Slobin, 1971), in the case of Finnish child language, the emergence of yes-no questions is very late. Here we might note, incidentally, that the Hawaiian Creole differs from Standard English in that it marks yes-no questions with a falling rather than a rising intonation, but to date there has apparently been no systematic study of child language in Hawaii to see if the yes-no question there also develops quite late.

Even when the child is learning to use a rising intonation to mark a yes-no question, negatives are indicated by the simple addition of "no" at the head of the string. At this stage, it appears that the child does not understand the construction of certain types of questions. In the second stage the questions are still produced by the rising intonation or by the use of question words ("what," "how," and so on), but the essential competence appears to have been achieved; this is indicated by the appropriateness of answers to questions. The third stage appears around ten months after the youngster has begun to form two-word utterances. It coincides with the appearance of functional auxiliary verbs and negative sentences, and is characterized by the production of well-formed questions.

One interesting observation noted by Bellugi was that there is a limitation on the number of transformations under control in the third stage. If a negative and a question appeared in a single utterance, only one or the other aspect was under good control. One child could ask "Can't it be a bigger truck?" in which it appears that he understood the negative question in both respects, but the same child revealed that the question aspect was less well controlled than the negative aspect when he failed to make the necessary inversion in the question "Why the kitty can't stand up?" After giving numerous examples from the speech of the child under study, the author concluded: "In his responses, all affirmatives were inverted, all negatives were not. The interpretation again fits the notion of a limit on the permitted complexity at one stage" (Bellugi-Klima, 1968, p. 40, quoted by Slobin, 1971, p. 52).

TOWARD A THEORY OF LANGUAGE ACQUISITION

The ability to induce meanings and to structure them is present very early in the ontogenesis of language. It should be apparent by now, even after this very cursory look at a few of the problems, that no theory that bases language acquisition on the concept of simple imitation is going to be very useful. An adequate theory will have to account for the structuring process. The child induces the grammatical and referential meanings from the utterances in the linguistic environment; these form the basis of the child's linguistic competence. But his or her linguistic performance is different from that of the adult, whose performances usually provide a more immediate demonstration of competence, and frequently correspond precisely with the model if the adult is given adequate time to prepare utterances (that is, if speech is not spontaneous).

The principal concern of the linguist is competence rather than performance, *la langue* rather than *la parole*, the abstract language code rather than the particular speech events. Children develop rules of their own, which the investigator can deduce from their performances, while the children's competence is always tested in terms of the model of the adults. Since we know the future result of the child's operations—mastery of the adult model—this probably creates no serious difficulties.

In brief, then, an adequate theory of language ontogenesis must account for the original and creative bridges constructed by the child to get from original experimental and maturational limitations to the rules that underlie adult linguistic performances. Such a theory will have to include and go beyond a theory that accounts for adult competence and performance, since that is only the final stage of ontogenesis. Very likely such a theory will have to be keyed to theories of cognitive development, what Carroll (1964) has described as "a child's capacity to recognize, discriminate, and manipulate the features and processes of the world around him" (p. 31).

BILINGUALISM

Bilingualism, or the "practice of alternately using two languages," as Weinreich (1953, p. 1) defined it, is extremely common around the world, and in many areas people are multilingual—that is, people command three or more languages.

It is customary to distinguish *compound* and *coordinate* bilingualism, but a third variety, *convergent* bilingualism, is also very important, and there are special cases, such as *diglossia* and the use of *lingua francas*, which need be mentioned.

Compound Bilingualism

Foreign-language study in the United States typically produces compound bilinguals, at least to the extent that the courses are successful. Instruction is usually in English and the target language is anchored to English. Thus a student of Korean would be taught that *cip* is "house," a student of Japanese would be taught that *-ta* marks the "past tense," and so forth. Unfortunately, the labels of two languages rarely correspond in a precise way. Thus, while "houses" in Korea are gradually becoming more like the sort familiar to most of us, traditionally a *cip* has been a reddish, dried-mud affair, L- or U-shaped, with plain oiled paper covering the floors and walls. While the *-ta* of Japanese often translates well as our past tense, it more precisely describes completed action and is used where we might not expect it, while not occurring where we should expect it based on our understanding of English usages of our past tense markers.

Compound bilingualism is probably most highly developed in professional translators, particularly those able to perform "simultaneous" translations required in the United Nations, even if the translators originally grew up as coordinate bilinguals (described below). The reason is that an inventory of verbal equations is important for speed, while components of the second language are related to each other in ways that may not correspond to anything in the first language; idioms may have no ready counterpart in the other language; and ambiguities can seldom be maintained in translation. Some features of the second language, in short, must be understood in terms of that language, *not* in terms of the original language. Where there is no real equivalent, some sort of convention must be adopted. For two useful discussions of translation problems from a general standpoint see Ervin and Osgood (1954) and Nida (1961).

Coordinate Bilingualism

Coordinate bilingualism is quite different from compound bilingualism because the coordinate form includes two languages that are maintained as separate systems; each language is learned with reference to its specific sociocultural environment, rather than with reference to the other language. Thus a Korean-English bilingual should directly associate *cip* with a typical Korean structure and *house* with a typical Western style structure. Presumably whatever considerations are relevant for first-language learning should apply to each of the coordinate bilingual's languages.

Because different languages are typically employed in different sociocultural contexts, it is nearly impossible for an individual to develop identical mastery of two or more languages. Robert Lowie, for example, had a superb command of English, but admitted that affairs of the kitchen were for him almost exclusively a matter of his native German, even though he had consciously attempted to maintain equal proficiency in both languages (Lowie, 1945).

Convergent Bilingualism

Convergent bilingualism describes a situation in which two languages have influenced each other to the point of virtual identity. This seems to be the case in many national border areas, where different language labels mark political facts more than they mark linguistic facts. A particularly nice demonstration of convergence has been provided by Gumperz (1967a) for two genetically unrelated languages of India that have converged to virtual structural identity, though they continue to sound quite different. That is, the two local varieties differ only in the rules that determine the phonetic shape of the corresponding words and affixes. Perhaps the basic idea of how the same underlying structure can be realized in rather different phonetic forms may be illustrated by comparing the English and Spanish forms of a simple equation:

English:	one	and	one	are	two
Spanish:	uno	y	uno	son	dos
Arithmetic	1	+	1	=	2
notation

Here the arithmetic notation represents the essential structure, which is verbally reflected in the structure of the English and the Spanish, even though the precise phonetic shapes of the 1, +, =, and 2 are quite different for the two speech varieties.

The Indian case represents convergence in a local community where the speakers of each language evidently cling to their "different" languages as ethnic identity symbols, or they might have gone the final step and developed a single set of rules for generating the same sound shapes for the underlying structures.

Diglossia

Ferguson (1956) originally coined the term *diglossia* to describe a situation in which within a single speech community there was both a "high" variety of speech used for most written or formal purposes, and which was not used as the medium of ordinary conversation by any group, and a "low" regional or standard vernacular which *is* used for ordinary verbal interaction. Classical Arabic, for example, is a high variety which is superposed over the local Arabic vernaculars. More recently, the term diglossia has been used to describe any situation in which there are high and low varieties used respectively for formal and informal communication (Fishman, Cooper, Ma et al., 1968, pp. 929ff.). An educated Puerto Rican in New York, for example, might use a literary-based variety of Spanish in formal situations, a local variety of Spanish in family and neighborhood interaction, and one or more varieties of English in non-Spanish contexts. There is a similar contrast in the use of the local variety of Standard English and the local pidgins and creoles or their derivatives.

Lingua Francas

A lingua franca is sometimes defined as a pidgin or creole (see Chapter 10), but more generally, perhaps, the term is used to describe any speech variety that is used as a medium of communication over a fairly wide range of speech communities. English is probably the language that is most widely used as a common medium of communication throughout the world today, but there are many other lingua francas around the world. Hausa, for instance, is important as a trade language in western Africa and Swahili serves a similar purpose in much of southern Africa.

INTELLECTUAL DEVELOPMENT OF THE BILINGUAL

We will conclude this chapter with a brief examination of the intellectual development of the bilingual because this is a lively academic issue, with serious implications for educational programs.

Many of the relevant studies are keyed to formal learning situations, and give the impression that bilingualism constitutes an intellectual handicap. One of the most influential reports to this effect is that of John Macnamara (1966), who claims that native-speakers of

English in Ireland who have spent nearly half their time learning Irish do not reach the same standard in written English as monolingual British children. There is an estimated lag of 17 months of English age. Nor do they achieve the standard in written Irish as monolingual Irish speakers. Here the lag is about 16 months of Irish age.

Peal and Lambert (1962), on the other hand, found that in Canada, bilinguals performed significantly better than monolinguals in both verbal and nonverbal tests. They argued that the bilinguals have a language asset, are more adept at concept formation, and have a greater mental flexibility. Macnamara (1964, cited in Lambert & Anisfeld, 1969) countered that the Canadians were brighter to begin with! Lambert and Anisfeld (1969) deny that this was the case.

Haugen (1956) has reviewed the evidence for many combinations of bilingual and concludes that general intelligence is not relevant to the question, and that many factors account for differences in language command, including the age of learning, different motivations, and different levels of opportunity to learn all aspects of the language.

REFERENCES

Bellugi, U. Development of negative and interrogative structures in the speech of children. In T. Bever and W. Weksel (Eds.), *Studies in psycholinguistics*. New York: Holt, Rinehart & Winston, Inc., 1966.

Bellugi-Klima, U. Linguistic mechanisms underlying child speech. In E. M. Zale (Ed.), *Proceedings of the conference on language and language behavior*. New York: Appleton-Century-Crofts, 1968.

Berk, J. The child's learning of English morphology. *Word*, 1958, *14*, 150-177.

Bernstein, B. Elaborated and restricted codes: An outline. *Sociological Enquiry*, 1966, *36*, 254-261.

Bloom, L. M. Language development: Form and function in emerging grammars. Unpublished doctoral dissertation, Columbia University, 1968.

Boas, F. *Race, language, and culture*. New York: The Macmillan Company, 1949.

Braine, M. D. S. The ontogeny of English phrase structure: The first phase. *Language*, 1963, *39*, 1-13.

Brown, R., & Bellugi, U. Three processes in the child's acquisition of syntax. In E. Lenneberg (Ed.), *New directions in the study of language*. Cambridge, Mass.: The M.I.T. Press, 1964.

Brown, R., & Berko, J. Word association and the acquisition of grammar. *Child Development*, 1960, *31*, 1-14.

Brown, R., & C. Fraser. The acquisition of syntax, In U. Bellugi and R. Brown (Eds.), The acquisition of language. *Monographs of the Society for Research in Child Development*, 1964, *29*, 1-191.

Bruner, J. Learning how to do things with words. In D. Aaronson & R. W. Rieber (Eds.), *Psycholinguistic research*. Hillsdale, New Jersey: Lawrence Erlbaum Associates, 1979.

Carroll, J. B. Language development in children. In Sol Saporta (Ed.), *Psycholinguistics*. New York: Holt, Rinehart & Winston, Inc., 1961.

Carroll, J. B. *Language and thought*. Englewood Cliffs, N. J.: Prentice-Hall, Inc., 1964.

Casagrande, J. B. Comanche baby language. *International Journal of American Linguistics*, 1948, *14*, 11-14.

Chomsky, N. Review of B. F. Skinner's *Verbal behavior*. *Language*, 1959, *35*, 26-58.

Chomsky, N. *Language and mind*. New York: Harcourt, Brace & World, Inc., 1968.

DeVilliers, P. A., & DeVilliers, J. G. *Early language*. Cambridge, MA: Harvard University Press, 1979.

DeVito, J. *The psychology of speech and language*. New York: Random House, Inc., 1970.

Eisenson, J., Auer, J. J., & Irwin, J. V. *The psychology of communication*. New York: Appleton-Century-Crofts, 1963.

Ervin, S. Structure in children's language. Paper presented at the International Congress of Psychology, Washington, D. C., 1963.

Ervin, S. Imitation and structural change in children's language. In E. Lenneberg (Ed.), *New directions in the study of language*. Cambridge, Mass.: The M.I.T. Press, 1964.

Ervin, S., & Miller, W. Language development. In *The sixty-second yearbook of the National Society for the Study of Education*. (Part I.) *Child Psychology*. Chicago, Ill.: University of Chicago Press, 1963.

Ervin, S. M., & Osgood, C. E. Second langauge learning and bilingualism. In C. E. Osgood and T. A. Sebeok (Eds.), *Psycholinguistics*, Bloomington, Ind.: Indiana University Press, 1954.

Ferguson, C.A. Diglossia. *Word*, 1956, *15*, 325-340.

Fishman, J. A., Cooper, R. L., Ma, R., *et al.* 1968. *Bilingualism in the Barrio*. Washington, D.C.: U.S. Department of Health, Education and Welfare, Office of Education, Bureau of Research. Final report on Contract No. OEC-1-7-062817-0297. (2 vols.).

Gumperz, J. J. On the linguistic markers of bilingual communication. *J. Social Issues 23* (No. 2, April 1967): 48-57.

Haugen, E. *Bilingualism in the Americas: A Bibliography and Research Guide*. American Dialect Society, Publication No. 26. Alabama: University of Alabama Press. (Pages 69-86 The Bilingual Individual, 1956, reprinted in Saporta, 1961.)

Hebb, D. O., Lambert, W. E., & Tucker, G. R. A DMZ in the language war. *Psychology Today*, 1973. *6*, 55-62.

Jakobson, R. *Kindersprache, Aphasie und allgemeine Lautgesetze*. Uppsala, Sweden: Uppsala Universitaets Aarsskrift, 1941.

Krech, D., & R. Crutchfield. *Elements of psychology*. New York: Alfred A. Knopf, Inc., 1958.

Kroeber, A. L. *Anthropology*. New York: Harcourt, Brace & World, Inc., 1948.

Labov, W. *Sociolinguistic patterns*. Philadelphia, Pa.: University of Pennsylvania Press, 1972.

Lambert, W. E., & Anisfeld, E. A note on the relationship of bilingualism and intelligence. *Canadian J. Behavioral Sciences*. In press.

Lenneberg, E. H. Understanding language without ability to speak: A case report. *Journal of Abnormal and Social Psychology*, 1962, *65*, 419-425.

Lenneberg, E. H. Speech as a motor skill with special reference to nonaphasic disorders. In U. Bellugi & R. Brown (Eds.), The acquisition of language. *Monographs of the Society for Research in Child Development*, 1964, *29*, 1-191.

Lenneberg, E. H. *Biological foundations of language*. New York: John Wiley & Sons, Inc., 1967.

Lenneberg, E. H. Of language knowledge, apes, and brains. *Journal of Psycholinguistic Research*, 1971, *1*, 1-29.

Linton, R. *The study of man*. New York: Appleton-Century Crofts, 1936.

Lowie, R. A case of bilingualism. *Word*, 1945, *1*, 249-259.

Macnamara, J. The commission on Irish: Psychological aspects. *Studies* (Summer) 1964, 164-173. Cited in Lambert and Anisfeld, 1969.

Macnamara, J. *Bilingualism and primary education*. Edinburgh, Scotland: Edinburgh University Press, 1966.

McNeill, D. *The conceptual basis of language*. Hillsdale, N.J.: Lawrence Erlbaum Associates, 1979.

Nida, E. A. *Some problems of semantic structure and translation equivalents*. In A William Cameron Townsend en el vigésimoquinto aniversario del Instituto Linguistico de Verano, Mexico, D. F., 1961.

Paivio, A., & Begg, I. *Psychology of language*. Englewood Cliffs, N.J.: Prentice-Hall, Inc., 1981.

Peal, E., & W. E. Lambert. The relation of bilingualism to intelligence. *Psychological Monographs*, 1962. *546* (Vol. 76, no. 27).

Salzinger, K. Ecolinguistics: A radical behavior theory approach to language. In D. Aaronson & R. W. Rieber (Eds.), *Psycholinguistic Research*. Hillsdale, N. J.: Lawrence Erlbaum Associates, 1979.

Sapir, E. *Language*. New York: Harcourt, Brace & World, Inc., 1921.

Skinner, B. F. *Verbal Behavior*. New York: Appleton-Century-Crofts, 1957.

Slobin, D. I. The acquisition of Russian as a native language. In F. Smith and G. A. Miller (Eds.), *The genesis of language*. Cambridge, Mass.: The M.I.T. Press, 1966.

Slobin, D. I. *Psycholinguistics*. Glenview, Ill.: Scott, Foresman & Co., 1971.

Smith, F., & Miller, G. A. (Eds.). *The genesis of language*. Cambridge, Mass.: The M.I.T. Press, 1966.

Templin, M. The study of articulation and language development during the early school years. In F. Smith and G. A. Miller (Eds.), *The genesis of language*, pp. 173-180. Cambridge, Mass.: The M.I.T. Press, 1966.

Velton, H.V. The growth of phonemic and lexical patterns in infant language. *Language, 1943, 19*, 281-292.

Vetter, H. J., & Howell, R. W. Theories of language acquistion. *Journal of Psycholinguistic Research*, 1971, *1*, 33-64.

Ward, M. C. *Them children: A study in language learning*. New York: Holt, Rinehart & Winston, Inc., 1971.

Weinreich, U. *Languages in contact*. New York: Linguistic Circle, 1953.

Weir, R. H. Some questions on the child's learning of morphology. In F. Smith and G. A. Miller (Eds.), *The genesis of language*, 172, Cambridge, Mass.: The M.I.T. Press, 1966.

Wiggins, J. S., Renner, K. E., Clore, G. L., & Rose, R. J. *The psychology of personality*. Reading, Mass.: Addison-Wesley, 1971.

Chapter 8

SPEECH PATHOLOGIES

The study of speech irregularities and problems of comprehension provides valuable clues toward an understanding of normal linguistic behavior; it also provides clues with which to trace the neurological correlates of speech, and frequently it has implications for learning theory.

The simplest type of irregularity is the nongrammatical pause, which may be silent or accompanied by an empty filler of the sort that we usually represent as "er" or "uh." The investigation of such phenomena helps us to deduce the processes that take us from concept to utterance. From a consideration of such normal aberrations of speech, we shall move into rather complex problems, such as the types of performance that result from brain damage and from severe emotional disturbances.

HESITATION AND PAUSAL PHENOMENA

In the course of a normal conversation we not only pause, but we also break off in the middle of an utterance, repeat ourselves, and in general present the listener with a highly fragmented stream of sounds. The listener, thanks to linguistic competence, is usually able

to follow the sense of the errant stream and make some suitable response.

Obviously the listener depends on a sufficient context to make an
interpretation, but how does the speaker generate an utterance? The
most naive psychological theory is that the speaker responds to some
stimulus with a word, with which the stimulus has been associated
previously, and then that first word serves as a stimulus for the elicitation of a previously associated second word, and so forth.

Lashley's classic statement on serial order in behavior (1951) and
Chomsky's criticisms (1957) stilled most discussions based on the notion that language is simply a matter of unit-by-unit sequencing, yet
some closely related ideas governed early approaches to the study of
hesitation phenomena: transition probabilities and the suggestion that
pauses are attributable to the relative unavailability of the next word
(Goldman-Eisler, 1958a, 1958b, 1961a, 1961b; Maclay & Osgood,
1959).

Transition Probabilities

In analyzing an extensive corpus of spontaneous speech, Maclay
and Osgood (1959) noted that pauses occurred more often before
content words (nouns, verbs, adjectives, adverbs) than before function words (connectives and other expressions that relate the more
substantive words to each other grammatically). This suggested that
the unfilled pauses were the result of difficulty in selecting the next
lexical, or content, word. Presumably because the function words are
used much more frequently than given lexical items, we have had
more practice with them and thus experience little difficulty in producing them. The less rehearsed content words, on the contrary, are
presumably not as readily available to the speaker—thus the pauses.

A very similar idea had been advanced somewhat earlier by Goldman-Eisler (1958a, 1958b), who was influenced by certain notions
derived from information theory. She argued that hesitations seemed
to occur before the relatively less predictable words in a sentence, the
words that have a low transition probability. While pauses do often
precede an increase in information, however, information just as
often increased without a preceding pause. Subsequently (1961a,
1961b, 1961c) she attributed the silent (unfilled) pauses to the speaker's monitoring his or her own speech and to verbal planning (see
Bernstein, 1962). Using a somewhat different approach, Boomer
(1965) also challenged the transitional probability theory of hesitations.

Hesitation and Speech Production

To test the specific hypothesis that hesitations were to be attributed to the unavailability of the next lexical item, Howell and Vetter (1968) demonstrated that very low-frequency nouns could be employed as readily as high-frequency nouns, thus supporting Deese's (1961) notion that once a word has been thoroughly learned, it usually remains available.

In the Howell and Vetter (1968) study, word frequency as such was much less important than the semantic and grammatical contexts of the words. Thus a very low-frequency word such as "caboose," which would have been troublesome if Maclay and Osgood (1959) were correct, posed no problem. But a more frequently used word, such as "grief" or "consequence," was very likely to involve obvious hesitation, apparently because an elaborate verbal context seems to be required by the word, while "caboose" and such nouns can be fitted to a simple frame: "It's a. . . ." Thus the construction of a sentence around some words involved more difficult grammatical and semantic considerations, while word frequency as such was not a consideration.

If word frequency does not account for most hesitation phenomena, what does? Since verbal planning and monitoring one's speech, as previously suggested, seemed reasonable, Howell and Vetter (1969) tried explictly to relate hesitations to the cognitive complexity of utterances. Subjects were required to form sentences based on certain stimulus nouns (as in the previous Howell and Vetter study), only this time the words were presented one, two, and three at a time. Presumably more hesitations would be noted when a subject had to fit two words into a single sentence than when only one word was presented, and yet more complexity should be implied when three words have to be fitted to a single sentence.

Howell and Vetter (1969) found that the actual time spent vocalizing was directly related to the number of stimulus words in the sentence. The ratio for preliminary hesitations (time from hearing the stimulus word to the time vocalization begins) was 3:1. Thus about 3 seconds elapsed before subjects began sentences with one stimulus word, 6 seconds before beginning sentences with two stimulus words, and 9 seconds before beginning those with three stimulus words.

Thus preliminary hesitation seemed clearly to be taken up with verbal planning, suggesting that the verbal planning time was a linear function of the cognitive complexity of the task.

The amount of pausing after the sentence was begun was roughly parallel to the vocalization time, but the placing of the pauses once the sentence was begun suggested that monitoring and sometimes additional verbal planning was taking place. An even more open-ended demonstration of the relationship between hesitation and cognitive complexity was provided by Goldman-Eisler (1961a), who compared the amount of hesitation observed when subjects described cartoons and when they had to abstract the meaning behind the cartoons; the latter task required a great deal of hesitation.

Comparative Study of Hesitation Phenomena

Most of the research reported in the professional literature has dealt with the investigation of hesitation phenomena among native speakers of English, while relatively little attention has been paid to such phenomena from a comparative standpoint.

Howell and Yamaguchi (1977) conducted a partial replication of the Howell and Vetter studies (1968, 1969) using native speakers of Japanese. The original study argued for a linear relationship between hesitation and the cognitive complexity of the speaking task; the Japanese study did not refute the argument, but it revealed a number of tactical differences in approaching the task that depend on sociocultural considerations as well as more strictly linguistic factors.

In Japan there seem to be sex differences which may derive from more general sociolinguistic differences in patterns of male and female speech. Further, preliminary and internal hesitation had to be redefined for the Japanese case in order to make comparisons with the American findings. In particular, for Americans the first vocalization after presentation of the stimulus words tended to occur shortly before beginning the sentence containing those words. At least the first part of the sentence had been planned before vocalizing began. The Japanese subjects began to vocalize almost immediately after hearing the stimulus words and only then began the appropriate verbal planning. This seems to reflect the different feedback patterns for Japanese in direct interaction.

Once these allowances had been made, the results accorded well with the findings for American subjects. But the experiment was extended to include verbs as stimulus words. When single verb stimulus words were presented, the results were virtually the same as when a single noun served as a stimulus word. But when two or three stimulus words had to be dealt with there was an unexpected tendency for subjects to use embedded constructions, in effect converting the verbs to noun phrases and treating the results as if nouns were the stimuli. Not only was there more hesitation than with the corresponding noun series, but there was nearly as much hesitation with two stimulus verbs as with three of them. While it would be premature to suggest that the results indicate that somehow "nounness" is more basic psycholinguistically than "verbness," it does suggest that the possibilities for enhancing our understanding of the relation of language and mental processes through studies of hesitation phenomena may be considerably greater than has been realized up to the present.

Early concern with the placing of hesitations in terms of lexical versus nonlexical items has given way to a current focus on the placing of hesitations in terms of words, phrases, clauses, and sentences (Goldman-Eisler, 1972; Cook, Smith, & Lalljee, 1974). The Howell and Yamaguchi study (1977) began with a perspective informed by the older material and concluded with questions relating directly to problems of syntactic complexity. Some efforts have been made to relate hesitation phenomena to problems of aphasis (Quinting, 1971; Spreen & Wachal, 1973). Dale (1974) has explored the idea that the placing of hesitations in the speech of mothers provides children with syntactic information; Jones (1974) has used hesitations as a way of testing certain aspects of Basil Bernstein's arguments regarding restricted and elaborated codes.

Hesitation and Anxiety

We have argued that in normal, spontaneous speech, pauses are mainly a function of verbal planning, but the spate of studies made on this subject during the last 15 years was largely stimulated by clinical observations that pauses appeared to be closely correlated with states of anxiety. There is no necessary contradiction in these views; the implication is that during the clinical interview, there may be more cognitive activity, which is not directly reflected in the patient's speech.

Mahl and Schulze (1969) cite a number of sources to the effect that prolonged silences (rather than brief hesitations) seem to reflect the inhibition or suppression of aggressive and erotic impulses, an editing out of the linguistic expression of such impulses, and an attempt to elicit responses from the therapist. In general, their interpretation is that long pauses imply conflict, fear, and anxiety. While the psychotherapy situation contains complexities that may not be directly relevant to more casual conversational situations, these observations do not contradict the concepts of monitoring and verbal planning. The differences seem to lie mainly in the content of the cognitive activity that is not reflected in verbalization.

STUTTERING

Stuttering usually appears first in childhood, between the ages of four and five. It usually involves repetition of a phoneme, syllable, or word often enough to disrupt easy communication. In addition the speech of the stutterer tends to be too rapid, too restricted in pitch range, is overtense, lacks expressive coloring, and is generally clumsy in articulation (Johnson & Moeller, 1967; Van Riper, 1973; Wingate, 1976).

Theories of Stuttering

Theories of stuttering fall into three main categories. Breakdown theories see a momentary failure of the complex coordinations involved in the production of speech. Repressed need theories maintain that certain neurotic needs are satisfied by stuttering. While anticipatory struggle reaction theories assume that the stutterer anticipates speaking difficulty, tenses the vocal apparatus, and thus precipitates the condition he has anticipated.

Most breakdown theories assert that a child must be predisposed to stuttering before speech can disintegrate. In general, the problem is thought to have a genetic basis (West, 1958), but still, stutterers do not have difficulty every time they try to speak. Most can be quite fluent in the absence of an audience, in the presence of an audience that poses no threat to the ego (household pets, small children), or when performing anonymously, as when singing or reciting aloud in a chorus (Eisenson, 1938). Thus stuttering is not simply a physical problem.

One theory that enjoyed support for many years was that of cerebral dominance, which postulated that if one hemisphere is not sufficiently dominant over the other, the two hemispheres tend to function independently with poor synchronization and a consequent breakdown in speech production (Travis, 1931, 1957). This theory presumably accounted for stuttering said to occur if handedness was changed, as when a left-handed person was forced to write with the right hand. But the vast majority of children whose handedness has been changed do not stutter. Thus the validity of the Travis theory is open to serious question, but the notion of cerebral dominance recurs when we deal with aphasia.

Anticipatory struggle reaction theories typically depend on the assumption that stuttering develops from normal hesitation phenomena found in children's speech when undue attention is called to them by impatient or anxious parents (Bloodstein, 1958; Bluemel, 1935, 1957; Johnson & Moeller, 1967).

Repressed need theories are largely psychoanalytic, drawing on the concept of the infantile need for oral erotic gratification or else seeing stuttering as an indirect expression of hostility or as a manifestation of an unconscious desire to suppress speech. Such theories find most of their support in clinical observations; to date they find little support from other sources.

Social Factors and Stuttering

A careful study of stuttering in different language areas is necessary not only for a fuller understanding of the linguistic events involved, but also for a more perfect understanding of the cultural and/ or genetic basis of stuttering. The incidence of stuttering in the United States population is about 0.7 percent (Conner, 1970). Similar figures have been reported for Denmark, Hungary, Belgium, Great Britain, and other European countries, though the claim is made that stuttering is rare or absent in so-called primitive societies (Bloodstein, 1969).

There are indisputable emotional aspects to the problem, so it seems likely that the absence of stuttering means a lack of the kinds of social situation that fosters stuttering. But if stuttering depends on a genetic predisposition, it should be possible to trace the distribution of the gene(s) responsible. Under the circumstances, it seems that preliterate peoples should serve as an excellent control for any investigation of the origins of the disorder.

But is stuttering really so rare in preliterate societies? If such reports depend to any appreciable extent on the reports of ethnographers, the issue is in considerable doubt. Most ethnographers go into the field to seek general social or cultural information and would see little reason to comment on the presence of an occasional stutterer; further, ethnographers all too frequently have a limited command of the language under study and tend, in any event, to work with a small number of adult informants for their data. The odds are against the appearance of reports that would provide reliable information on the incidence of stuttering among preliterates. The information could be obtained, of course, if ethnographers had some reason to check specifically on the question.

Social factors appear to be critical in stuttering. In the United States, at least, public-school speech therapists report that in large metropolitan areas, the "better" neighborhoods have a disproportionately high number of stutterers. Similarly, college students show an incidence two or three times higher than that of the grade-school population. Thus in the United States, stuttering seems to be mainly a middle- and upper middle-class problem (Bloodstein, 1969).

In addition to the factors of social class and parental pressures that promote stuttering, the disorder is most typical of childhood and is predominantly found among males. There is some variation with the age and educational status of the groups surveyed, but generally there are two dozen male stutterers to one female stutterer; and males tend to experience a more severe form of stuttering than females, and are less likely to grow out of it (Schuell, 1946).

A substantial number of stutterers recover without resorting to the services of a speech therapist. Wingate's (1976) careful review of published reports on stuttering remission indicates that about half (42 per cent) of identified stutterers recover; even if untreated, stuttering does not "grow" or "develop;" and prospects for remission are best in childhood and poorest in adult years.

APHASIA

Damage to the brain from traumatic injury or disease can result in various kinds of language and related sensorimotor disturbances. The vocabulary to describe specific manifestations of the disorder seems practically without limit, so here we will deal mainly with those aspects of the problem that have been informed by a linguistic orientation.

Ruth Lesser (1978), in a review of linguistic studies of aphasia, notes that the interdisciplinary field of aphasiology—the study of how brain damage can disrupt the use and system of language in adults—"offers unique opportunities to find out more about the anatomo-physiological organization of the human brain; it gives scope for the distinguishing of psychologically separate components in mental operations of language; it provides a testing ground and inspiration for linguistic theory" (p. ix). And it is hoped that its findings may contribute directly to the rehabilitation of those who have suffered aphasic disorders.

Varieties of Aphasic Behavior

Since head wounds are often untidy, involving damage to more than a single area of the brain, the most controlled opportunity for study appears in the course of brain surgery, when aphasic behavior can be induced by electrical stimulation of specific areas. Penfield and Roberts (1959) have provided a map of the localization of functions in the brain, based on a survey of the clinical literature on aphasia (see Figure 2.1 in Chapter 2).

Two gross categories of aphasia are illustrated by the following samples from Goodglass (1968). The first is commonly associated with damage to Broca's area (shown in Figure 2.1):

> Yes . . . ah . . . Monday . . . ah . . . Dad and Peter Hogan (pseudonym for the speaker), and Dad . . . ah . . . Hospital . . . and ah . . . Wednesday, nine o'clock and ah Thursday . . . ten o'clock ah doctors . . . two . . . two . . . an doctors and . . . ah . . . teeth . . . yah. And a doctor . . . an girl . . . and gums, and I. (p. 178)

The speech is telegraphic, with few inflectional endings or function words, and a virtually complete loss of syntactic complexity. That is, there is little in the way of coordinating and subordinating constructions.

This "agrammatic" aphasia contrasts with a "fluent" variety, in which the most striking characteristic is difficulty in producing specific words, usually nouns:

> Well, I had trouble with . . . oh, almost everything that happened from the . . . eh, eh . . . Golly, the word I can remember, you know, is ah . . . When I had the . . . ah biggest . . . ah . . . that I had the trouble with, you know . . . that I had the trouble with, and I still have a . . . the ah . . . different . . . The things I want to say . . . ah . . . The way I say things, but I understand mostly things, most of them and what the things are. (p. 179)

It would be most convenient if we could simply assign the first type of disorder to Broca's area and the second to Wernicke's area (see Figure 2-1), but the matter is not that simple. Penfield and Roberts (1959) argue that there are no really pure forms of defect. The aphasic may be relatively less capable in one aspect of language than the other, but is seldom completely capable in any aspect. Moreover, the popular idea that multilingual aphasics may suffer disturbances in one language while having normal control of speech in another language is very doubtful. At least, Penfield is convinced (Penfield & Roberts, 1959, p. 221), on the basis of 30 years' experience with French-English bilinguals in Montreal, that careful testing always shows defects in both languages. The point is important to the issue of whether different areas of the brain are used for different languages.

The whole of the cerebral cortex seems to participate in the various language processes, but not all locales are equally important in this respect. The superior cortical speech area (see Figure 2.1) is most dispensable. If this area in the dominant hemisphere is removed, the result is an aphasia that disappears in a few weeks. If Broca's area is removed, the resultant aphasia eventually clears up completely in some cases, but possibly not in all cases. On the other hand, any large destruction of the posterior (Wernicke's) area has lasting and serious effects. In the case of a child, a major lesion in the posterior speech cortex or in the underlying thalamus results in the transfer of language processes to the opposite hemisphere. In the case of adults, it is doubtful that a similar transfer is possible. We are again reminded of the recurring argument that puberty marks important developmental changes in language ability.

The terminology found in discussions of aphasia is bewildering, but we have already seen that there are at least two characteristic problems of language production: grammatical and lexical. In addition, we should expect to see problems of comprehension. Jakobson (1966) has indicated some important differences between the tasks of the aphasic speaker and the listener. The speaker begins with certain basic notions, represented by his or her content words, and must then build a context for these by means of the function words. The agrammatic type of aphasia disturbs the second part of the process, while the fluent type disturbs the process of selecting the content words, but leaves the basic syntactic constructions intact. The use of content words in the absence of a grammatical context is what gives the agrammatic type the appearance of telegraphic speech. While the speaker knows what he or she wants to say, the listener depends on the whole to understand the parts. The listener, says Jakobson,

> is a probabilist to a much greater extent than the (speaker). Thus there are no homonyms for the speaker; when he says "bank" he knows perfectly whether he is speaking about the shore of a river or a financial establishment, whereas the listener, as long as he is

not helped by the context, struggles with homonymy and has to
use a probability test. The identification of the constituents is the
second stage. (p. 72)

Thus the speaker may have trouble dredging up key words, or may
be able to produce the words but not to relate them grammatically.
In the first case the listener must guess the missing lexical items, and
in the second must guess how the items are supposed to be related.

Studies of the sort conducted by Goodglass and Hunt (1958) and
Goodglass and Berko (1960) seem particularly well suited to an at-
tack on the question of how encoding (speaking) and decoding (interpreting or listening) are related. In the former study, 24 aphasic
subjects answered questions based on a statement read to them by the
examiner:

Examiner reads: "My sister lost her gloves." (This is repeated.)

Question 1.   What did she lose?

Question 2.   Whose gloves were they?

The subjects thus have to understand the statement and respond
to two aspects. The first requires production of the plural marker
(gloves); the second requires production of the possessive marker
(sister's). According to their interpretation of Jakobson's position,
Goodglass and his associates felt the patients with agrammatism
(contiguity disorder, telegraphic speech) should have more trouble
with the possessive than with the plural; and as predicted, the possessive /s/ was much more frequently omitted than the plural /s/. While
it may not be critical, it should be noted that the sample item given
above (from Goodglass, 1968) requires that the subject just repeat the
plural form of the original, while the possessive does not appear in
the original, and thus must be supplied as well as articulated by the
subject.

By asking subjects to indicate whether certain sentences are correct or incorrect, it is possible to determine whether aphasics can realize that various features are missing such as the missing plural
marker in "three book," the missing possessive marker in "ship an-
chor," or the missing third person marker in "he run." On the basis
of these and similar experiments, Goodglass concluded that there was
no correspondence between the inability to use a form and the inability to recognize it auditorily. The two processes appear to be
somewhat independent.

Earlier, Jakobson (1955) had suggested that in aphasia, grammatical features are lost in the opposite order to that of acquisition. That
is, the features mastered last by the child are the first to be lost

through aphasia. This is usually called the "regression hypothesis" (but see Wepman & Jones, 1964, for another regression hypothesis). Jakobson's hypothesis received some support from experiments conducted by Goodglass and Berko (1960), but Goodglass (1968) found that aphasics also "showed a wide range of difficulty with grammatical operations that had already been well mastered by Berko's young children" (p. 188).

The question of whether there really are different types of aphasia has also been linked to the old but continuing argument over the "equipotentiality" versus "localization" of brain functions. Howes (1967), depending on experiments that were based on written rather than spoken forms of language, concluded that there are two distinct types of aphasia, and at least one of the neural systems that underlie these types must be an equipotential system. (Equipotentiality is implied when recovery takes place because the functions of the damaged tissue have been taken over by some other tissue.)

As Lenneberg has pointed out (in Wepman & Jones, 1966), in addition to the problems of grammatical relationships and lexical availability, there is an emotional component. Some patients do better when alone or relaxed, while others do better when greatly exercised. In one case, a patient with global injuries and severe disturbances of both types, who could say nothing, was about to be sent home to a relative whom he could not stand: he became very excited and suddenly spoke quite fluently.

Finally, Luria (1959, 1962) has argued that in aphasia it is not so much the signals that are lost as the significance of the signals. Jakobson (1966) expounds the idea thus: there is "no question of inability to hear or articulate vowels of longer or shorter duration (in languages such as Czech or Hungarian): what is lost is the distinctive semantic value of the difference between long and short signals in the phonemic code" (p. 71).

SCHIZOPHRENIC SPEECH

The other major area of speech pathology is the range of disturbances associated with schizophrenic disorders. In the case of stuttering or aphsaia, we assume that the speaker desires to communicate in normal terms, and that the cognitive processes are essentially intact. In the case of schizophrenia, there is often reason to doubt that the patient desires to communicate in the normal sense, and the cognitive processes frequently appear to be distorted. Indeed, there is a lively and perennial debate over whether the phenomena that have been identified as "schizophrenic language" are actually the symptoms of "schizophrenic thought." These two issues—the peculiarities of schizophrenic communication and the relationship between disordered thought and disordered language—have dominated a good deal of the research and theory on schizophrenic speech.

Schizophrenic Communication

Many clinicians would probably subscribe to Ferreira's (1960) notion that the schizophrenic manipulates or disguises language in order to conceal thoughts known to be dangerous and forbidden: "in the privacy of his language, the schizophrenic finds the much looked-after opportunity to say a piece of his mind about a relationship the nature of which he could not state publicly" (p. 136).

Bateson, Jackson, Haley, and Weakland (1956, 1963) have advanced the theory that schizophrenia has its origin in the "double bind" in which a younster finds him or herself when a parent consistently conveys simultaneous but incongruent messages. That is, the mother says words to the effect, "come here, I love you," but at the same time communicates rejection by her tone of voice, gestures, and other subtle cues. If the child discriminates accurately between the messages, he or she will be punished by the realization that the mother does not really love him or her, but if the child does not discriminate accurately between them, and takes the verbal message at face value, he will then approach her. When the child approaches, the mother will become hostile, so the child will withdraw; then the mother will rebuke her son or daughter for withdrawing, because that signified that she was not a loving mother. Either way the child loses, and thus is in a double bind.

So far the double bind concept has been pretty well received, and if Bateson et al. are correct, it may be more than a coincidence that schizophrenic verbalizations are frequently ambiguous, difficult, or impossible to interpret. That is, the schizophrenic frequently offers difficult messages to those with whom he or she appears to be interacting.

The schizophrenic's apparent flatness of affect, inappropriate expression of affect combined with withdrawal, or loss of interest in the social and physical environment, are probably the most widely cited characteristics of the disorder. It is typically withdrawal that seems to be expressed in schizophrenic speech. Tangential responses and the pursuing of irrelevant details are easily interpreted as an avoidance of direct communication.

The omission of transitional expressions and joining of disparate ideas (called scattering) is less readily interpreted in the same way, though the effect is still poor communication. The following written example of scattering (from Maher, 1966) seems almost like a third or fourth approximation to English:

> If things turn by rotation of agriculture or levels in regards and "timed" to everything; I am re-fering to a previous document when I made some remarks that were facts also tested and there is another that concerns my daughter she has a *lobed* bottom right ear, her name being Mary Lou . . . Much of abstraction has been left unsaid and undone in this product/milk syrup, and others due to economics, differentials, subsidies, bankruptcy, tools, buildings, bonds, national stocks, foundation craps, weather, trades, government in levels of breakages and fuses in electronic too all formerly "stated" not necessarily *factuated*. (Italicized words are considered to be neologisms) (p. 395).

The idea that the schizophrenic employs language in order not to communicate is an interesting one, but there is a contrary school of thought that also finds considerable support. Ullman and Krasner (1969), for example, argue that in a sense the deficiency is in the listener rather than in the patient. The listener, if able to fill in the gaps, would "understand" the patient. We shall take up this idea in relation to the distinction between "schizophrenic thought disorders" and "schizophrenic language disorders" because it bears significantly on the kinds of inferences that lead to the former or the latter. At any rate, Ullman and Krasner seem to be suggesting that material which seems unintelligible on the surface may actually make some sort of sense. Of course, the patient and the normal listener are not observing the same interactional rules, but according to this view, the desire to communicate in normal terms may actually be present.

Language Disorder or Thought Disorder?

Clinicians have tended to regard speech as a direct reflection of thought. Thus, schizophrenic patients whose speech is disrupted to the point of incoherence and unintelligibility are identified as showing the symptoms of "formal thought disorder." Attention has been drawn to some of the problems created by treating speech and thought as isomorphic by Chaika (1974), LeCours and Vanier-Clement (1976) and others. But Rochester (1979) emphasizes that the issue is further complicated by this "inferential tradition":

> To say that a speaker is incoherent is only to say that one cannot understand that speaker. So to make a statement about incoherent discourse is really to make a statement about one's own confusion. It is therefore just as appropriate to study what it is about the listener which makes him or her "confusable" as it is to study what it is about the speaker which makes him or her "confusing." The focus of study simply depends on the direction of attribution. (p. 3)

One of the consequences of the inferential tradition is that the assessment of "thought disorder" in both clinical and experimental contexts has been based on speech, not thought. A second consequence is that "talk failures" are inferences based on the listener's own experience of confusion. As Figure 8-1 from Rochester's book *Crazy Talk* (1979) demonstrates, thought disorder and incoherent talk constitute parts of a tautology.

Leaving aside for the moment the question of how to distinguish between language and cognition in the psychopathological setting, are there any features by which "schizophrenic speech" or "schizophrenic language" can be identified with any degree of consistency or reliability?

In his presidential address to the Eastern Psychological Association in 1973, Roger Brown reminisced about a period of 3 weeks of "total immersion in schizophrenia" he had spent at several hospitals in the Harvard locality and at least one meeting of the Cambridge Chapter of Schizophrenics Anonymous. He stated that he found "plenty of schizophrenic thought" but nothing that qualified as "schizophrenic speech." From this he was led to conclude that there is no such critter. If this conclusion raises the eyebrows of those who have spent a good deal longer than 3 weeks observing and studying persons diagnostically labeled schizophrenic, the explanation might lie in Brown's definition of schizophrenic speech. Brown equates schizophrenic speech with regressed speech, which suggests childlike speech, and tells us:

> While I fairly often heard patients spoken to with what I call nursery school intonation, a kind of exaggerated prosody that

Figure 8.1. Imaginary conversation between student and textbook writer. From Rochester, S., and Martin, J.R. *Crazy Talk*. New York: Plenum Press, 1979, p. 5. Reproduced by permission of the authors and publisher.

most adults use with children, I have to report that in my three weeks I never heard anything childlike from a patient nor indeed anything I would want to set apart as schizophrenic speech. (p. 397)

The concept of schizophrenia as a "regression psychosis" has been popular with theorists of a psychoanalytic persuasion. Among psychopathologists whose orientation is behavioral rather than psychodynamic, the concept has largely been discredited. As Maher (1966) has noted, the mere demonstration of a superficial resemblance between some feature of schizophrenic behavior and that of child behavior does not bring us appreciably closer to an understanding of the psychotic behavior. He concludes that the concept of schizophrenia as a psychosis of regression has not been demonstrated with respect to language, and expressed doubt as to the potential usefulness of such demonstrations in psychopathological investigations.

If schizophrenic speech is not childlike or regressed, what are its salient characteristics?

Analyses by Linguists and Aphasiologists

In 1974, linguist Elaine Chaika reported the results of an analysis of a taped interview with a thirty-seven-year-old female schizophrenic patient, who was under medication with thorazine—a major tranquilizer—at the time of the recording. The patient's record indicated that she spoke normally for periods ranging up to several weeks, but that her deviant language coincided with "psychotic episodes." The excerpts presented below were taken from what Chaika describes as "virtually a monologue:" the patient's intonation did not allow intrusions and she often seemed to be talking to herself.

Preceded by 20 second pause
(2) a. My mother's name was Bill. (pause)
     b. (low pitch, as in an aside, but with marked rising question intonation) . . . and coo?
     c. St. Valentine's Day is the official startin' of the breedin' season of the birds.
     d. All buzzards can coo.
     e. I like to see it pronounced buzzards rightly.
     f. They work hard.
     g. So do parakeets.
(3) a. This is a holy smoke (Dr: that's a cigarette you're holding)
     b. It's a holy one. (pause)

    c. It goes in one hole and out the other and that makes it holy.

Preceded by 45 second pause

(4) a. In a month I've been upstairs, they've been taking my brains out a piece at a time or all together.

     b. Federal case doesn't mean communication.

     c. Steal from Mrs. Gotrocks, she can afford it.

     d. I've got something (inaudible).

     e. Did that show up on the X-rays?

     f. You'll see it tonight.

     g. I've been drinking phosphate.

     h. You'll see it in the dark (inaudible)

     i. Glows.

     j. We all glow as we're glowworms.

Preceded by 30 second pause

(5) a. Oh, it's that thorazine. I forgot I had it.

     b. That's Lulubelle. (pp. 260-261)

Chaika suggested on the basis of the corpus excerpted here and on the basis of samples of schizophrenic speech reported in the literature that there were half a dozen characteristics of such language, and raised the possibility that speech judged to be "schizophrenic" by researchers results from an intermittent, cyclical aphasia. But another linguist, Victoria Fromkin (1975) has challenged Chaika's conclusions on the grounds that with the exception of disruption of discourse (as seen in 4a-4i), the phenomena identified as characteristics of schizophrenic speech can be found in normal speech performance. As evidence she cites some excerpts from *The White House Transcripts* (Gold, 1974) to show that normal productions "are filled with incorrect deletions, repetitions, syntactic rule misapplications" and other deviant properties (p. 501):.

4. a. D. The fact that the civil case drew to a halt—that the depositions were halted he is freed. (p. 60)

    b. P. Going on to the interrogatory thing—we shall see—your view would not to give any further ground on that? (p. 79)

    c. H. That is the kind of thing that, you know, we really ought to do is call the Speaker. (p. 64)

    d. D. I suppose the other area we are going to see some publicity on in the coming weeks because I think now that the indictments are down there will be a cresting on that—the whitewash—the civil rights cases in advance. (p. 64)

    e. D. I was talking the '68 incident that occurred. (p. 84)

In her rebuttal to Fromkin, Chaika (1977) contrasts the samples from *The White House Transcripts* with a specimen of schizophrenic "word salad" reported by Lorenz (1961):

> The honest bring-back-to-life doctors agents must take John Black out through making up design meaning straight neutral under-world shadow tunnel.

The structure of the syntax errors in this passage cannot be easily identified, while the deviance in the White House passages is "caused by piling sentence upon sentence, often failing to embed subsequent sentences into the matrix, or to finish the matrix" (p. 466). But within each utterance, the phrases and sentences are understandable and, for the most part, syntactically correct.

The possibility raised by Chaika that schizophrenic speech may reflect an intermittent aphasia has been of interest and concern to aphasiologists, as indicated by the attention this issue has received in the professional literature (Benson, 1973; Gerson, Benson, & Frazier, 1977). LeCours and Vanier-Clement (1976) contributed to the discussion with a review of "schizophasia," which is characterized by various paraphasias (inappropriate placement of phonemes, morphemes, or larger syntactic units) and other inappropriate practices (each with a technical label which need not concern us here).

The Rochester and Martin Analysis

In reviewing descriptive analyses such as the study by Lecours and Vanier-Clement, Rochester and Martin (1979) noted that (1) not every schizophrenic patient is schizophasic and (2) not every schizophasic patient is schizophasic all of the time. According to the authors:

> These facts have been responsible for great confusion in experimental investigations. Experimenters have behaved as if "schizophasia" could be sampled at random from unselected schizophrenic patients. It is no wonder that there have been so many failures to replicate even the simplest "verbal behavior" studies (p. 43).

They draw the conclusion that if schizophasia is episodic, then investigators must seek to capture the episodes and describe them. Further, more precise descriptions must be given of patient characteristics in order to determine whether some sorts of patients are more likely than others to show different types of discourse failure.

> In their own research with thought disordered (TD) and non-thought disordered (NTD) schizophrenics, Rochester and Martin (1979) found no instances of the severe agrammatism that has sometimes been identified in earlier studies, though their TD patients were young, relatively intact persons, while much of the literature on the language of schizophrenics deals with chronic schizophrenics, generally older patients, who may have been suffering the adverse consequences of organic brain damage.

Two aspects of discourse failure which distinguished TD speakers from other speakers in the Rochester and Martin study were: (1) a strong dependency on the lexical meanings of words to achieve cohesion between clauses and sentences; and (2) a tendency to rely on the prosodic features of clauses and words to link these clauses to the prior context. These findings confirm previously reported results of a similar kind. They appear to be closely related to a third feature of TD discourse noted by Rochester and Martin: the difficulties posed for the listener in comprehending the TD speaker as a consequence of the tendency for the latter to rely on high proportions of implicit reference in which the referents are frequently obscure to the point of inaccessibility.

Rochester and Martin have sought to interpret their findings within the theoretical/analytical framework provided by Halliday (Halliday, 1978; Halliday & Hasan, 1976) on "phoricity systems." These systems structure utterances on the basis of what speakers assume their listeners know; thus, the study of phoricity systems supplies an analytical approach to reference and referential processes. Based on Halliday's work, Rochester and Martin "assume that the speaker processes meanings into expressions by making choices within a number of language systems" (p. 177): phonological/written expressions, lexicogrammatical forms, and semantic meanings within text. It is assumed that the fully competent adult speaker can produce coherent texts by making appropriate decisions at each of the three levels or strata mentioned above.

If the speaker is subjected to fatigue, stress, or some other factor or factors which result in the reduction of control over language processing, he or she begins to fail to produce coherent discourse in certain orderly, predictable ways:

The first failures occur at the level of sentence-to-sentence links and may be seen in a lack of topic direction, in failures to establish major and minor role actors and clear event lines, and in a lack of certain kinds of cohesion between clauses. Later failures would include the earlier ones and, in addition, involve mistakes at the lexicogrammatical stratum of language use. In this case, one would see the use of neologisms, inadequate grammatical forms, and the use of inappropriate wordings of various kinds. However, the intonation patterns and pausing and other prosodic features of normal speech would be more or less intact. Finally, a complete breakdown in language operations would be signaled by the speaker's inability to match intonation patterns or select rhyming words when asked. (pp. 177-178)

Rochester and Martin use the concept of "stratal slips" to summarize this interpretation of discourse failures at the various successive levels of linguistic functioning. Stratal slips can occur *within-text* (when cohesion based on semantic linkage is replaced by cohesion based on lexicogrammatical forms or prosodic features) or *outside-of-text* (when connections within the text are reduced and connections between the text and the verbal or nonverbal aspects of the situational context are increased).

The significance of the Rochester and Martin analysis is that it directs attention toward the process or processes that adversely affect the control of language operations. The "depth of processing" formulation the authors have adopted is not restricted to dealing narrowly with linguistic functions, but is concerned with a much broader range of cognitive activities. As Rochester and Martin have stated, it seems essential "to add onto studies of language processing simultaneous studies of other aspects of cognitive and perceptual functioning so that one can assess the extent to which incoherent discourse occurs with disrupted functioning in other domains" (p. 186).

While recognizing the importance of this approach, we feel that it is unduly restrictive in its focus upon the individual schizophrenic person. People can talk to pets, small children, inanimate objects, or even to themselves, but most human speech takes place in the context of linguistic interaction between adults, i.e., communication. Failure to relate speech to the communicative context can result in some questionable interpretations of schizophrenic speech production. For example, Brown (1958) refers to a study in which the investigator found that schizophrenics would accept an unusually large number of synonyms for words. Not only is it clear that giving a large range of meanings to words is an exercise in abstraction, but in more or less typical examples of what is described as a penchant for dealing concretely with questions, there may be a clear awareness of conceptual categories of kind and type, as Maria Lorenz (1968) observed after citing the following example:

> A patient is asked to define certain terms:
> Q. Book
> A. It depends on what book you are referring to.
> Q. Table.
> A. What kind of table? A wooden table, a porcelain table, a surgical table, or a table you want to have a meal on?
> Q. House.
> A. There are all kinds of houses, nice houses, nice private houses.
> Q. Life.
> A. I have to know what life you happen to be referring to. *Life Magazine* or to the sweetheart who can make another individual happy. (p. 36)

Linguistically, of course, there is no difficulty. The problem is, in part, one of differing assumptions about the nature or purpose of the communicative act. The questioner expects an abstract, dictionary-type definition to cover the general case, while the subject rejects that expectation. Compare the apparent perversity of the schizophrenic in the above exchange with one of the examples reported by Garfinkel (1967):

> The victim waved his hand cheerily.
> (S) How are you?
> (E) How am I in regard to what? My health, my finances, my school work, my peace of mind, my . . .?
> (S) (Red in the face and suddenly out of control.) Look! I was just trying to be polite. Frankly, I don't give a damn how you are (p. 44).

Garfinkel's experimenter (E) was not schizophrenic: he was dramatizing the fact that assumptions or common understandings that underlie interaction lack properties of strict rational discourse as these are idealized in rules that define an adequate logical proof:

> For the purposes of *conducting their everyday affairs* persons refuse to permit each other to understand "what they are really talking about" in this way. The anticipation that persons *will* un-

derstand, the occasionality of expressions, the specific vagueness of references, the retrospective-prospective sense of a present occurrence, waiting for something later in order to see what was meant before, are sanctioned properties of common discourse (p. 41).

If Garfinkel is correct, a good deal of our daily interaction depends upon ambiguous or vague communication that seems designed to bind two parties while actually insuring their separation. The particular example quoted from Garfinkel illustrates what Malinowski called *phatic communion*, in which it is the mere fact of exchanging utterances which is important and the content of the utterances is virtually irrelevant. By insisting on a literal interpretation of the greeting, the experimenter was behaving in a way that was perceived as hostile. In other examples, the experimenters were seen as ill or in a "bad mood."

It is possible to account for discourse failures by positing some pathological process within the central nervous system that disrupts information processing and thus operates to produce the kinds of language behavior that Rochester and Martin have described as distinguishing TD speakers from NTD speakers. This explanation does not rule out the possibility that certain features of communicative contexts may pose stress and anxiety for the schizophrenic individual which, together with the disruptive aspects of the underlying pathology, distort the schizophrenic's language processing and thus result in severe distortions in communication. Schizophasic speech, as Rochester and Martin have emphasized, is episodic in nature, i.e., varies from situation to situation. It may well be that the clue to this variation must be sought in the varying demands on the schizophrenic in different communicative contexts, along with whatever sources of cognitive disturbance can be attributed to schizophrenic pathology.

REFERENCES

Bateson, G., Jackson, D., Haley, J., & Weakland, J. Toward a theory of schizophrenia. *Behavioral Science*, 1956, *1*, 251–264.

Bateson, G., Jackson, D., Haley, J., & Weakland, J. A note on the double-bind. *Family Process*, 1963, *2*, 154–157.

Benson, D.F. Psychiatric aspects of aphasia. *British Journal of Psychiatry*, 1973, *123*, 555–556.

Bernstein, B. Linguistic codes, hesitation phenomena and intelligence. *Language and Speech*, 1962, *5*, 31–46.

Bloodstein, O. Stuttering as an anticipatory struggle reaction. In J. Eisenson (Ed.), *Stuttering: A symposium*. New York: Harper & Row, 1958.

Bloodstein, O. *A handbook on stuttering*. Chicago: National Society for Crippled Children and Adults, 1969.

Bluemel, C. *Stammering and allied disorders*. New York: The MacMillan Co., 1935.

Bluemel, C. *The riddle of stuttering*. Danville, Ill.: Interstate Publishing Co., 1957.

Boomer, D.S. Hesitation and grammatical encoding. *Language and Speech*, 1965, *8*, 148–158.

Brown, R. *Words and things*. New York: The Free Press, 1958.

Brown, R. Schizophrenia, language and reality. *American Psychologist*, 1973, *28*, 397–403.

Chaika, E. A linguist looks at "schizophrenic" language. *Brain and Language*, 1974, *1*, 257–276.

Chaika, E. Schizophrenic speech, slips of the tongue, and jargon-aphasia: A reply to Fromkin and to LeCours and Vanier-Clement. *Brain and Language*, 1977, *4*, 464–475.

Chomsky, N. *Syntactic structures*. The Hague: Mouton & Co., 1957.

Conner, B.J. A study of the availability of data on incidence of stuttering among various nations. Unpublished M.S. thesis, Tulane University, 1970.

Cook, M., Smith, J., & Lawlee. Filled pauses and syntactic complexity. *Language and Speech*, 1974, 17, 11–16.

Dale, P. Hesitations in maternal speech. *Language and Speech*, 1974, *17*, 174–181.

Deese, J. From the isolated verbal unit to connected discourse. In C.N. Cofer & B.S. Musgrave (Eds.), *Verbal learning and verbal behavior*. New York: McGraw-Hill, 1961.

Eisenson, J. *The psychology of speech*. New York: F.S. Crofts, 1938.

Ferreira, A.J. The semantics and the context of the schizophrenic's language. *Archives of General Psychiatry*, 1960, *3*, 128–138.

Fromkin, V.A. A linguist looks at "A linguist looks at 'schizophrenic' language." *Brain and Language*, 1975, *2*, 498–503.

Garfinkel, H. *Studies in ethnomethodology*. Englewood Cliffs, N.J.: Prentice-Hall, Inc., 1967.

Gerson, S.N., Benson, D.F. & Frazier, S.H. Diagnosis: Schizophrenia vs. posterior aphasia. *American Journal of Psychiatry*, 1977, *134*, 966–969.

Gold, G. (Ed.). *The White House transcripts*. New York: Bantam Books, 1974.

Goldman-Eisler, F. Speech production and the predictability of words in context. *Quarterly Journal of Experimental Psychology*, 1958a, *10*, 96–106.

Goldman-Eisler, F. Speech analysis and mental processes. *Language and Speech*, 1958b, *1*, 59–75.

Goldman-Eisler, F. Hesitation and information in speech. *Information Theory, Fourth London Symposium*, 162–174. London: Buttersworth, 1961a.

Goldman-Eisler, F. A comparative study of two hesitation phenomena. *Language and Speech*, 1961b, *4*, 18–26.

Goldman-Eisler, F. The distribution of pause durations in speech. *Language and Speech*, 1961c, *4*, 232–237.

Goldman-Eisler, F. Pauses, clauses and sentences. *Language and Speech*, 1972, *15*, 103–113.

Goodglass, H. Studies on the grammar of aphasics. In S. Rosenberg & J.H. Koplin (Eds.), *Applied psycholinguistics research*. New York: The Macmillan Company, 1968.

Goodglass, H., & Berko, J. Agrammatism and inflectional morphology in English. *Journal of Speech and Hearing Res.*, 1960, *3*, 257–267.

Goodglass, H., & Hunt, J. Grammatical complexity and aphasic speech. *Word*, 1958, *14*, 197–207.

Halliday, M.A.K. *Language as a social semiotic: The social interpretation of language and meaning*. London: Edward Arnold, 1978.

Howell, R.W., & Vetter, H.J. High and low frequency nouns as sources of hesitation in the production of speech. *Psychonomic Science*, 1968, *12*, 157–158.

Howell, R.W., & Vetter, H.J. Hesitation in the production of speech. *Journal of General Psychology*, 1969, *81*, 261–276.

Howell, R.W., & Yamaguchi, M. Hesitation phenomena in English and Japanese. In F. Peng & M. Hori (Eds.), *The hidden dimensions of communication (Kotoba no Shosô)*. Tôkyô: Bunka Hyôron, 1979.

Howes, D. Some experimental investigations of language in aphasia. In K. Salzinger & S. Salzinger (Eds.), *Research in verbal behavior and some neurophysiological implications*. New York: Academic Press, Inc., 1967.

Jakobson, R. Aphasia as a linguistic problem. In H. Werner (Ed.), *On expressive language*, Worcester, Mass.: University Press, 1955.

Jakobson, R. Linguistic types of aphasia. In E.C. Carterette (Ed.), *Brain Function*. (Vol. III). *Speech, language, and communications*. Berkeley, CA: University of California Press, 1966.

Johnson, W., & Moeller, D. (Eds.). *Speech handicapped school children*. New York: Harper and Row, 1967.

Jones, P.A. Elaborated speech and hesitation patterns. *Language and Speech*, 1974, *17*, 174–181.

Lashley, K.S. The problem of serial order in behavior. In L.A. Jeffress (Ed.), *Cerebral mechanisms in behavior*. New York: John Wiley & Sons, Inc., 1951.

LeCours, A.R., & Vanier-Clement, H. Schizophasia and jargonaphasia: a comparative description with comments on Chaika's and Fromkin's respective looks at "schizophrenic" language. *Brain and Language*, 1976, *3*, 516–565.

Lesser, R. *Linguistic investigation of aphasia*. New York: Elsevier, 1978.

Lorenz, M. Problems posed by schizophrenic language. In H.J. Vetter (Ed.), *Language behavior in schizophrenia*. Springfield, Ill.: Charles C. Thomas, Publisher, 1968.

Luria, A.R. Disorders of "simultaneous perception" in a case of bilateral occipito-parietal brain injury. *Brain*, 1959, *82*, 437–449.

Luria, A.R. *Higher cortical functions in man and their disturbances in local brain lesions*. (In Russian). Moscow: University Press, 1962.

Maclay, H. & C.E. Osgood. Hesitation phenomena in spontaneous English speech. *Word*, 1959, *15*, 19–44.

Mahar, B.A. *Principles of psychopathology*. New York: McGraw-Hill, 1966.

Mahl, G.F. & G. Schulze. Psychological research. In N. Markel (Ed.), *Psycholinguistics: An introduction to the study of speech and personality*. Homewood, Ill.: The Dorsey Press, 1969.

Penfield, W., & Roberts, L. *Speech and brain mechanisms*. Princeton, N.J.: Princeton University Press, 1959.

Quinting, G. *Hesitation phenomena in adult aphasic and normal speech*. The Hague: Mouton and Company, 1971.

Rochester, S., & Martin, J.R. *Crazy talk: A study of the discourse of schizophrenic speakers*. New York: Plenum Press, 1979.

Schuell, H. Sex differences in relation to stuttering: Part I. *Journal of Speech Disorders*, 1946, *11*, 277–298.

Travis, L.E. *Speech pathology: A dynamic neurological treatment of normal speech and speech disorders*. New York: D. Appleton and Company, 1931.

Travis, L.E. *Handbook of speech pathology and audiology*. New York: Appleton-Century-Crofts, 1957.

Ullman, L.P., & Krasner, L. *A psychological approach to abnormal behavior*. Englewood Cliffs, N.J.: Prentice-Hall, Inc., 1969.

Van Riper, C. *The treatment of stuttering*. Englewood Cliffs, N.J.: Prentice-Hall, Inc., 1973.

Wepman, J.M., & Jones, L.V. Five aphasias: a commentary on aphasia as a regressive linguistic phenomenon. *Assoc. Res. Nervous and Mental Disease*, 1964, 42: 190–203.

Wepman, J.M., & Jones, L.V. Studies in aphasia: a psycholinguistic method and case study. In E.C. Carterette (Ed.), *Brain Function (Vol. III). Speech, language, and communication*. Berkeley, CA: University of California Press, 1966.

West, R.W. An agnostic's speculations about stuttering. In Jon Eisenson (Ed.), *Stuttering: A symposium*. New York: Harper & Row, 1958.

Wingate, M.E. *Stuttering: Theory and treatment*. New York: Irvington, 1976.

Chapter 9

DERIVED SYSTEMS

Linguists consider language to be primarily a system of vocal communication, but it can be transposed into nonvocal forms in various ways. The transpositions may correspond rather closely to the spoken forms; in our writing system, for example, we may say in a very general way that each graph (letter) corresponds to a sound, and the sequencing of the graphs corresponds to the sequencing of the sounds in the spoken form of the message. On the other hand, the transposition may be very global; a signal may correspond to a whole message, as in our legendary warning to Paul Revere that one signal light would indicate that the British were approaching by land, while two lights would indicate that they were approaching by sea. One could argue against describing this sort of case as a transposition of language, but we shall keep the example as marking one extreme (the other being, perhaps, a very precise phonetic transcription of a spoken message). Among the types of derived system to be discussed here are scripts, the manual communication system of the deaf, various kinds of secret language, "Pig Latins," drum and whistle languages, and glossolalia, which is a kind of pseudolanguage.

SCRIPTS

The first attempts at graphic communication may have been of the global variety, rather than being isomorphic with spoken language.

The magnificent cave paintings from the Upper Paleolithic period in Europe, which date from about 10 to 15 thousand years ago (Clark, 1967), imply very strongly that mimetic magic was used. The famous masked dancer known as The Sorcerer, for example, who is wearing a wolf's tail and a deerhead mask, seems to be prancing in a ritual dance, which Hoebel (1972, p. 187) compares with the Deer Dance that is performed today by Pueblo Indians. In the same vein, Clark (1967) looks to the Australian aborigines to show that primitive hunters seek an edge in survival and reproduction, and that art is used as a magical device to get that edge.

Of course Upper Paleolithic art does not reflect language, but in the Near East, within a few thousand years, pictures had become pictograms, and had formed the basis for a true system of writing: what Trager (1972) describes as "any conventional system of marks or drawings or analogous artifacts which represents the utterances of a language as such" [p. 180]. The oldest such system, so far as we know, was the cuneiform writing of the Sumerians, developed some 5 to 6 thousand years ago (Trager, 1972, p. 193). The cuneiform messages consisted of wedge-shaped components that were formed into conventionalized pictograms and scratched into clay tablets. Figure 9.1 shows how pictograms (at the top of each sequence) developed into the cuneiform characters. The slightly more recent and perhaps independently invented Egyptian hieroglyphs (Trager, 1972, p. 19) remained more obviously pictorial (Figure 9.2), and were painted onto surfaces, including paper (papyrus), with a brush and ink. By 4 thousand years ago the Chinese were inscribing pictographic characters on bones for purposes of divination, and by the beginning of the Christian Era the Maya were inscribing and painting characters that were basically pictographic, but in many cases were so stylized as to render interpretation difficult or impossible. Trager (1972) and Kroeber (1948) both give helpful discussions of the Maya system; Friedrich (1957) deals with most of the Old World early writing systems, including many that have never been appreciably deciphered. Trager (1972) gives the most comprehensive and concise recent treatment of the nature and development of scripts; Gelb (1963) has produced the classic study of writing systems from a theoretical, as against a historical-descriptive, standpoint, but Trager (1972) cautions against Gelb's conclusions, while conceding that the factual material Gelb has assembled is useful.

In both the Near and the Far East, pictographic writing developed into a kind of rebus system, in which a picture could be used for its phonetic value. Rebus writing based on English would include, for example, successive drawings of an eye, a tin can, and waves (to im-

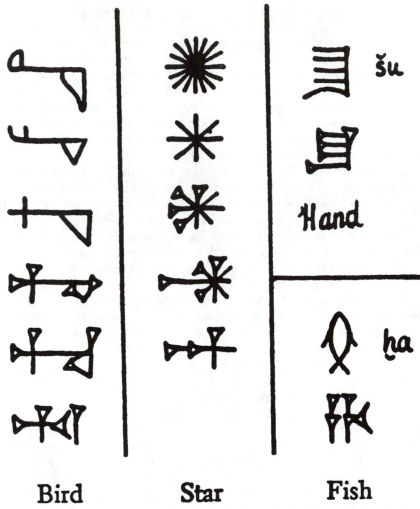

Bird   **Star**   **Fish**

Figure 9.1.   Old Sumerian Pictograms and Their Development into Cuneiform Symbols. From Friedrich, *Archiv Orientálni*, Vol. 19, Table XI. (Reprinted by permission from J. Friedrich, *Extinct Languages*. New York: Philosophical Library, 1957, p. 34)

ply the sea), to render the sentence "I can see." We do this now for entertainment, but in the development of scripts this was a valuable move toward the development of systems based directly on the graphic representation of sound: syllabaries and alphabets.

Kroeber (1948) called the rebus writing a mixed -phonetic or tran-

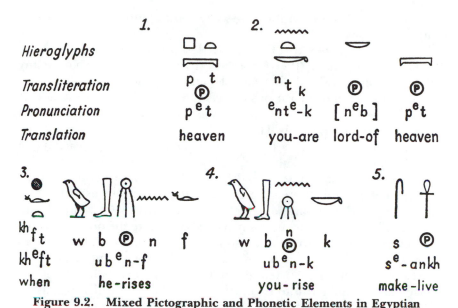

Figure 9.2. Mixed Pictographic and Phonetic Elements in Egyptian Hieroglyphs. Phrases from a page of Egyptian hieroglyph papyrus. The circled P denotes a pictograph or ideograph; the rest of the writing is by pictorial *consonantal letters*. In I, heaven is written alphabetically and confirmed by a conventionalized pictographic "determinative" (the vault of heaven); in 2, by pictograph alone. The first words of 2 and 3 are wholly phonetic: pictographs for the ideas of "when" and "you are" would be hard to devise. The grammatical suffixes -*l* and -*k* added to *uben*, "rise," in 3 and 4 illustrate another reason for the development of consonant letters. In the first of these, the confirming pictograph (sun with rays) is put in the middle of the stem *uben*; in the second, between it and the suffix. In the first words of 2 and 3, the letters in the word read downward; elsewhere, mostly horizontally. The true alphabet was devised by a process of *segregative reduction* out of mixed-method writing such as this. (Reprinted by permission from A. L. Kroeber, *Anthropology: Race, Language, Culture, Psychology, Prehistory*. New York: Harcourt Brace Jovanovich, 1948, p. 371.)

sitional system, in which pictures of "ideographs" were used alongside other pictures that were used for their phonetic value. Such systems are very cumbersome, of course, by comparison with alphabetic systems, yet custom has been powerful enough to foster long-term retention: the Egyptians retained theirs for 3 thousand years (Figure 9.2), including a thousand years after their neighbors had begun to use alphabets (Kroeber, 1948, p. 512). In the case of China, retention has been even longer—some 4 thousand years and counting.

Chinese characters are frequently described as having a general semantic component (there is a "wood radical" under which many characters are classified, for example, and they include words for the names of trees and for various objects that are or have been made of wood, as well as words that lack any obvious "wood" meaning) and also phonetic components. Historically, each character represented a word; hence the script is technically described as *logographic*. When the Japanese borrowed the Chinese script, which they began to do perhaps 1500 years or so ago, they simply read and wrote Chinese. Eventually, around the eighth century, they began to use the characters to render Japanese, which is quite a different kind of language. This involved the use of markers to indicate the order in which the characters were to be read, so as to get them into Japanese syntax; at about the same time, characters which for the most part had already been used for their phonetic values were deliberately selected and simplified into two forms of a syllabary (which is reasonably convenient for Japanese). Karlgren (1923) gives a lucid account of how the Chinese script developed; the introduction of the Chinese script into Japan has been readably described by Sansom (1928); and the general problem of how Chinese writing was used by surrounding groups is discussed by Trager (1972).

Some Egyptian hieroglyphs were used for their consonantal value, independently of whatever pictographic value they may have had before. Various surrounding Semitic peoples carried the phonetic principle further, developing the alphabetic principle between perhaps 2000 B.C. and around 1200 B.C., when the form we recognize as "ancestral" (that of the Phoenicians) became established. Virtually all forms of all the alphabets found in the world can be traced back to this period in the Near East, though which specific group, Phoenician or some other, deserves credit for the idea of an exclusively phonetic use of graphs may never be known with certainty. Once the idea was established, however, that idea could generate alphabets which bear no formal resemblance to the ancestral form. The Cherokee Indian Sequoya, an illiterate of the early nineteenth century, got the idea of an alphabet from seeing how books were used by literate Americans, and used the letters of our alphabet to depict the sounds of his native Cherokee language (though, of course, the values he assigned to these letters had nothing to do with the phonetic values that we assign to them).

One of the earliest examples of the Phoenician alphabet is on the

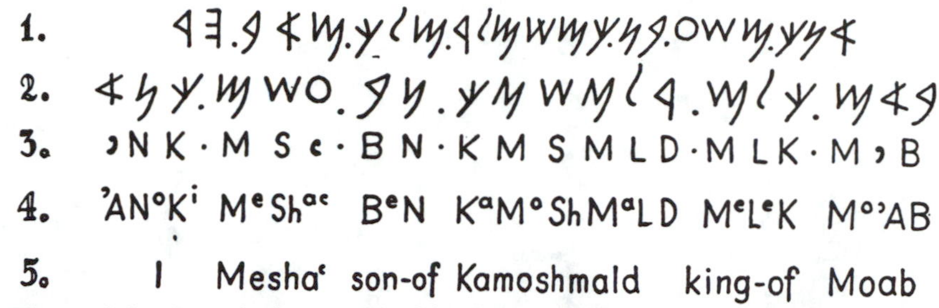

1.   ꝗ꜒.ꝑ ꜀ꟼ.ꝩ ꜀ꟼ.꜀ ꜀ꟼꟽꟽꝩ.ꝩꝩ.Оꟽꟽ.ꝩꝩ꜀

2.   ꜀ꝺꝩ.ꟽꟽWО.ꝺꝩ.ꝩꟽꟽ Wꟽꟽ꜀ꝗ.ꝩ꜀ꝩ.ꟽꟽꝗꝺ

3.   ꓛN K · M S є · B N · K M S M L D · M L K · M ꓥ B

4.   ꓥAN°Kⁱ MᵉShᵃᶜ Bᵉ N KᵃMᵒShMᵃLD MᵉLᵉK MᵒꓥAB

5.   I Meshaᶜ son-of Kamoshmald king-of Moab

Figure 9.3.   Inscription on Moabite Stone, 860 B.C. 1, First line of actual inscription, read right to left. 2, Same, reversed, left to right, words slightly spaced. 3, Transliteration into modern Roman capitals. 4, Unwritten vowels supplied, to give full pronunciation. 5, English translation.—Note resemblance of letters of line 2 with those of 3 and 4, slightly disguised by originals facing opposite from ours (B, D, K), lying on side ('A, S), extra stroke or lengthening of a stroke ('A, D, M). (Reprinted by permission from A. L. Kroeber, *Anthropology: Race, Language, Culture, Psychology, Prehistory*. New York: Harcourt Brace Jovanovich, Inc., 1948, p. 470.)

famous Moabite Stone of King Mesha (see Figure 9.3). Note carefully the familiar forms of some of the original letters, such as the A that heads line 2 (though it is on its side from our standpoint). The actual inclusion of specific letters for vowels was a Greek contribution, but that original sign for the glottal stop is the character that later became our A. Then compare the letters on line two of Figure 9.3 with the letters in Figure 9.4, which is a passage in Manchu. (The Manchu form of the alphabet is virtually the same as that of the Mongols, from whom they received it, adding a few diacritical marks; the Mongols, in turn, received the alphabet from the Uighurs, and they received it from the Sogdians, who received it from the Aramaeans; Aramaean was probably the language of Christ, since Hebrew had already ceased to be a spoken vernacular by that time.) For example, in Figure 9.4 the initial letter of the first word of the first line (read top to bottom, left to right) is D. The initial of the second-last word in line 4 is a B, while the word just above it begins with a double-toothed A, which is the form it takes in initial position; after the D (which is also a little different when not initial) there is another A, which would look quite similar to the A on line two of Figure 9.3 if it were carved in the older, wood-block style. The L of the same word still resembles the original on line 2 of Figure 9.3, as does the M (line 1, word four; line 2, word three, etc.). The S may be a little less obvious (line 1, word two), but the resemblance is there. The

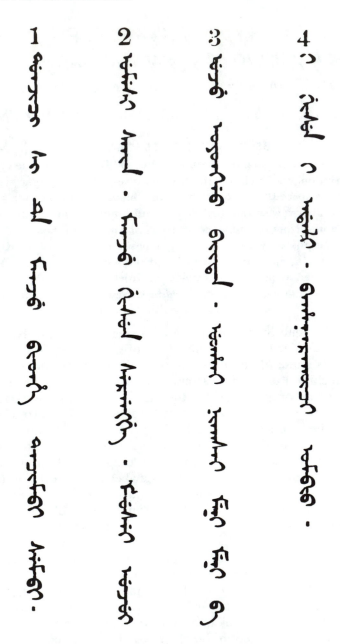

Figure 9.4.   Passage in Manchu. (Reprinted from P. G. von Möllendorff, *A Manchu Grammar.* **Shanghai: American Presbyterian Mission Press, 1892, p. 15.)**

extended example is offered simply to demonstrate the ultimate affinity of our alphabet and one as exotic as that of the Manchus (which is one of the few that Trager does not describe).

Scripts, if they are to be maximally serviceable, must be transparent representations of language. Of course no script is immediately transparent—we must learn to equate the vocal units with the graphic units, and this is more difficult with some scripts than with others. The Spanish and Finnish alphabets, for example, are employed in a way that poses minimal difficulties, because they do a pretty good job of reflecting the phonemic realities of their languages. Our spelling, on the other hand, presents difficulties even to native speakers of English, because of its departures from the principle that one symbol should represent one significant unit of sound (the unit here is the phoneme; we are ignoring the suprasegmentals, which ideally would also receive graphic expression). But any alphabetic system is probably potentially more serviceable than a nonalphabetic script. Syllabic systems such as the *kana* of Japan may work well enough for the languages to which they have been adapted, but no technical difficulty would be involved in substituting an alphabet; there might be psychological problems, simply because change is involved, but an alphabet would do the job at least as well as the syllabary alone. In practice, the Japanese use their syllabary in conjunction with the Chinese characters, which has the advantage of disambiguating homonyms, but the syllabary offers no advantages over an alphabet in the matter of homonyms. Furthermore, in the case of loanwords from languages with different sound patterns (English words taken into Japanese, for example), an alphabet provides the necessary flexibility. Even Chinese, which has phonemic tones that are theoretically part of every syllable (though only a few syllables in each spoken sentence may receive full tonal value), can be handled easily with the alphabet. The student of Chinese writing must learn hundreds of characters to gain even a minimal understanding of Chinese printed materials, and a highly literate individual will number an inventory in thousands of characters.

Why have the Chinese not cast aside such a cumbersome system in favor of the alphabet? The main reason is of course the force of tradition, but the visual diversity of characters also has some advantages. We can perhaps appreciate the visual advantage of spelling differently the homophones "pair," "pare," and "pear," which a truly phonemic spelling would obscure. The American student of Chinese may be confronted with pseudo-problems, because of the ways in which Chinese is frequently Romanized. The Yale system depends on diacritical marks to indicate tones, while the Wade-Giles system uses superscript numbers. In both cases, the tendency of the student is to learn the letter groupings (as we all do with the Chinese names that appear in the newspapers—Mao, Shanghai, and so on), and then try to recall what the appropriate tones are. This might be nearly as cumbersome for the Chinese as it is for an American, but the National Romanization System employs an ingenious notion, which Chao (1947) attributes to Lin Yutang: the spelling is varied to indicate difference in tone. Thus *mai, mae,* and *may* would in other systems be spelled the same, and diacritics or superscripts would indicate the tones. In the National Romanization System the *-ai* indicates a high rising tone, the *-ae* a low rising tone, and the *-ay* a falling tone, no matter what the initial consonants may be. In this case *mai* is "to bury," *mae* is "to buy," and *may* is "to *sell*" (Chao, 1947, p. 10). Chao's students, at least, seem to remember tones relatively easily with this system, but not even the current Chinese government, which emphasizes mass education, has managed to replace the traditional logographic system with an alphabet. Perhaps because characters serve so well to symbolize the Chinese identity, the administration seems content for the present to simplify characters and to restrict their variety.

SECRET LANGUAGES

While most scripts aim at maximum clarity (given the restrictions of tradition), secret languages are designed to obscure meanings for the outsider. In his recent general treatment of secret languages, Joyce Hertzler (1970) was concerned more with their social than their linguistic aspects. Socially, Hertzler distinguishes codes that enhance and support the mystery, grandeur, and exclusiveness of all kinds of secret societies, and codes that consist mainly of the cants of the half-world and the underworld. After considering some aspects of such argots, we shall look at some more high-powered disguises of communication.

Argot

Argot is the secret language of thieves and tramps (Fowler, 1926, p. 307). Its colorful and often intricately contrived vocabulary serves to mask the meaning of communications that take place between members of the "in-group," particularly those that occur in the presence of the uninitiated, but it has the additional purpose of promoting feelings of security and camaraderie among those who employ such verbal camouflage. Fowler notes that in earlier usage, the term "cant" was the English equivalent of argot, the designation for the "special vocabulary of the disreputable," although its current meaning is more restricted to "the insincere or parrotlike appeal to principles . . . that the speaker does not believe in or act upon, or does not understand" [p. 307].

One of the most famous varieties of argot, *jobelin*, the secret language of the medieval crime society called the "Coquillards," was immortalized in the poems of François Villon. Six *ballades* composed in argot have been recognized by scholars as the authentic work of Villon; another group of five *ballades en jargon*, of the Stockholm Manuscript, were published for the first time in 1884 by A. Vitiu, but the authenticity of these works has been seriously challenged (Sainéan, 1913).

The secret language of the Coquillards was racy, earthy, occasionally quite bawdy, and thoroughly appropriate to the society of the *coquille* (meaning shell, or more figuratively the rounded hilt of a sword), whose members, according to Wyndham-Lewis (1928), included "the best card-sharpers, brigands, footpads, dice-coggers, crimps, Mohocks, mumpers, pimps, ponces, horse-stealers, confidence-men, bruisers, thugs, lock-pickers, coin-clippers, house-breakers, hired assassins, and all-round desperadoes in Europe" [p. 6]. Perhaps its most outstanding characteristic, as exemplified in Villon's work, was the richness of its metaphors, which recall the characterization of slang as the poetry of everyday language. Thus criminals whose ears had been lopped off were described as having been "circumcised of their handles" (*des ances circoncis*), a figure of speech which, as Fox (1962, p. 106) observes, seems particularly appropriate in a language whose word for head had originally meant "earthenware pot." The *jobelin* was especially given to irony. Fox notes:

> . . . *le mariage* meant "hanging"; *montjoye* ("Hill of Joy," originally the name given to a hill near Paris where St. Denis was martyred) meant "gibbet"; *un ange* was a hangman's assistant; *dorer* meant "to lie," literally "to cloak beneath a bright exterior"—a little like English "to gild the pill;" a *vendeguer* was a thief, as was also *gagneur*, recalling the euphemistic use of "to win" in modern English. [p. 106]

There are some remarkable parallels with modern English slang. *Ne pas sçavoir oignons peller* seems to have meant much the same as "not to know your opinions," the *estre sur les joncs* ("to be on the rushes") meant "to be in prison," an expression that is close to the English "to be on the mat" (to be in trouble).

Although some of the *jobelin* terms are rather obvious (e.g., *le coffre* for prison, *la dure* the ground), we can only guess at the meanings of many of the words that Villon used in poems such as this:

> Spelicans
> Qui en tous temps
> Advancez dedans le pogois
> Gourde piarde
> Et sur la tarde
> Desbousez les povres nyais,
> Et pour soustenir vos pois
> Sans faire haire
> Ne hault braire,
> Mais plantez ils sont comme joncs
> Par les sires qui sont si longs.

Similarly, we can catch tantalizing glimpses of illicit activity in W. E. Henley's verse:

> Fiddle, or fence, or mace, or mack,
> Or moskeneer, or flash the drag;
> Dead-lurk a crib, or do a crack,
> Pad with a slang, or chuck a fag;
> Bonnet, or tout, or mump and gag,
> Rattle the tats or mark the spot:
> You cannot bag a single stag,
> Booze and the blowens cop the lot.

Villon, one believes, would have agreed fervently with the hedonistic fatalism of those last two lines, for he had often enough "dropped a big score" on booze and broads himself.

The insular and isolated life-style of the professional criminal tends to preserve intact many terms of the argot vocabulary. A good deal of the language used by the professional thief even in the twentieth century resembled the argot spoken by members of the Elizabethan underworld (Aydelotte, 1913; Judges, 1930). Elizabethan professional criminals ("conny-catchers") were subjects of interest to Shakespeare, whose character Autolycus in *A Winter's Tale* is the most noteworthy example of the pickpocket in English literature. As Judges (1930) points out, some of these argot terms (for example, "cut-purse" for pickpocket) can be traced back to the time of Geoffrey Chaucer and the emergence of the English language itself, and perhaps even further back, to an Anglo-Saxon root.

We are indebted to the work of David Maurer (1940, 1941, 1969) for more recent studies of argot among professional pickpockets, forgers, and confidence men. Pickpockets ("cannons") belong to a "whiz mob" and speak the "whiz lingo." The training process whereby a youth is indoctrinated into the whiz subculture and instructed in the use of its argot is part of an apprentice-journeyman relationship between a "new stall" and a "tool." Maurer (1960) describes it thus:

> Many a night in a hotel room they *punch gun* or *punch whiz* and the whole lore of the subculture is gradually made clear to him. "Guns like to punch whiz when they get together and they tell funny things about eggs they have pushed around. Peter men don't punch much guff as a rule, but sometimes the scat will loosen them up . . ." [p. 450]

The tool may have more than one prospect, or protégé, that he is grooming to become a "class cannon." He may "muzzle around" a bit "single o," then come back to complete the training of the "new stall." Now, as Maurer puts it:

> The boy has *busted out*. He has been *joined out*. He is part of a mob. He has *mobbed it up*, though he might be stretching this phrase a bit to apply it to a boy making his debut in a two-handed *outfit*. He is a *cannon* now and *on the whiz*. [p. 450]

As a secret language, argot is devoid of any features that would be of compelling interest to the linguist. The etymologist would undoubtedly find his curiosity aroused by problems of word origins, in the case of some of the more obscure terms and phrases in argot; and the literary analyst cannot help being intrigued by the expressive use of simile and metaphor in which the argot abounds. But apart from purely lexical considerations, the argot poses no linguistic challenges at the syntactical level. It is this aspect of the matter, together with the obvious problems involved in gaining access to the criminal subculture that employs the argot, that has largely accounted for the relative dearth of linguistic studies in this area.

Drum Language

While drum messages in Africa may be limited to phrases such as "danger, return to village" and "end of danger" (van Valen, 1955), and thus need not depend on the forms of spoken language, the drums are more commonly used for any type of message, including gossip, announcements, hunting calls, jokes, and entertainment. Doob (1961, p. 284) has described the awe and mystery that may surround the drums associated with high office among the Nhole of Uganda; Armstrong (1954) has described how drums are used to instruct the dancers in the warlike secret societies of the Oglemye or Ichahoho.

In the groups described by van Valen (1955), every male member of the community may have a drum name, with three components: first, a drum phrase or epithet characteristic of the individual; second, the first part of the father's name; and third, the village of maternal origin. The name is given either at initiation ceremonies or when the boy is first old enough to understand the drum (around five or six years old). In the latter case the name is sometimes changed at his initiation. The drum name for a woman consists of the expression for "girl" or "wife" plus the drum name of either the father or husband. Most women understand the drum language but do not send messages, and thus never touch the drums.

The chief of a tribe may have the prerogative of silencing all other drums in the area by sounding his special name, to ensure the clear transmission of his message. In some areas only the chiefs and their close male relatives are permitted to use the drums at all. A complete message usually consists of five parts (van Valen, 1955):

1. a signal for attention or a chief's refrain
2. the name of the desired recipient (repeated three or four times)
3. the name of the sender (omitted if the chief's refrain is used)
4. the message itself (repeated three times or more)
5. the signal for the end, either a single sharp beat or a series of low notes.

There are regional variations, of course; the entire message usually takes 5 to 15 minutes, but it may continue for an hour if the drummer is in the mood to play the drums for effect.

The maximum audible range for one drum is usually 5 to 7 miles, though under optimum conditions (especially early in the morning or late in the evening, when thermal convection currents are reduced), the messages may carry as far as 20 miles (Carrington, 1949). It is theoretically possible to relay messages hundreds of miles, but this rarely happens, because most messages do not warrant it, and it would require what in effect are bilingual drummers.

The drums themselves may be grouped into two major types: the more common all-wood slit drums, which are usually called gongs (or bells, by Herzog, 1964) since they have no tensed membranes, and those that have a skin. The latter often occurs in pairs and are called, appropriately enough, twin drums. The types vary regionally, but each tribe customarily uses only one variety for signalling purposes. For more technical accounts of the drums, see Good (1942), Armstrong (1954), Herzog (1964), or the summary in Vetter (1969).

The general principle that governs the actual language of the drum seems to lie in the tonal quality of most of the spoken languages: the drum reproduces the tones, stresses, and number of syllables in the various utterances (Armstrong, 1954). That is, every syllable has its own tone, subject to variations in accordance with grammatical and phonological contexts. What the drums transmit, then, is an abstraction from the total speech utterance; thus it is not usually a code or cipher. The messages seem to be analogues of the suprasegmentals of the spoken forms. Messages tend to be standardized and fairly long, since short, nonstandard transmissions are more likely to be ambiguous unless there is a sufficient social context to make their meanings clear.

Van Valen (1955) distinguishes *grammatical* tone, which evidently has an analogous function to that of intonation and stress in English, and *semantic* tone (the tonal character of the words themselves); the semantic tone is typically more important than the grammatical tone.

Each syllable has a definite relative pitch or tone, which is either high or low, although one or more middle levels may be related in some way to these. The tone is part of the word, so that if we let (') represent a high tone and (.) represent a low tone, we can see how the tones are phonemic: in one area *lisaka* (. . .), *lisaka* (. .), and *lisaka* (. ") mean respectively "puddle," "promise," and "poison."

Since the drum beats are discontinuous, problems arise in the representation of tonal glides and vowel length, which are phonemic in many of the languages concerned. The Luba of the Belgian Congo try to avoid words that contain tonal glides, but when that is impossible they reduce them to one of two register tones; the Yaunde, when in the same situation, use two quick successive strokes that represent the termini of the glide (Stern, 1957, p. 497). For vowel length the Yaunde use two short strokes, which are distinguished from successive short vowel representations by the tempo with which they are administered; the Tshi signals of the Ewe indicate length by extending the interval between strokes (Stern, 1957, p. 497).

The range of individual styles is about the same as that in the speech of individuals (Clarke, 1934).

Herzog (1964) has provided a useful case study of how the drums are used to transmit messages by the Jabo of Eastern Liberia. Jabo is essentially monosyllabic and tonal; vowel length and voicing are also phonemic. Where duration is critical, it is customary to speak of the duration of a short vowel as consisting of one *mora*, while a long vowel might be one-and-a-half or two *morae* in length. In Jabo drum language, then, each beat on the wooden signal drum represents a single *mora*. If two full vowels follow each other, one beat may be omitted or both beats may be shortened. In addition, a technique called "scraping" is sometimes used to represent duration. This consists of two quick beats, given by the two sticks in alternation. Since the scraping occasionally occurs when the drum grammar does not seem to require it, it seems to have an element of style or artistry about it. Scraping is also used to represent true diphthongs, though a single beat is more common, and the variation again may be governed by aesthetic qualities.

While the spoken language of the Jabo is basically a four-tone system, in the drum language the two lower tones are generally treated as if they were one (yielding a three-tone drum language), even though the two lower tones could be kept distinct without too much technical difficulty. The two higher tones are less frequently treated as the same on the drums, and the two middle tones are consistently distinguished. The correlation and variation of the spoken tones and the drum tones led Herzog (1964) to conclude that the Jabo four-tone language grew out of an older three-tone system, with the splitting of the lower register. Most of the surrounding tribes, including the Grebo, from whom the Jabo derived their signalling system and much of their music, employ a three-tone language.

On the true, or skin-covered, drum, only the two middle tones are reflected, probably for technical reasons. Since considerable force is required to beat the drums effectively, the drummer tends to make his strokes with the right hand and left hand alternately, which leads to a mechanical alternation of the two middle tones. In any event, because of the concomitant simplification of the sound patterns, most messages tend to be stereotyped, or coded.

In the Jabo area there are comparatively few drummers, and they tend to be specialists; but in other regions of Africa, for instance the Cameroons or the Congo, many men know how to play the signal drum.

Whistle Speech

Whistle speech, which is employed by the male speakers of several tonal Indian languages in Oaxaca, Mexico, shares some interesting parallels with the drum languages of Africa. For example, in both cases the underlying languages are tonal, so that it is the supraseg-mental pattern that provides the basis of communication. Again, it is typically the prerogative of the male to engage in whistle language, though the women understand it. In both cases, since the segmentals are absent, there is considerable danger of ambiguity. And in both cases the derived systems tend to be employed over distances that are not suitable for normal conversation.

The whistle language seems to have greater flexibility than drum language, however. At least among the Mazateco, in Oaxaca, all males use the whistles regularly, not only in the fields and in other areas where they are separated by considerable distance, but even when within conversational range (Cowan, 1948). Cowan provides several examples of business and social transactions of some complexity that were conducted without difficulty by means of whistles, and he was able to get consistent translations from different informants for his whistle texts.

One of the most common occasions for ambiguity is the whistling of proper names. This follows, Cowan says, from the way in which Spanish names are assimilated into the Mazateco tonal system.

> The stressed syllable of the Spanish word becomes semi-high in tone, syllables preceding the stressed syllable become semi-low, syllables following the stressed syllable become low. The word loses its Spanish stress on the last syllable of the word. Thus names such as *Modesto, Gustavo, Frederico,* and *Ricardo* would all take an identical tone pattern: semi-low, semi-high, low. There is no way, aside from the context of the company present, to tell which name is being whistled. [p. 283]

For a more extended discussion of this interesting phenomenon, with some technical elaboration, see Cowan (1948). More recently, Busnel and Classe (1976) have produced a wide-ranging study of *Whistled Languages*, which not only deals in detail with tonal and nontonal language representations, but also with whistling in the infrahuman part of the animal kingdom.

Pig Latins

Hertzler (1970) notes that linguistically, the secret languages of so-called primitive societies are variations on the everyday language, rather than completely novel systems. In the case of the Eskimo and Dakota Indian secret languages, for example, ordinary speech is modified by unusual accentuation, the use of special figurative or symbolic expressions, and the addition of archaic words and phrases.

Most of us have had experience at some time in our childhood with some form of "Pig Latin," or *igpay atinlay*, in which the initial consonant or consonant cluster is removed from the initial position and suffixed with /ey/ to the end of each word, or in the case of a word that begins with a vowel sound, the /ey/ or /yey/ is suffixed alone to achieve the thin disguise. The conversion of normal speech to Pig Latin is essentially a matter of applying a simple morphophonemic rule, linguistically a very low-order event—far less complex than applying the interrogative, negative, or "do" transformations in everyday speech. Yet, as Saporta (1967) has pointed out (following the discussion in Halle, 1962), Pig Latin would differ from normal English in having infixes where English has suffixes, as in [óyzbey] rather than [bóyz] for the plural of *boy*. Further, Pig Latin lacks initial and final consonants, but has extremely complicated medial clusters and so forth. The point is worth emphasizing, because typologically English and Pig Latin would seem rather different, even though their actual language differences are minimal, as measured by the number of rules required to convert English into Pig Latin.

The composition of "secret" languages through the application of a simple morphophonemic rule seems to be rather widespread throughout the world, even though the phenomenon has not received a great deal of attention in the literature. Very likely there are several such systems even within the United States. College students at Oglethorpe University in Atlanta, Georgia, for example, were using "Easy Talk" in the 1950s. Before words that begin with a vowel, [iyəz] is employed as the initial; otherwise it follows each consonant sound except a final one. Thus, "This is a table" would be [ɗiyəzis iyəzəz iyəzə tiyəzeybiyəzl]. On the island of Hawaii, a [g] plus reduplication of the preceding vowel is used, so that "book" would be [buguk]. "Nothing" would be [nəgəθigŋ], and so forth.

One form found in Japan simply requires the insertion of *nosa* after every syllable but the last. Thus *kono hon*, "this book," becomes *konosano honosan* (final *n* is syllabic in Japanese). It requires very little practice to catch on to such a simple system, even though it can seem quite alien the first time it is encountered. Jeffreys (1956) has compiled several passing descriptions, from various sources, of low-order systems of disguised language in Africa. A number of accounts refer to languages that are spoken backwards, but it is unlikely that whole utterances of sentence length are precisely reversed. A Swahili system is approximately the reverse of our own Pig Latin: the final syllable of each word is prefixed to the beginning. Also, some of the Congo peoples are said to reverse the syllables of their words. But reversing syllables or transposing a final syllable to the first position of a word is not the same as speaking backwards. The difference can be illustrated with our word "backward": [bǽkwɪrd] would have to become [drɪwkǽb], not an impossible switch, of course, but rather difficult to handle fluently, especially if longer sequences are involved. On the other hand, [wɪrdbǽk] is relatively simple; this is an operation that can be applied automatically to one word at a time, rather quickly. A sentence-length reversal would require conscious control of the whole sequence before one started.

At any rate, in all cases where details are spelled out at all, it is apparent that relatively low-order rules are applied. The Boloki of the Congo seem to have a system very similar to the Japanese secret language described above: *sa* is inserted after each syllable. While working with Ibo groups in Nigeria, Jeffreys came across many allusions to such secret languages, but he was unable to obtain particulars. This is, of course, one of the hazards of trying to investigate something that is supposed to be "secret." Of potential interest, however, is the remark that the secret speech of one town is unintelligible in the next town, and the secret speech of one age group might even be unintelligible to another age group. In the absence of clear evidence to the contrary, we would be wise to assume that any "secret" language that can be learned quickly and used fluently involves only a few, very low-order linguistic rules.

Codes and Ciphers

There really are some secret languages of a very high order of sophistication. Most notably these are found in use between diplomatic and military posts. There are many levels of system, including the theoretically unbreakable one-time pad system, which depends on the use of additive pages that are never reused again, and thus do not provide the outsider with the kinds of statistical information that provide the key to breaking lesser systems. Cryptanalysts rely on a knowledge of letter frequencies (/e/ is the most frequent letter in written English, so the most frequently occurring symbol in the cipher text is likely to be an /e/, and so forth) and a familiarity with stereo-typed expressions, particularly at the beginnings and ends of messages. But only the very simplest systems can be carried in the head of the user, and any system as simple as that will be broken very quickly by the expert, with relatively little data. To devise high-level systems, on the other hand, requires nearly as much ingenuity as is required to break them.

On November 19, 1941 the Japanese Foreign Ministry cabled the Japanese Embassy in Washington, saying that if an apparent weather message, "East wind, rain," were inserted in the middle of the daily Japanese language news broadcast, all code papers and the like were to be destroyed, because Japanese-American diplomatic relations would have reached the breaking point (Wohlstetter, 1962, p. 51). The three-word weather message was a code, in which a limited signal represented a whole message; there was no direct representation of the language of the message in the signal that was to be concealed in the news broadcast. As with other codes, the recipient must have the inventory of messages or message components (words and phrases that equate to the arbitrary signals) in advance of transmission. Since the code units are representations not of language, but rather of messages or message units (note the use of international codes of various sorts, such as flags to indicate weather conditions, or sema-phore signals, which can be interpreted the same way by speakers of different languages), they are not of particular interest here.

Ciphers are quite a different proposition. Ultimately the signal units represent the language units. The Chinese Telegraphic Code Book, for example, contains approximately 9,999 four-digit numbers, which correspond to that number of Chinese characters. A message that consists of four-digit numbers converts directly into a message of Chinese characters, which are read as if the message had originally been transmitted in the Chinese script. By far the most common systems, however, depend on ciphers that convert to alphabetic letters and directly represent the language of the message. The breaking of ciphers depends on a practical understanding of specific features of written language, such as letter frequencies and frequencies of letter sequences; and of course specific frequencies will vary from one language to the next. Gaines (1956) gives examples:

> Finding, for instance, an unexplained cryptogram in which a count of the letters show that about 40 percent of these are vow-els (with or without *Y*), we may classify it, not only as a transpo-

sition, but as one enciphered in English or German, since one of the Latin languages can hardly be written with so low a vowel percentage. Then, if we note the occurrences of the letter E, and find that this makes up about 12 percent of the total number of letters we may discard the possibility of German, in which the letter E is far more likely to represent 18 percent of the text. Or, if the vowel percentage is high enough to point to one of the Latin languages, French would be distinguished from the others by the outstanding frequency of its letter E, sometimes as great as that of the German E, while the Spanish, Portuguese, or Italian language will not always show it as the leading letter, its place having been taken by A. In the Serb-Croat language, the letter A always predominates, and in Russian the letter O. [pp. 14–15]

Gaines (who wrote originally in 1939) mentions only European languages, but obviously the logic would apply to any language that is alphabetically rendered. On the matter of sequences of letters, lists of the digrams, trigrams, and commonest words in English are readily available (see the appendices in Gaines, 1956, for example). Thus "the" is far and away our most popular word, being more than half again as frequent as the next most popular, "of," and 15 times more frequent than "this" or "my." The English trigram *the* is about three-and-a-half times more frequent than the next most popular, *ing*. The frequency of *the*, of course, reflects not only the popularity of the word with that spelling, but also words such as "these," "there," "breathe," and "mother."

It is easy to see, then, that a monoalphabetic substitution system, in which the letters are given an arbitrary but consistent value, would hardly stump a third-grader who was armed with even the most elementary statistical information on his language. The problem became more interesting, however, around the middle of the fifteenth century, when the Italian architect Leo Battista Alberti introduced the notion of multiple alphabets (Kahn, 1966). Alberti began with a scrambled alphabet, say *rpqemy* . . . , from which the first letter of the message would be taken. Suppose we want to send the message "Face them down." The f would be represented by y; then to get the second value, the scrambled alphabet would be shifted one place to produce a second scrambled alphabet. Thus the second alphabet would begin *pqemy* . . . *r*, and the a in "Face" would be represented by p. Shifted again, the alphabet becomes *qemy* . . . *rp*, and the c in "Face" is represented by m; so "Fac . . ." would appear in the enciphered message as "Ypm . . . ." On the basis of a single scrambled alphabet, shifting yields as many alphabets as there are letters in the alphabet being used (in this case, obviously, 26).

Since each letter of the alphabet will have 26 values, it would be necessary to have a lot of traffic (messages) in order to compute the letter frequencies, and very likely the starting point for the sequences of alphabets would be changed periodically. The original alphabet *(rpqemy . . .)* might be used for the first letter of the messages on the first of the month, but the second alphabet might be used to begin messages on the second of the month, and so forth, for 26 days, after which the cycle might begin anew. But certain shortcuts in deciphering are provided by our tendency to use stereotyped beginnings. If, for example, we were intercepting messages from Naval Headquarters for the Pacific Theater, and had reason to believe that the majority of messages originating there would begin "Cincpac" (Commander-in-Chief, Pacific), we would assume that if a majority of messages on a given date all began "Xaqibbs" we might have our foot in the door for seven alphabets. Then, if we knew that a fair number of Cincpac messages contain the word "directive" followed by a number, we would have a lead on another nine or more alphabets. The different letter sequences that would represent these same assumed values on succeeding days would provide the means of calibrating the several alphabets, and this would lead eventually to the recovery of the whole sliding-alphabet table.

This overly casual description should not deceive the reader into underestimating the ingenuity needed to devise and break code and cipher systems. The polyalphabetic system was modified in the sixteenth century by Belasco (Kahn, 1966), so that an easily remembered keyword was repeated over the plain text for encipherment, to indicate the specific alphabet to be used, and according to Kahn it remained essentially impregnable for 300 years. Today there is an international battle of computers among the major powers, each of which is seeking more clever systems than the other powers.

While considerable genius has been involved in the development and solution of ciphers, there has been little systematic exploitation of them for any psychological insights they may contain. We know that there is remarkable consistency in an individual's letter frequencies. Kahn (1967) notes the *tour de force* of Wright (1939), who wrote a 267-page novel without using the letter *e*. The difficulty of the task can be appreciated when one realizes that Wright had to avoid most verbs in the past tense, because they end with /-ed/; he could not use such popular words as "the," "there," "these," "those," "when," "then," "more," "after," or "very"; the pronouns "he," "she," "they," "we," "me," and "them" were out; and certain forms of "be" and "have," which function both as main verbs and auxiliaries, had to be ducked—

namely "be," "have," "are," "were," or "been." And Wright was a sufficient purist to avoid using the numbers 7 through 29 inclusive, because if they were spelled out, they too would contain at least one *e*, and for the same reason he avoided the abbreviated forms "Mr." and "Mrs."

Ignoring letter-frequency statistics can result in such economic outrages as our standard typewriter keyboard. Thus, as Kahn (1967) notes, 56 percent of the action is on the left-hand side, even though ours is largely a right-handed world; and 48 percent of all motions for successive letters use only one hand rather than two.

> Thus words like *federated* and *addressed* force the left to leap frantically among the keys while the right hand languishes in unemployed torpor. Much more efficient is the even rhythm of the two-handed *thicken*. As if to emphasize the problem, touch-typing places the two most agile fingers of the right hand directly on keys for two of the least frequent letters of the alphabet, *j* and *k*. [p. 741]

Certain more recently designed keyboards, which take into consideration the relative frequency of letters, can cut the learning time in half. Samuel Morse, on the other hand, assigned his dot-dash values to letters on the basis of his count of the letters in a Philadelphia newspaper's typecase: thus *e* is simply one dot, *t* one dash, and so forth. Kahn (1967) maintains that because Morse was so rational in his approach, it is possible to handle nearly 25 percent more traffic on a telegraph line in a rush period than would have been possible if Morse had made up his code haphazardly. As to why the manufacturers of typewriters do not mend their ways and produce rational keyboards, the answer is simple enough. Typists who have learned the old system are not much interested in learning a new one, and the people (especially in business) who own typewriters are not much interested in making the expenditure necessary to obtain the new machines. The problem is perhaps similar to that of our spelling system: we all recognize that it is cumbersome, but there is too much lethargy in the system to permit a change.

Until recently the world of cryptology was considered to be quite esoteric, but now both business and academe have become so interested in its applications that the National Security Agency has become alarmed over the likelihood of a serious compromise that would work against the interests of the country. Efforts to censor cryptologic research have resulted in a furor over academic freedom. At the moment a voluntary system of review by NSA of manuscripts produced by academicians is in effect, but there is a possibility of restrictive legislation being enacted in the future (see Begley, Lord, Carey, & Hall, 1981; Knight, 1981).

Anyone interested in the history of codes and ciphers should consult David Kahn's (1967) *The Codebreakers*, an enormous volume (containing nearly a thousand pages of text) written for the layman. For those who would try their hand at some cipher systems, Gaines' (1956) little introduction is useful; it contains problems—and solutions!

GLOSSOLALIA

One of the (socially) more interesting "secret" languages is not really a language at all. This is glossolalia, or the practice of "speaking in tongues." In the United States the so-called gift of tongues was until recently found mainly among various Pentecostal groups (Samarin, 1972), but now enthusiastic glossolalists are to be found among Catholics, Lutherans, Baptists, Presbyterians, Pentecostals, Episcopalians, and even the "Jesus People" (Grabbe, 1971). Very briefly, the speaker of tongues vocalizes in a way that is unintelligible to most listeners, and perhaps even to himself, but the vocalization is presumed to be divinely inspired, and typically there is someone in the audience who renders a "translation" of the glossolalia.

Glossolalia is of greater social and psychological than linguistic interest, since the vocalizations do not constitute language (Samarin, 1969, 1972; Goodman, 1969a). Jaquith (1967) has provided two samples of glossolalia, which were produced by a young, white, adult male, raised in a large Midwestern city, a product of Anglo-American and Pentecostal traditions. The first of 13 strings marked by a terminal contour was "kow hi na ya ka yow a na"; the last was "pa rey ney ə kə rey ə rey ne ki ya la re ya na la re a ro o re ne kiy ya le ya ka tuw." (Only the segmental phones, syllable boundaries, and contour-final junctures have been indicated; stress, vowel length, and intonation are unmarked, to simplify presentation.) All of the phones in both samples occur in the casual speech of the informant, and the distribution patterns of the phones are compatible with those of his ordinary speech. Jaquith correctly notes that the strings are not amenable to phonemic analysis, precisely because they are not examples of language. The "translations" are unitary semantic blocks, nearly always a very generalized praise of God, and could in no way be treated as languages are when translated from one to another (morpheme by morpheme or phrase by phrase).

A useful survey of glossolalia and of similar phenomena in non-Christian religions has been conducted by May (1956). There seems to be some disagreement on the extent to which glossolalia is associated with a trance or some other special psychic state. Worldwide, of course, we should expect to see considerable variation, but even within the American Midwest there seems to be significant variation. Goodman (1969b), for example, maintains strongly that trance is the type of state associated with glossolalia, but Jaquith (1967) saw little evidence of this in his material (see also Hine, 1969). Again, it need not be the case that one investigator is correct and another mistaken. Very likely there is actual variation, depending on cultural considerations and even local social expectations. But if Kildahl (quoted by Grabbe) is correct, it is at least necessary that the individual should be able to relinquish some measure of mental self-control. The following rather detailed account of glossolalic behavior, gathered by Salas (1967), is probably typical of many experiences.

The account is that of a young woman who was first exposed to the Pentecostal religion when she was eight years of age, in the Spanish Harlem section of New York City.

> It has been five years since I stopped speaking in tongues. I do not know what I meant when I was speaking, but I do know that I said repetitions of syllables, vowels, and consonants. To acquire the gift, I was told by a young preacher . . . to repeat rapidly several praises to the Lord, as *Cristo, Dios mio,* and Halleluja. I felt afraid, because the people who were seated next to me expected me to start speaking in tongues right away. The lady next to my father kept saying *pecado, pecado.* I could not let my father think I was in sin, so I did what (the preacher) told me to do. I began repeating Halleluja, and *Cristo.*

Gradually, as she repeated the phrases, her vocalizations underwent a change, until they became unintelligible, as if she were a babbling baby.

> I just felt large amounts of energy pouring from my system. The joy I felt made me jump all over the church. I fell on the floor, but it would not hurt me.

While thus possessed she would from time to time take hold of someone, with her eyes closed, and pull him to the altar. This implied that he was in sin, and if he was not, then he would have to testify to that effect in public.

The atmosphere of the church seems to have had a great deal to do with whether or not glossolalia would occur. One evening, in an unfamiliar Pentecostal church, she noted that few people were present, the pace of the service was slow, the opening prayer was delivered without much energy, and the hymns were all subdued. No tongues were spoken that night, but a week later the situation was quite different. There was a large congregation, the music was spirited, and even the prayers were rather lively.

> Even the children were attentive. The hymns sung were full of life, and so cheerful and hearty that on the singing of *El espiritu de Dios se mueve*, a lady came out of the back seat with the Holy Spirit, and began throwing herself all around the place and speaking in strange tongues. I could not understand it, but this language sounded beautiful, very loud and clear.

Soon many voices were heard, particularly those of women and children, and the lively atmosphere was maintained by continued singing and praising of the Lord.

Visits to various Pentecostal churches in New York, including some in the Bronx and Brooklyn, all revealed the same experience. When the service was lively and a sense of unity held the congregation, someone would begin to speak in tongues, and the rest would soon join in. When the service was very slow there was no speaking in tongues. Further, glossolalia was most likely to begin while hymns were being sung, especially the fast ones and those that mentioned the Holy Spirit, for example *Ese cielo azul es mi cielo, es la biblia sagrada mi historia, el Espiritu Santo me guia, y con Cristo me voy a la gloria*.

We can gather from this young woman's experience that there may be a considerable anxiety component among those who do not engage in glossolalia, because they fear they will be accused of sin by the glossolalists. When the glossolalia begins, there is a sudden increase in traffic to the rest rooms—particularly, it seems, on the part of teenagers, who show a sudden urgent need to comb their hair and wash their hands. Those who cannot escape in this fashion are strongly motivated to speak in tongues. In one congregation of approximately 60, nearly half were speaking in tongues at the same time.

Children in the churches could be observed looking around, attending to those speaking in tongues, and then they would imitate them. One little girl said that she liked to speak in tongues, because people in the church were always so nice to her afterwards. Older people generally treated glossolalic children with respect, and even their nonglossolalic peers treated them deferentially, usually declining, for example, to tell dirty jokes in front of them.

In brief, in this woman's experience, glossolalia is unlikely when the congregation is small, the preacher is not lively in his presentation, the singing leader is monotonous, and the hymns are slow; and the individuals are not likely to participate if they are unduly troubled. Given the proper atmosphere and even a minimal exposure to the phenomenon, anyone who is interested in developing the techniques of glossolalia can do so. Samarin (1969) maintains that "the only necessary, and perhaps sufficient, requirement for becoming a glossolalist seems to be a profound desire on the part of an individual for a new or better religious experience." Perhaps a small qualification of both of these statements is required. Some of Goodman's informants never seemed to catch on, and Jaquith's informant seems to have sought the experience for many years before gaining it. In view of Kildahl's argument that the individual must relinquish some meaure of conscious control over his behavior, perhaps we should say that the individual must be able to free himself of any inhibitions he may have with respect to relinquishing that control.

REFERENCES

Armstrong, R. G. Talking drums in the Benue-Cress River region of Nigeria. *Phylon*, 1954, *15*, 355–363.

Aydelotte, F. *Elizabethan rogues and vagabonds*. London: Clarendon Press, 1913.

Begley, S., Lord, M., Carey, J., & Hall, L. NSA's cryptic alliance, *Newsweek*, August 24, 1981, p. 51.

Busnel, R. G., & Classe, A. 1981, *Whistled languages*. Volume 13, Communication and Cybernetics (Series). New York: Springer-Verlag, 1976.

Carlisle, R. C., & Siegel, M. I. Some problems in the interpretation of Neanderthal speech capabilities: A reply to Lieberman. *American Anthropologist*, 1974, *76*, 319–322.

Carrington, J. F. *Talking drums of Africa*. London: Cary Kingsgate Press, 1949.

Chao, Y. R. *Cantonese primer*. Cambridge, Mass.: Harvard University Press, 1947.

Clark, G. *The Stone Age hunters*. New York: McGraw-Hill Book Company, 1967.

Clarke, R. T. Drum language of the Tumba people. *American Journal of Sociology*, 1934, *40*, 34–48.

Cowan, G. M. Mazateco whistle speech. *Language*, 1948, *24*, 280–286.

Doob, L. W. *Communication in Africa*. New Haven, Conn.: Yale University Press, 1961.

Fairservis, W. A., Jr. *Cave paintings of the great hunters*. New York: Marboro Books, 1955.

Fowler, H. W. *A dictionary of modern English usage*. London: Clarendon Press, 1926.

Fox, J. *The poetry of Villon*. London: Thomas Nelson and Sons Ltd., 1962.

Friedrich, J. *Extinct languages*. New York: Philosophical Library, Inc., 1957.

Gaines, H. F. *Cryptanalysis*. New York: Dover Publications, Inc., 1956. (Originally published, 1939.)

Gelb, I. J. *A study of writing*. (Rev. ed.) Chicago: University of Chicago Press, 1963.

Good, A. L. Drum talk is the African's wireless. *Natural History*, 1942, *50*, 69–74.

Goodman, F. D. 1969a. Phonetic analysis of glossolalia in four cultural settings. *Journal for the Scientific Study of Religion, 1969, 7,* 227–239.

Goodman, F. D. 1969b. The acquisition of glossolalia behavior. Paper presented at the 68th Annual Meeting of the American Anthropological Association, New Orleans, November 20, 1969.

Grabbe, L. L. Glossolalia: The new "tongues" movement. *The plain truth 36*, No. 10, October 1971, 20–24.

Halle, M. Phonology in a generative grammar. *Word*, 1962, *18*, 54-72.

Hertzler, J. O. *Laughter: A socio-scientific analysis*. Jericho, N. Y.: Exposition Press, Inc., 1970.

Herzog, G. Drum signaling in a West African tribe. In Dell Hymes (Ed.), *Language in culture and society*. New York: Harper & Row, 1964.

Hime, V. H. Pentecostal glossolalia: Toward a functional interpretation. *Journal for the Scientific Study of Religion*, 1969, *7*, 211–226.

Hoebel, E. A. *Anthropology: The study of man*. (4th ed.) New York: McGraw-Hill Book Company, 1972.

Jaquith, J. R. Toward a typology of formal communicative behavior: glossolalia. *Anthropological Linguistics*, 1967, *9*, No. 8, I–8.

Judges, A. V. (Ed.) *The Elizabethan underworld*. London: Routledge, 1930.

Jeffreys, M. D. W. Letter on disguised languages to *Man*, 1956, *56*, no. 19, 15–16.

Kahn, D. Modern cryptology. *Scientific American*, 1966, *215*, No. 1, 38–46.

Kahn, D. *The codebreakers*. New York: The Macmillan Company, 1967.

Karlgren, B. *Sound and symbol in Chinese*. London: Oxford University Press, 1923.

Knight, J. Introduction to report of the Public Cryptography Study Group. *Academe*, 1981, *67*, 371–382.

Kroeber, A. L. *Anthropology*. New York: Harcourt, Brace & World, Inc., 1948.

Lieberman, P., & Crelin, E. S. Speech and Neanderthal Man: a reply to Carlisle and Siegel. *American Anthropologist*, 1974, *76*, 323–325.

Maurer, D. W. *The big con*. Indianapolis: Bobbs-Merrill Co., 1940.

Maurer, D. W. The argot of forgery. *American Speech*, 1941, *16*, 243–250.

Maurer, D. W. The skills and training of the pickpocket. In D. R. Cressy & D. A. Ward (Eds.), *Delinquency, crime, and social process*. New York: Harper & Row, 1969.

May, L. C. A survey of glossolalia and related phenomena in non-Christian religions. *American Anthropologist*, 1956, *58*, 75–96.

Mollendorff, P. C. *A Manchu grammar*. Shanghai: American Presbyterian Mission Press, 1892.

Sainean, L. *Les sources de l'argot ancien*. Paris: Champion, 1913.

Salas, J. E. Learning to speak in tongues. Unpublished paper, 1967.

Samarin, W. J. Glossolalia as learned behavior. *Canadian Journal of Theology*, 1969, *15*, 60–64.

Samarin, W. J. Glossolalia. *Psychology Today*, August 1972, 48–50, 78.

Sansom, Sir G. *An historical grammar of Japanese*. London: Oxford University Press, 1928.

Saporta, S. Linguistics and communication. In L. Thayer (Ed.), *Communication theory and research*. Springfield, Ill.: Charles C. Thomas, Publisher, 1967.

Stern, T. Drum and whistle language: An analysis of speech surrogates. *American Anthropologist*, 1957, *59*, 487–506.

Trager, G. L. *Language and languages*. San Francisco: Chandler Publishing Co., 1972.

Van Valen, L. Talking drums and similar African tonal communication. *Southern Folklore Quarterly*, 1955, *19*, 252–256.

Vetter, H. J. *Language behavior and communication*. Itasca, Ill.: F. E. Peacock Publishers, Inc., 1969.

Wohlstetter, R. *Pearl Harbor*. Stanford, Cal.: Stanford University Press, 1962.

Wright, E. V. *Gadsby, a story of over 50,000 words without using the letter E*. Los Angeles: Wetzel Publishing Company, 1939.

Wyndham-Lewis, D. B. *François Villon*. New York: Coward-McCann, 1928.

Chapter 10

PIDGINS AND CREOLES

When speakers of one language come into contact with the speakers of another language and must find some way to communicate, the result is likely to be a makeshift vernacular that we call a *pidgin*. Until recently, pidgins were either ignored or were treated as amusing curiosities, but now it is becoming clear that there are important theoretical issues in this area.

One of the more important and interesting issues is whether pidgins are a particularly direct means of identifying language universals, as Kay and Sankoff (1974) suggest, or whether the quest for universals is more profitably pursued through the study of *creoles*, as Bickerton (1977, 1981) argues. Creoles are languages which may develop in a pidgin community in the second and subsequent generations. Pidgins are improvised vehicles used by people who have a "natural language" to fall back on for most of their communicative needs. But if children are born into a community that relies heavily on a pidgin for communication among different groups in the community, then the pidgin becomes the first language of the children. But because pidgins are only adequate for a limited range of purposes, the children must convert them into a vehicle capable of serving all their communicative needs. At this point we no longer speak of a pidgin, but rather a creole, which has native speakers and is much more elaborate than the pidgin out of which it grew.

In brief, since pidgins are so elementary, it seems reasonable to suppose that they depend on very basic features of language in general, but Bickerton (1981) argues persuasively that creoles are quite different from their antecedent pidgins, while resembling each other in a surprising number of ways: thus, he says, it is to the creoles that we must look for the most basic features of language in general.

PIDGINS

The controversy over linguistic universals stems in part from another controversy: the origin of pidgin languages. When the First International Conference on Creole Language Studies was convened in 1959 it provided the first opportunity for most of the world's authorities on pidgins and creoles to meet and compare views. Most were impressed by the number of similarities to be found among pidgins and creoles spoken so widely around the globe. One way to account for the similarities was to attribute the spread to the peregrinations of Portuguese traders and explorers of the fifteenth and sixteenth centuries. Presumably the mariners carried a variety of Mediterranean Lingua Franca to the New World in one direction, and in the other direction they carried it down the west coast of Africa, then across the Indian Ocean to the Far East (DeCamp, 1977). This is known as the *monogenetic* theory, according to which all pidgins would have a common origin and this would account for the similarities.

While diffusion has clearly played a part in the formation and spread of some pidgins, most students of the subject now accept the *polygenetic* theory which recognizes that a pidgin may arise whenever and wherever the need occurs. Thus, as we shall see below, a pidgin developed in Japan shortly after the end of the Second World War and a very similar pidgin developed in South Korea about the same time. No Portuguese mariners were involved in even the most indirect way, even though they had an impact in the fifteenth and sixteenth centuries that is reflected in a number of loan words that have retained their currency to the present day. Now the Korean version of the pidgin has a heavy contribution from the Japanese version that is best accounted for by diffusion (via American military personnel) from Japan to Korea. While this accounts for the occurrence of many Japanese loan words in the Korean pidgin, other problems remain, not only in this area but more generally. That is, even where diffusion can be ruled out, enough similarities remain to suggest that perhaps the speakers are guided by some underlying principles that transcend specific languages.

> From a structural point of view, the essential characteristic of a pidgin language is that it is sharply reduced in its pronunciation and grammar and in its vocabulary. In general, this reduction is in the direction of whatever features are common to the languages of all those using the pidgin, for mutual ease in use and comprehensibility, thus arriving at a kind of greatest denominator . . . . (Hall, 1966: 25)

The commonality factor that Hall refers to may be rephrased as "shared surface structures" which, if Kay and Sankoff (1974) are correct, will be close to universal underlying structures. In a similar vein, but somewhat earlier, Smith (1972) suggested that many of the similarities to be found among pidgins and creoles might be explained by "the isomorphism of the surface structures to the underlying structures, which appear to be universal in nature" (p. 55).

Sometimes universals are treated very generally—all languages have ways of forming negatives and questions, for example. But Kay and Sankoff (1974) as well as Smith (1972) see universal deep structure as being semantic structure, and this appears to be the case for Bickerton (1977) as well. Bickerton agrees with Kay and Sankoff that there is little transformational depth to pidgins (deep and surface structures are close), but rejects the notion that the shared surface structures of pidgins are close to linguistic universals, even though the idea has a superficial plausibility. We shall return to the argument when we come to creoles as such.

Aside from purely linguistic considerations, social factors have been widely discussed in the literature on pidgins and creoles. In general, the feeling seems to be that if the speakers of one donor language are socially superordinate—a colonial power, for instance—they will tend to simplify the grammar of their language, limit their vocabulary, and perhaps incorporate words from the language(s) of the subordinate group of speakers. This means that most of the learning and accommodation is the onus of the subordinate group. Since the basis of the resulting pidgin is said to be the language of the superordinate group, we speak of most pidgins as being X-based, where "X" is for historical reasons more often than not a European language. While this may be a fair statement in many cases, in some it is surely an over-simplification.

Thus Leland (1887), referring to the Chinese pidgin of the day, commented that "Pidgin is a very rude jargon, in which English words, strangely distorted. . . are sent forth according to the principles of Chinese grammar" (p. 1). In fact, there are a fair number of Chinese words in the pidgin, and many sentences could as easily be described as in accordance with the principles of English grammar, while some do not quite fit the grammars of either donor.

At any rate, in the absence of a colonial or other situation in which one side is dominant, the contributions and accommodations may be rather evenly distributed. We can illustrate this with some examples from the postwar pidgins of Japan and Korea, often called "Bamboo English." (The technical "dominance" of the Americans was not particularly obvious at the level of most male-female interaction, where the pidgin developed.)

BAMBOO ENGLISH

During the months that followed the beginning of the occupation of Japan by American and some British Commonwealth troops at the end of August 1945, informal communication between the two sides involved a great deal of gesturing, radical simplification of English by the Americans, while the Japanese engaged in considerable *relexification*—substituting English words for Japanese words while preserving Japanese word order. Thus, "Me tomorrow Saseho go," from a young Japanese woman in mid-1946, in which the local pronunciation of Sasebo is given, with the verb in final position. The time expression is not normally placed for either language; in Japanese the use of the pronoun would not be mandatory here, in which case the time expression would be in the normal initial position. No verb is offered in, "You tonight pass?" from the same woman, but again the pronoun would not be required here in Japanese. Another woman of the period asked *Doko* [where] go? *Kyanpu* [camp] go?" without any pronoun but with the verb relexified. While Japanese can use intonation to convey an interrogative meaning, in the present case it is misleading to use a question mark after the "camp," because the American misunderstood and thought he was being advised to return to camp.

The Japanese interrogative particle *ka* appears in a set question that was popular in 1945 and 1946: *Nan desu ka* you? "What is [it with] you?" which was used more or less interchangeably with "Watsamattayou?" The question *Nan desu ka* "What is [it]?" is perfectly normal Japanese and has the same meaning as the English equivalent that is offered. With the addition of "you," it takes on the somewhat different meaning of "What's the matter with you," alluding to behavior or motivation rather than to physical health in most cases.

Sometime after the first year of the American occupation but by the end of the second the pidgin had developed most of its characteristic forms. Relexification is less obvious, but some of the early features, such as *reduplication*, became "anchors" for the pidgin. Thus *testo-testo* "to try out," from English "test," or *miru-miru* from Japanese *miru* "to see or look" were established virtually from the beginning of the occupation.

While the pidgin was well established by the end of the 1940s, it was not until 1955 that it was noted in the literature, and then basically as an example of Japanese influence on the speech of Americans in Japan (Norman, 1955, who recoined "Bamboo English" to describe the phenomenon. The term had been used originally by George G. Struble in 1929 to describe the result of classroom English-teaching in the Philippines—that is, it did not describe a pidgin). The same English perspective was reflected in the discussions of "Korean Bamboo English" by Algeo (1960) and Webster (1960). Goodman (1967) was the first to deal with the contact vernacular primarily in terms of a pidgin, drawing on his own experiences at Hamamatsu in 1955.

While in official situations the American forces occupying Japan after the war enjoyed clear dominance, more or less from the beginning the male-female relationships that gave rise to the pidgin in its ultimate form were essentially egalitarian. Eventually there was widespread cohabitation, in many cases leading to marriage. The resulting pidgin represents a compromise system that generally follows four rules of simplification, though these are only statistical tendencies and the forms observed varied widely, while individual speakers differed considerably in their approximations to the "norms" implied below. The examples were collected between 1958 and 1961, mostly from the Fukuoka area of Japan (Howell, 1978). Standard spellings are used for both the Japanese and the English, though actual pronunciations varied widely.

The first rule of simplification is the commonality factor that has been noted frequently. In the present case, if Japanese and English have a common syntactic solution to a problem, such as posing a question, it will become fixed in the pidgin. Thus both languages have the option of using a rising intonation to mark a simple (non-tag) yes-no question:

(1)   You want fight? (Japanese speaker)
(2)   You buy for me? (American speaker)

While it might be possible to develop a measure of complexity for

syntactic solutions, perhaps in terms of the number of transformations required to produce a given surface structure, it will probably
suffice here to rely on our intuitions to follow the other three simplification rules.

The second rule is that if one donor has a simple solution and the
other a complex solution, the simple one will tend to become fixed
in the pidgin. English tag questions, for example, require that an affirmative assertion be followed by a negative tag and vice versa (It's
complicated, isn't it? It's not easy, is it?). Japanese has an extremely
simple tag construction (among others which are not so simple) that
does not depend on the polarity of the assertion: the simple addition
of the particle *ne*. This is the only tag observed for American (male
speakers, while it was one of several used by the Japanese (female)
speakers:

   (3)   He's stinko, ne? (American speaker)

   (4)   Dame [bad], ne? (Japanese speaker)

The third rule is that if both donors have solutions that are quite
easy to pick up by the other side, then we may expect to find both
solutions in the pidgin. Thus English normally introduces a non-yes-
no question with an interrogative expression. Japanese is more variable in this respect, usually having the same option but with other
placements possible. Thus,

   (5)   Boysan [His] house doko [where]? (Japanese speaker) which
is normal order in Japanese but exceptional in English, and it is usually the Japanese who use it in the pidgin. On the other hand, placing the interrogative word first occurs in the speech of both sides,
even though *doko* does not ordinarily come first in Japanese:

   (6)   Doko you home? (Japanese speaker)

   (7)   Doko husband? (American speaker)

Some interrogative expressions do come initially in Japanese, and they
retain that position in the pidgin:

   (8)   Dôshite [How come] Japanese speak? (Japanese speaker, but
similar examples could be cited for Americans.

The fourth rule is that where neither donor has a simple solution
to a syntactic problem a novel and simple solution is found. To form
negatives normally in the plain style in Japanese requires some
knowledge of verb conjugations and is thus not simple; similarly, in
English, to negate "He went" we must introduce the auxiliary "do,"
to which the negative and the tense are added, while the past is sub-
tracted from the main verb to yield "He didn't go," which is again,
not simple. The preferred solution in the pidgin is to use "no" plus
verb (including modal):

   (9)   I no speak English (Japanese speaker)

(10)   I no can learn language (American speaker)

(11)   No isogashii [busy] (Japanese speaker)

Again, these are just tendencies and do not reflect the full range of observed usages. Some Japanese speakers would use "don't" or "not," often as part of set expressions, just as some Americans learned to treat Japanese -nai as a negative particle on the basis of set expressions such as "jôtôjanai" for "no good." (In Japanese *jôtô* is literally "high class" and the informal negative would be *jôtô ja nai*. In the pidgin "jôtô" designates anything warranting approval, and "jôtônai" designates anything warranting disapproval.)

Two cautionary notes are in order here. The first has to do with alternate solutions. While the postwar pidgin produced a novel and simple solution to formation of the negative, a different solution, based on Japanese, was utilized in port cities during the second half of the nineteenth century as the country was being opened to the West after two and a half centuries of nearly total isolation from the outside world. While there were lexical contributions from a number of languages, the word order was essentially Japanese and most of the non-Japanese vocabulary was English. That is, the principal donors were, as in the case of the postwar pidgin, Japanese and English. But the pidgins are quite different in many respects. In the nineteenth century case there were two ways to form a negative. One was the use of *nai* as a postposed particle, as used by a few Americans in the postwar Bamboo. The other was to suffix -*en* to all verbs ending in -*mas*. (In Japanese the polite ending for verbs is -*masu*, but the final -*u* is normally unvoiced and thus not heard by the foreigners.) The result was a form that looked like the normal negative of verbs with the polite suffix even though it was reached by a substantial "shortcut" by comparison with the rules the Japanese would use to produce that form. See Daniels (1948) for a study of the nineteenth century pidgin vocabulary and a discussion of sources for the pidgin material.

The other cautionary note has to do with ambiguity. If simplification would introduce an awkward ambiguity, it is likely to be sacrificed in favor of the need to control the ambiguity, as E.B. Woolford (personal communication) has noted on the basis of experience with Tok Pisin, otherwise known as Neo-Melanesian, an important pidgin used primarily on New Guinea, the Bismarck Archipelago and neighboring island groups, and the Solomon Islands (Hall, 1943).

The use of intonation to mark a question may be widespread enough to qualify as universal, and it may be that marking the question at or very near the end of the sentence when there is no specifically interrogative word is also worthy of consideration as a universal.

But the use of a specifically rising intonation to mark a question is not universal, since a falling intonation is used in some varieties of English, in the so-called Hawaiian Pidgin, evidently in Hawaiian, possibly in Finnish, which at least does not use the rising intonation (Slobin, 1971), and probably other languages as well. Some sort of tag question, inviting concurrence on the part of the listener, is no doubt widespread also. While the use of interrogative words is universal, their relative placement is variable. The most interesting of the Japanese Bamboo English excerpts are probably those involving the negative, with the *no plus verb*, which does not fit the pattern of either donor and may imply a universal deep structure feature that is not so general as to be trivial.

In the case of the Korean Bamboo English, as noted earlier, the influence of the Japanese version is striking. One reason for the close similarity may be that the Koreans are receptive to the same possibilities of linguistic adaptation: structurally Korean and Japanese are almost identical. That is, if Korean were completely different from Japanese, Japanese-type contributions might seem "complex" enough to be resisted and a pidgin of rather a different nature might have developed, even though the influence of English might still have been powerful.

KOREAN BAMBOO ENGLISH

Americans moved into Korea about the same time they moved into Japan in late 1945 and, except for the short period between the establishing of the Republic of Korea in the southern half of the peninsula in 1948 and the outbreak of the Korean War in mid-1950, have been there ever since. The Japanese influence on the Korean version of Bamboo English is striking, while no Korean elements are found in the Japanese version. Occasionally troops coming to Japan from Korea will attempt to apply terms derived from Korean, but such attempts are rejected. The Korean *caki* "over there," rendered "chogey" by Webster (1960) and "chogi" by Algeo (1960), is one such term that troops sometimes try to use, in the sense of "go," with little luck. The reason for the cool reception of Korean elements in the Bamboo in Japan is probably to be found in the relatively low prestige enjoyed by Korea and Koreans in Japan and the greater prestige of Japan in the eyes of the Americans. Since Korea was under Japanese control for 35 years, until the end of the Second World War, most older Koreans knew Japanese quite well in 1960. But the younger barmaids knew little or none, and in any event, the Japanese expressions appear to be the same as those found in the Japanese Bamboo English. That is, it appears likely that most expressions derived from Japanese were introduced by the Americans. Thus Algeo (1960) mentions *benjo* (latrine, now considered inelegant in Japan), *biiru* (beer), *puresento* (gift, from English, "present"), *watashi* (I), and several expressions warranting a brief commentary here. The term "moose", for a female consort, is from Japanese *musume,* "daughter," and in that bald form would only be used for one's own offspring. In the Japanese version of the pidgin it was used mainly in the sense of "girl friend." A more general term for young unmarried women was *jôsan* in both versions of the Bamboo. The polite Japanese suffix *-san*, attached to names and titles generally in Japanese, is found in both versions of Bamboo English primarily in a few set expressions. Thus "boysan" could describe a young male in general; in Japan, at least, it could include young soldiers. In Korea, *mamasan* and *papasan* were used to designate an elderly female and male respectively, while *mamasan* could also mean the madam of a brothel (Algeo, 1960). In Japan the usage may have been a little more involved. In the normal Japanese-language world, *mama* and *papa* are used by some families as parental terms, and *mama* is the usual term to designate the proprietress of a drinking establishment (her male counterpart is the "master"). In the Japanese version of the pidgin a *mamasan* could be the proprietress of a bar, but more generally she could be one who sold goods or services, while a *papasan* would be a male who sold goods or services. The usage closely parallels the Japanese *-yasan* of *hanayasan* (one who sells flowers), *yasaiyasan* (one who sells vegetables), and so forth. Thus in Japanese a *sakanayasan* is a fishmonger, while in the pidgin a woman who brought fish around to military homes was the "fish mamasan." The man whose job was to stoke fires to provide Americans with hot water in and around military bases was the "water papasan" or the "boiler papasan."

Webster (1960) mentions "skivvy honchô" as the leader of a Korean working party, deriving it from the Navy term for underwear, but this is a folk etymology. The first term is from Japanese *sukebei* "lecherous," and the *hanchô* is literally a "squad leader," a term Miller (1967) associates with the old Imperial Army, but the term survives in the civilian world to designate a relatively low-ranking supervisor. In the Japanese version of Bamboo English a *sukebei hanchô* was a sexually ambitious soldier. More generally, the *hanchô* designated anyone in charge of an office or function, and in this sense has become part of the American English lexicon, usually with the spelling "honcho."

Another set of terms found in both versions of the Bamboo English are *takusan* and *sukoshi*, Japanese words meaning respectively "a large quantity of" and "a small quantity of" something. In the pidgin they are used more widely, with *sukoshi* also designating small size, while *takusan* functioned as a general intensifier.

The relatively few Korean terms mentioned by Algeo (1960) and Webster (1960) are not presented in a form that makes identification immediate and certain. Thus Algeo (1960) offers for "house" (cip) "chibee," in which the "-ee" presumably represents a particle designating the subject of a verb. Webster (1960) sees "edewa" as a verb; it derives from *iri* "hither" and a form of *ota* "come." In any case, to judge from their examples and comments, the Korean contribution to the pidgin is minor by comparison with those from English and Japanese.

To provide a sample of continuous text we offer the opening passage from *Cinderella* (anonymous, from Webster, 1960, pp. 264–265) with a brief commentary:

> Taksan[1] years ago, skoshi[2] Cinderella-san[3] lived[4] in hootchie[5] with sisters, poor little Cinderella-san ketchee[6] no fun, hava-no[7] social life.[8] Always washee-washee,[9] scrubee-scrubee, make chop-chop.[10] One day Cinderella-san sisters[11] ketchee post cardo[12] from Seoul. Post cardo speakie[13] so: one prince-san[14] have big blowout,[15] taksan kimchi,[16] taksan beeru,[17] play "She Ain't Got No Yo Yo,"[18] Cindy-san sisters taksan excited, make Cinderella-san police up[19] clothes.

1. taksan, Japanese *takusan*, "a lot of"; note that in Tokyo Japanese the -u- is unvoiced and virtually inaudible.

2. skoshi, Japanese *sukoshi*, "a small quantity of," with the -u- again unvoiced and barely audible.

3. -san, the most common Japanese polite suffix.

4. lived, less likely than "stay" in the pidgin and the past tense marker is usually omitted.

5. hootchie, "pad," a term popular in Korea but not in Japan; the etymology is uncertain.

6. ketchee, "catch," a staple of the pidgin in Japan as well, meaning "get, obtain," including such extensions as "catch jôsan" in the sense of making an arrangement with a prostitute.

7. hava-no, "lack," much less common than "no have"

in Japan and in Korea as well (if we may rely on Webster, 1960).

8. social life, an improbable phrase for the pidgin.

9. washee-washee, "wash," probably obsolete in Japan: scrubee-scrubee may not be a regular feature of either version of Bamboo English.

10. chop-chop, "food, meal," is not common in Japan.

11. the plural marker tends to be omitted in Japan and probably in Korea.

12. post cardo, improbable for the pidgin.

13. speakie, "speak," is the usual word for "say, tell," but it is not normally followed by "so."

14. prince, unlikely for the pidgin.

15. blowout, not common in Japan.

16. kimchi, pickled vegetables, a Korean staple.

17. beeru, "beer," from Japanese *biiru*.

18. the song title is a parody of *Shina no Yoru*, "China Nights," a Japanese favorite during and after the Pacific War.

19. police up, a military expression for cleaning or straightening up an area.

While there appear to be many expressions not characteristic of the pidgin in the foregoing excerpt, the flavor is correct and the uncharacteristic entries help make the point that pidgins are usually for limited purposes. When the anonymous author ventured outside the normal realm of coversational topics, he had to go outside the normal pidgin vocabulary.

The comments for notes 4, 6, and 13 (stay, catch, and speak) illustrate the lack of synonymy discussed by Smith (1972) in connection with the reduced functional load of pidgins. Eliminating synonyms reduces a form of redundancy typical of more developed languages, but the extreme reduplication (notes 9 and 10) injects redundancy without really expanding the lexicon. Thus, it is an economical redundancy from the standpoint of the learner.

Since pidgins, most generously defined, can develop whenever there is a need and fade even more quickly when the need is gone, it is not possible to set a figure on the number of pidgins, but there are probably several hundred around the world at any given time.

(See the extensive bibliography compiled by John E. Reinecke and others, 1975.) In many cases pidgins give rise to creole languages, where children are born and raised in a pidgin community.

CREOLES

At the beginning of the chapter we mentioned the controversy over whether pidgins or creoles more closely tapped linguistic universals, and mentioned the lack of transformational depth in pidgins (about which there is no controversy). A similar notion was offered by Smith (1972), who suggested that "the surface structures of pidgins appear to be much more isomorphic with the underlying semantic structures than in the case with vernaculars" (p. 54), but he sees this as a likely explanation for the similarities among pidgins and seems to be thinking in terms of linguistic universals.

In the view presented by Kay and Sankoff (1974), the process of creolization involves "the creation of transformational machinery which moves the surface structure progressively further away from universal deep structure" (p. 66).

Bickerton (1977) argues for the greater importance of creoles for getting at universals. He divides the pidgin-creole world into two groups. In one, where the original population has remained more or less intact, pidgins remain and creolization has taken place only belatedly or not at all. This area includes West Africa, the China coast, Melanesia, and the Pacific Northwest. The pidgins have attained considerable range in the sense of topics that they can deal with and, Bickerton says, they all differ markedly from one another in their grammatical structure.

Where the populations have been largely displaced, on the other hand—the Caribbean, the Bight of Benin Islands, the Indian Ocean, and Hawaii—creolization seems to have taken place rapidly. All are now creole- or post-creole speaking and all except Hawaii have lost all trace of any antecedent pidgin. Most crucially, these creoles show grammatical similarities that constitute virtual identity in several areas.

The first similarity is in having three articles that cover the same semantic areas in each language. Thus, by way of illustration, Guyanese Creole has a definite article, *di*, which presupposes that the speaker knew in advance what the particular item was, in *mi bai di buk* (I bought the book). In *mi bai wan buk*, the indefinite article, *wan*, indicates that the speaker did not know in advance what book he was going to buy, while *mi go bai buk* lacks an article, but the zero-marking may be considered to signify a "nonspecific" article, so that the sentence can mean that the speaker intends to buy one book, or perhaps several books.

The second similarity concerns ten characteristics of tense and aspect in the creoles. To take just the tenth one to give an idea of their flavor, there is an *anterior plus irrealis plus nonpunctual*, which has the meaning of "an unrealized condition in the past, of a nonpunctual nature," as for example, "I would have been looking for something else" (Bickerton, 1977, p. 59).

There are other areas of similarity, some more obvious than others, but except for the rule *no plus verb*, noted for the Bamboo English and commonly found in pidgins and creoles, Bickerton (1977) feels that pidgins are not the place to look for language universals. While the shared characteristics of creoles have not been immediately apparent to all students of the subject (see Rickford, 1977, for example), and some nonspecialists seem to take the pidgin argument for granted (Crane, Yeager, and Whitman, 1981, p. 200, comment that "The type of simplification that takes place in pidgins is characteristically universal"), the issue may soon be resolved in Bickerton's favor. He has now marshalled a formidable array of arguments and evidence to back his claims (Bickerton, 1981), which have now been extended to deal not only with creoles as such, but first-language acquisition by children and the very origin of language.

To consider only the part of the argument that pertains to creoles for the moment, Bickerton notes that in the case of pidgins it is usually easy enough to detect the ethnic background of the speakers. In Hawaiian Pidgin English, for instance, the Japanese characteristically place the verb in final position, where it belongs in Japanese, while Filipino speakers often place the verb before the subject, again reflecting the influence of the native language. But these differences disappear in the first creole generation. Thus the speech of the creole speaker does not reflect his ethnic background, though this is not to deny any input from the antecedent pidgin. Since the arguments are rather technical, we may close this section with Bickerton's (1981) own summary statement:

> . . . the more we strip creoles of their more recent developments, the more we factor out superficial and accidental features, the greater are the similarities that reveal themselves. Indeed, it would seem reasonable to suppose that the only differences among creoles at creolization were those due to differences in the nature of the antecedent pidgin, in particular to the extent to

which superstrate features had been absorbed by that pidgin and were therefore directly accessible to the first creole generation in the outputs of their pidgin-speaking parents. Finally, the overall pattern of similarity which emerges . . . is entirely consonant with the process of building a language from the simplest constituents—in many cases, no more than S[entence], N[oun], and V[erb], the minimal constituents necessary for a pidgin. (p. 132)

BLACK ENGLISH VERNACULAR

The creole of greatest contemporary interest for many Americans is the one popularly called "Black English" (BE), though Labov (1972) argues for the term "Black English Vernacular" (BEV). The BE is better reserved for

> the whole range of language forms, used by black people in the United States: a very large range indeed, extending from the Creole grammar of Gullah spoken in the Sea Islands of South Carolina to the most formal and accomplished literary style. A great deal of misunderstanding has been created by the use of this term, "black English," which replaced our original "Nonstandard Negro English" when the latter became less acceptable to many people. (Labov, 1972, p. xiii)

The BEV includes the relatively uniform grammar that is typified in the speech of black youth in their teens or late preteens, who participate fully in the street culture of the inner cities. It is found in many urban centers of the United States, but Labov specifically refers to New York, Boston, Detroit, Philadelphia, Washington, Cleveland, Chicago, St. Louis, San Francisco, and Los Angeles.

The BEV, then, is a "northern" urban speech variety, but it derives from a southern regional variety. Labov (1972) says that nearly every feature of BEV can be found among some white speakers in the south, but the forms are more characteristic among black speakers. He cites Stewart (1968, 1970) to the effect that there are many structural aspects and marginal phenomena of BEV that indicate a strong creole influence or origin, or at the least suggest that BEV was in the past more divergent from other dialects than it is today. The creole origin of BEV has not been universally accepted, though for most contemporary scholars the main questions are matters of detail. In general, as Rickford (1977, p. 197) notes, "creolists usually devote a great deal of their argument to establishing how different BE [here more broad than the urban restriction of BEV] always has been from SE [standard English] and other white dialects, and noncreolists argue that BE is and always was no different from Southern or colonial white dialects" (Kurath, 1949).

One feature that seems to have been reliably traced to an African origin is *say* as a complementizer, "that" in the sentence "They told me say they couldn't get it" (Rickford, 1977, p. 212). The form is found in at least some of the BEV areas. Rickford (1977) found it used by adults twenty to forty years old in Philadelphia and notes that Dillard (1972) found the form in use among older people in Washington, D.C. It is found in Gullah and many West African and Caribbean creoles with a wide variety of verbs, such as *tell, believe, think, know* and evidently others (Rickford, 1977). Cassidy (1961) and Dillard (1972) suggest that it is derived from Akan *se* (Rickford, 1977). Akan is a language used over much of Ghana and in parts of the Ivory Coast.

While ritual insult games widely played by black youth in BEV areas have not, apparently, been reliably traced to an African origin, they do appear commonly in Caribbean creole areas (Rickford, 1977) and thus constitute another apparent link between the BEV and creoles.

Many of the BEV features are widely shared with creoles, but here we shall content ourselves with a few of the better known examples. One is the omission of the copula, as in "he sick." This may equate to SE "he is sick," but it carries the specific implication that he is sick at the moment, and it contrasts with "he be sick," which implies that the individual is the victim of a long-term illness. Similar considerations govern the use of the auxiliary "be": "he workin' " (he is working at the moment) contrasts with "he be workin' " (he is always working). Dillard (1972, p. 45) cites several examples of acceptable and unacceptable forms, the latter of which are marked with an asterisk.

Thus in the sentence "He be waitin' for me every night when I come home," the "be" agrees with "every night" in specifying duration. "He waitin' for me right now," without the auxiliary, correlates with the "right now" in indicating "at the moment." Thus it would be semantically anomalous to say "*He waitin' for me every night" or "*He be waitin' for me right now."

Similarly, to negate "He waitin' for me right now," the negator "ain' " is appropriate: "He ain' waitin' for me right now." But the negator "don' " is required for the durative marker "be"; "He don' be waitin' for me every night." The forms "*He ain' waitin' for me every night" and "*He don' be waitin' for me right now" are not grammatically acceptable. To give so few examples of the grammatical differences of BEV from SE is not to slight the number and the complexities of the differences; rather, it is testimony to the intricacy of the problem. A brief appreciation of the difficulties may be obtained from Bailey's (1974) review of Dillard's book; a full appreciation would require a volume at least the size of this one. Labov (1972) devotes a 65-page chapter just to the "Contraction, Deletion, and Inherent Variability of the English Copula," with specific reference, of course, to BEV.

Whether we look at BEV or any other area where several speech varieties are employed, there are likely to be serious problems of description. Nagara (1972), for example, studying the pidgin of Japanese plantation workers in Hawaii, had to be a little arbitrary in considering all utterances to be pidgin unless their predicate words were derived from Japanese, in which case the utterances were classified as Japanese. Thus the utterance "You study *sura ka?*" (Do you study?) is classified as Japanese rather than pidgin. Nagara honored the dichotomy because none of his informants could produce a sentence without relying upon the morphophonemic rules of Japanese when the sentence included a predicate word derived from that language. Further, in the case of Nagara's informants, when a Japanese predicate word occurred, the terminal juncture always conformed to the Japanese norm.

Nagara's reasoning is quite understandable, but others might handle the problem a little differently. Dealing with an ethnically more diverse group, Carr (1972) dealt with the local varieties of speech in Hawaii in terms of a continuum (from pidgin through standard English) with five stages, while Bickerton (1977) shows a single speaker (of Japanese extraction) varying from utterances in which all words are from English to utterances in which most of the words are from Japanese, the differences depending on the speaker's emotional involvement with the topic.

Finally, a note on social considerations playing a part in decreolization, in which creole speakers come to abandon the creole in favor of another language (usually the language of the "establishment"). It is likely that pidginization, creolization and decreolization are all governed by the same social factor: the relationship between the peer group and the reference group. We suggest that when the peer group and the reference group are the same there is no serious tendency toward language change, and if the peer group and the reference group are different, then there is a tendency for language to change in the direction of that of the reference group (Howell, 1978), an idea at least strongly implied in Labov's study of Martha's Vineyard (1963) and in various of his studies of speech in New York City. In addition, the idea seems to answer Roger Brown's (1973) question as to why a child continues to elaborate its speech in the direction of the adult model when its restricted speech forms seem to get the job of communciating done pretty well.

Bickerton (1977) has suggested that if there are target models of the standard language available and if the speaker interacts mainly with those who speak the language natively, then the speaker will make a pretty fair approximation to the standard. Otherwise the result will be a pidgin. But there seem to be many cases of lost opportunities that are understandable if the speaker will not or cannot sufficiently identify with (take as a reference group) the native speakers of the language in question. Certainly in the case of Bamboo English, the speakers each identify primarily with their own sides and there is a limited interest in mastering the language of the other side. The pidgin is a convenient compromise for both sides. Similarly, in cases where some communication is necessary in the language of the other side, so the speakers undertake the formal study of the target language, there is often a tendency to settle for a level of competence that falls far short of mastery (Nida, 1957).

Even in the case of creolization, it seems highly probable that the second- and subsequent generations are not identifying as strongly with the parental generation as with the generation of their peers (of different language backgrounds). If there is, then, a creole community that lacks the ambition or opportunity to assimilate into the politically, socially, and economically dominant stratum of the larger society, then the creole may be perpetuated. But if pidgin or creole speakers are motivated (and are permitted) to join the dominant segment of society they will tend to change their speech to fit that of the dominant members of the society. That is, there will be depidginization or decreolization (Howell, 1978). But taking on the speech forms of the reference group does not *assure* acceptance into that group.

REFERENCES

Algeo, J. T. Korean Bamboo English, *American Speech*, 1960, *35*, 117–123.
Bailey, C.J. Review of J.L. Dillard, *Black English, Its History and Usage in the United States. Foundations of Language*, 1974, *11*, 299–309.

Bickerton, D. Pidginization and creolization: Language acquisition and language universals. In A. Valdman (Ed.) *Pidgin and Creole linguistics*. Bloomington: Indiana University Press, 1977.

Bickerton, D. *Roots of language*. Ann Arbor, Mich.: Karoma Publishers, Inc., 1981.

Brown, R. Development of the first language in the human species, *American Psychologist*, 1973, *28*, 97–106.

Carr, E. B. *Da Kine Talk*. Honolulu: The University Press of Hawaii, 1972.

Cassidy, F. G. *Jamaica talk*. London: Macmillan, 1961.

Crane, L., Yeager, E. & Whitman, R.L. *An introduction to linguistics*. Boston: Little, Brown & Co., 1981.

Daniels, F.J. The vocabulary of the Japanese ports lingo, *Bulletin of the School of Oriental and African Studies, University of London*, 1948, *12*, 805–823.

DeCamp, David. The development of pidgin and creole studies. In A. Valdman (Ed.) *Pidgin and Creole linguistics*. Bloomington: Indiana Univ. Press, 1977.

Dillard, J.L. *Black English, its history and usage in the United States*. New York: Random Hosue, Inc., 1972.

Goodman, J. S. Development of a dialect of English-Japanese pidgin, *Anthropological Linguistics*, 1967, *9*, No. 6, 43–55.

Hall, R. A., Jr. *Melanesian pidgin English*. Baltimore, Md.: Linguistic Society of America, 1943.

Hall, R. A., Jr. *Pidgin and Creole languages*. Ithaca: Cornell University Press, 1966.

Howell, R. W. Linguistic reflections of sociocultural differences in the pidgins of Japan and Hawaii. In Haruo Kozu and Ramesh Mathur (Eds.), *Proceedings [of the] Language, Thought, and Culture Symposium, 1976*. Hirakata City, Japan: Kansai University of Foreign Studies. Intercultural Research Institute Monograph Series No. 5, 1978.

Kay, P., & Sankoff, G. A language-universals approach to pidgins and creoles. In D. DeCamp & I. F. Hancock (Eds.), *Pidgins and Creoles: Current trends and prospects*. Washington, D.C.: Georgetown University Press, 1974.

Kurath, H. *A word-geography of the eastern United States*. Ann Arbor: University of Michigan Press, 1949.

Labov, W. The social motivation of a sound change. *Word*, 1963, *19*, 273–309.

Labov, W. *Language in the inner city: Studies in the black English vernacular*. Philadelphia: University of Pennsylvania Press, 1972.

Leland, C. *Pidgin-English sing-song*. (2nd ed.) London: Trübner & Company, 1887.

Miller, R. A. *The Japanese language*. Chicago: University of Chicago Press, 1967.

Nagara, S. *Japanese pidgin English in Hawaii*. Honolulu: University Press of Hawaii, 1972.

Nida, E. A. *Learning a foreign language*. Ann Arbor: Friendship Press, 1957.

Norman, A.M.Z. Bamboo English, the Japanese Influence upon American speech in Japan. *American Speech*, 1955, *30*, 44–48.

Reinecke, J. E., Tsuzaki, S. M., DeCamp, D., Hancock, I. F., & Wood, R. *A bibliography of pidgin and creole languages*. Honolulu: University Press of Hawaii, 1975.

Rickford, J. R. The question of prior creolization in black English. In A. Valdman (Ed.), *Pidgin and creole linguistics*. Bloomington, Ind.: Indiana University Press, 1977.

Slobin, Dan I. *Psycholinguistics*. Glenview, Ill.: Scott, Foresman & Company, 1971.

Smith, D. Some implications for the social status of pidgin languages. In D. M. Smith & R. W. Shuy (Eds.), *Sociolinguistics in cross-cultural analysis*. Washington, D.C.: Georgetown University Press, 1972.

Stewart, W. Continuity and change in American Negro dialects. *Florida Foreign Language* Reporter 6 Spring 1968, 3–4, 14–16, 18.

Stewart, W. Toward a history of Negro dialect. In F. Williams (Ed.), *Language and poverty*. Chicago: Markham, 1970.

Struble, G. G. Bamboo English. *American Speech*, 1929, *4*, 276–285.

Webster, G. Korean bamboo English once more. *American Speech*, 1960, *35*, 261–265.

Chapter 11

LANGUAGE AND SOCIETY

In 1935 J. R. Firth declared sociological linguistics to be "the great field for future research," but until the 1960s the prophesy was largely unfulfilled. Sociolinguistics, the study of how linguistic and social events covary, was represented by isolated articles that more often than not were the by-products of research in linguistics, anthropology, sociology, or psychology. The situation has changed dramatically in the past two decades. Many universities now offer courses in sociolinguistics; and a body of literature specifically on sociolinguistics has fully emerged and is growing rapidly.

Just as there are grammatical constraints on speech (rules that permit some sequences and preclude other sequences), there are also social constraints on speech. And much as grammatical relationships are marked in certain ways, for example through the use of the plural *s* or the past tense *-ed*, social relationships are linguistically marked. They are marked in many ways, as through the choice of pronouns (*tu* versus *vous*), terms of address (first name versus title plus last name), special verb forms (in languages such as Japanese and Korean), the local versus the standard dialect, or through the choice of language in a multilingual community. Changes in social relationships are marked by changes in the patterns of verbal interactions, whether those changes are momentary or enduring; and social change

233

can be considered over a wide range of levels, from the momentary falling-out of intimates to sweeping changes that transform the society and take millennia to be fully realized. Yet at all levels we may expect to see the changes reflected in altered patterns of verbal interaction, and in the options for linguistic choice.

DIMENSIONS OF VERBAL INTERACTION

Social aspects of verbal interaction are conducted along at least two dimensions, which seem to have validity not only for humans, but also for most other animals (see Brown, 1965, and Callan, 1970, for useful discussions). The first dimension is that of relative closeness or familiarity; the second is that of relative power. Familiarity can be thought of as a horizontal dimension, ranging from solid or intimate relationships to relationships of complete nonfamiliarity or extreme social distance. The power dimension is vertical, in that it marks degrees of dominance and submissiveness. In general, if there is no question of relative power or social rank, then the vertical dimension is not immediately relevant, and interaction takes place on the horizontal dimension in accordance with the relative "closeness" of the parties concerned.

The two dimensions are related to each other in that they employ the same verbal markers, but they differ in the patterns by which the markers are used. Perhaps this relationship of the dimensions was first recognized by Garvin and Riesenberg (1952), in their study of respectful behavior in the finely stratified Micronesian society of Ponape. They found it necessary to distinguish between verbal and nonverbal manifestations of attitudes toward superiors in title (power dimension) and respected equals (intimacy dimension) on the one hand, and attitudes toward inferiors in title (power) and intimate equals (intimacy) on the other. That is, with equals one speaks the way one is spoken to: there is reciprocal use of given forms and the pattern of usages is symmetrical. But one addresses superiors differently from the way one is addressed by them: there is a nonreciprocal use of given forms, and the pattern of usages is asymmetrical. Moreover, the way one behaves toward intimates is the way one behaves toward inferiors, and the way one behaves toward non-intimates is the way one generally behaves toward superiors.

The expression of social distance and social rank in terms of symmetrical and asymmetrical patterns of linguistic choice was more broadly discussed 8 years later by Brown and Gilman (1960). They argued that the use of the pronouns *tu* and *vous* (or their equivalents) in some 20 languages of Europe and India vary along the dimensions of solidarity and power. The nonreciprocal use of *tu* (T) and *vous* (V) is associated with a disparity in social status, the higher-ranking individual being addressed as V and the lower as T. The reciprocal use of T is associated with relative intimacy, and the reciprocal use of V with relative distance or formality. Brown and Ford (1961) found that the same patterns of usage existed in terms of address in American English. The use of the first name (FN) and of the last name plus title (TLN) correspond respectively to the use of T and V. That is, the reciprocal use of FN implies intimacy, reciprocal use of TLN implies distance, and nonreciprocal use of FN and TLN implies a difference in the social ranks of the speakers.

The evidence, though almost exclusively based on Indo-European languages, led Brown and Ford to formulate a concept of the relationship between the power and solidarity dimensions. They suggested that the abstract link of intimacy/condescension and distance/deference may be a [socio]linguistic universal. They were limiting their formulation to matters of personal address, and apparently did not know about the Garvin and Riesenberg (1952) study, but a series of independent characterizations all support the formulation and its generalization. Clifford Geertz (1960), for example, described levels of polite speech in Java, which fitted their formulation, as did Foster's (1964) study of pronouns of address in a Mexican village and Howell's (1965) study of the utterance endings in Korean translations of Blondie cartoons. Further support for the principle has been found in Japanese pronouns of address (Brown, 1965), the uses of Spanish and Guarani in Paraguay (Rubin, 1962), and Yiddish pronouns of address (Slobin, 1963). Finally, the principle is supported by Howell's (1973) general treatment of familiar and nonfamiliar behavior.

There is considerable evidence, then, that interaction can be usefully described in terms of symmetrical and asymmetrical patterns that involve dimensions of relative closeness and relative power. Now Brown and his associates were dealing with very broad patterns, so it is not surprising that some difficulties have arisen with specific applications. Friedrich (1966), for example, found it impossible to understand pronominal usage in nineteenth-century Russian literature on the basis of the two-dimensional model, and pointed out that *switching* of patterns occurs in accordance with a number of variables, including the topic and the setting. Friedrich underscored how difficult it is to predict linguistic choice when one considers the full range of options generally available with which to show various degrees of familiarity or respect. The problem is not so much in the model offered by Brown and associates as in the fact that terms of address or pronouns tend to be polar, while it is possible through the use of nicknames, diminutives, and the like, to register relationships that fall between the poles of familiarity and respect symbolized by T-V, FN-TLN, and other markers.

DYADIC RELATIONS

The simplest social interaction involves only two parties, a dyad. We can observe how specific people interact together, and learn something about the nature of their relationship from the way they speak to each other, or we can look at the speech that characterizes "identity relationships" (Goodenough, 1965) or role relationships, such as physician-nurse, physician-patient, and so forth. It often happens that two individuals will stand in more than one identity relationship, as with two schoolteachers who are married to each other, and thus are at once colleagues and spouses. In private they may exchange pet names, while in front of students they may use rather formal terms of address.

In considering dyadic interaction, it is helpful to realize that any two parties will have a basic pattern that characterizes their normal interaction, and any departure from that basic pattern signals a shifting in some aspect of the relationship. Multifaceted social relationships and the different interaction patterns associated therewith are not directly included in Brown's model, though he does discuss semantic conflict in dealing with sociolinguistic change (Brown, 1965). To cite an actual example of a shift in linguistic choice in accordance with the changing salience of identity relationships, a Korean sergeant found himself working for a captain who had gone to the same high school some years earlier. In settings where the military aspect of their relationship was salient, the sergeant addressed the captain by his military title, but in the absence of third parties, he used the term for "elder brother," thus marking the more basic and enduring aspect of their relationship. In general, it is likely that the more facets there are in a given dyadic relationship, the greater the likelihood will be of shifting patterns of verbal interaction.

Thus there is a basic pattern of interaction for any dyad, but that pattern shifts in accordance with changes in the salience of different aspects of the total relationship. This is analogous to the way departures from "normal" intonation and stress patterns in English signal differences in meanings.

THE AMBIGUITY OF PATTERNS

It is convenient to think that when the higher-status member of a dyad uses T or FN while receiving V or TLN, he is exercising a unilateral privilege, but the meaning of such an asymmetrical pattern varies with the circumstances under which it is established. When a pattern that was originally TLN-TLN becomes TLN-FN, as so frequently happens with university faculty members and certain students, the implication is that a degree of intimacy has now been attained which was not there originally. When the professor who used to call the young woman Miss Taniguchi now calls her Dolores, it signals a reduction in social distance. But suppose he had from the start called her Dolores? It would not be immediately apparent from the use of the terms alone whether he wanted to be chummy, or whether he was simply flexing his higher-status muscle. Of course, if he also issues an invitation to the student to call him Humbert, he is clarifying the situation. That is, the TLN-FN pattern is ambiguous unless the faculty member has explicitly invited the reciprocal use of the first name. The reason that the asymmetry which develops from an initially symmetrical TLN-TLN pattern is not ambiguous is that respect for the lower-status individual has been established by the initial use of the TLN. Once the respect has been symbolized, the subsequent use of FN clearly implies friendliness or solidarity on the part of the higher-status member.

Reciprocal use of TLN, then, may symbolize either social distance or mutual respect. A similar ambiguity arises when a higher-status member invites FN but continues to receive TLN. While the subordinate member of the dyad may wish only to signal respect, the higher-ranking individual may interpret the use of TLN as a deliberate attempt to maintain social distance.

Just as the mutual expression of respect may not symbolize extreme distance—diplomatic correspondence aimed at a rapprochement of governments is typically expressed in the most elaborately polite language—so the reciprocal use of familiar markers may not symbolize either solidarity or intimacy. Antagonists may abuse each other in the foulest terms—obviously, each is thereby denying respect to the other.

All three patterns are thus potentially ambiguous. Mutual V-V signifies that neither member of a dyad wishes to presume upon the privilege of familiar expression; mutual T-T means either that both parties grant the privilege of familiar expression, or that both have taken it unilaterally. The asymmetrical V-T means that the higher-status member of a dyad is exercising the privilege of familiarity, with or without the consent of the lower-ranking member.

POWER AND INTIMACY DIMENSIONS

The most detailed account of changes of pattern in verbal interaction over time is by Brown and Gilman (1960). They found that in Europe, prior to the fourth century, the second-person singular pronoun (T) was used only to address one person, and the second-person plural pronoun (V) was used only to address more than one person. Then people began to use the V when addressing the emperor (of whom there were then two), whence the practice spread to European court circles in general, until around the seventeenth century (and much earlier in certain areas), V was *the* second-person pronoun employed between members of the upper classes of Europe, and T was *the* second-person (singular) pronoun employed among the lower classes. Thus there was symmetrical V for the upper classes, symmetrical T for the lower classes, and asymmetrical V-T between classes. This asymmetrical "power" relationship was followed by the later development of a "solidarity" dimension, in which, for both classes, T was used between intimates and V between persons who were distant but socially equal. European society was then operating on two sociolinguistic dimensions: an asymmetrical status dimension and a symmetrical intimacy dimension. Thus, in the use of the second-person pronoun as a linguistic status marker, there were a status dimension, a simultaneous status and intimacy dimension, and an intimacy dimension. We should bear in mind, however, that there were other status markers, such as terms of address, in which the older pattern was (and is) still to be discerned.

Evidently a unidimensional system based on power obtained in Europe, until for some reason, a second dimension developed to differentiate forms of address among power-equals. The two dimensions coexisted in equilibrium for an unspecified, but certainly long, period of time. But reciprocal and nonreciprocal relationships are mutually exclusive and thus may involve structural incompatibilities, or "semantic conflict," to use Brown and Gilman's term (1960, pp. 258–261). Thus there is a power differential between father and son, and yet they are intimates in the same household. When it somehow became possible that persons separated on the basis of power could be joined on the basis of intimacy, the two-dimensional system became unstable, but it continued to exist well into the nineteenth century. Since then the semantic conflicts have been resolved in favor of reciprocal address patterns, until today there is in effect a unidimensional system based on intimacy or solidarity.

Brown sees the asymmetrical patterns as products of a relatively static, or closed, society, in which status is largely ascribed, and is closely tied to the feudal and manorial systems in Europe. The reciprocal solidarity norm has grown with the open-class society and the egalitarian ideology. The semantic conflict in the norms of address was resolved by the suppression of status in favor of solidarity, presumably because of its congruence with other far-reaching changes in European society (Brown, 1965, pp. 61–62). With the suppression of the status norm in favor of the solidarity norm, Brown notes a decline in shifting use of the pronouns to express transient sentiments—transient shifts between T and V—and an expansion of the areas regarded as appropriate for the use of T. The expanded use of the familiar pronoun is important to the idea that there has been a reduction in the proportion of asymmetrical identity relationships, which corresponds generally with an increase in the possibilities for upward mobility.

While broad treatments such as those of Brown and others are often so abstract that they may lack a direct behavioral validity, they do provide important clues for our understanding of the establishment and expression of social relationships, and may be used as guides in our examination of contemporary interaction among smaller groups. If, for example, steps are taken to establish an equal basis for possible upward mobility, the effect of those steps should subsequently be reflected in changed patterns of verbal behavior.

Thus, in parts of the American South, two generations ago, the social boundaries of the asymmetrical black-white relationship were marked, among other ways, by a general pattern that required blacks to use respect language (including TLN) toward whites, while receiving familiar language (including FN) in return. There were finer expressions of social relationship within the general pattern, as in the use by blacks of TFN toward a former preadolescent white companion or toward an employer, but we lack the documentation to discuss these distinctions in detail. Brown's logic would suggest that if the recent moves to improve the status of blacks in the South are proving effective, then there should be a discernible tendency toward the development of a symmetrical pattern of white-black verbal inter-action. The following account was given by a white participant ob-server in a federally-sponsored program to train rehabilitation personnel. The informant was identified as a Californian rather than a Yankee, and he was specifically concerned to observe interaction patterns. His background includes previous training and fieldwork in anthropology. The observations were made in Knoxville, Tennes-see, in 1964. Unfortunately, no information is available on specific interactions in that particular setting a generation ago. The picture given here, then, is an "after" picture, and we have no comparable "before" picture other than what is generally assumed to have been the case for "the South" (Howell, 1967, pp. 80–83).

1.   About 1 hour was spent observing white and black employees of the city engaged at the same rate of pay for the same unskilled la-bor on a street-repair project. There was no apparent racial dishar-mony. The whites addressed their black peers by FN. If the blacks had replied with TLN, they would have been acknowledging a status differential, while to use FN would have been to claim overtly that if there was a status differential, it was at least secondary to a relation-ship characterized by intimacy or solidarity. During the relatively short period of the observation, no black used *any* address term to a white.

2.   A black woman was employed as a teacher at an all-white school for the handicapped, and her interaction with her white colleagues was observed over a period of months. In formal situations she would be addressed by TLN, and in informal situations by FN. Again, she seemed to avoid using any terms of address to her co-workers.

3.   At a formal reception of the visiting faculty from the black school (which was supervised by the director of the local white school for handicapped children), all parties were introduced by TLN and all shook hands. In less than half an hour, however, the black con-tingent took leave of the gathering, evidently to minimize the oppor-tunity for awkward interaction. While the interaction of the two faculties was quite polite and formal, the early departure of the vis-itors seemed again to be a manifestation of avoidance behavior.

More casual observations, including informal conversations with various local blacks and whites, suggest that the evident use of avoid-ance does indicate a departure from earlier practices, in which blacks, here as elsewhere, had contributed to the linguistic marking of asymmetrical social relationships by using TLN or TFN toward whites.

Avoidance also probably enters the picture in the contrary case, where black and white youngsters have been close companions, exchanging FN or nicknames, but as adulthood approaches they are required to conform to an asymmetrical pattern. There is probably a period in which the black adolescent avoids the use of any address term to his former white chum, although he will continue to be addressed by FN.

SOCIOLINGUISTIC CHANGE IN JAPAN

The Knoxville case is particularly interesting as an example of a specific linguistic manifestation of rather sweeping social changes. A somewhat different example is provided by a particularly well-documented case study of a small Japanese agricultural village (Yoshida, 1964).

Until the turn of the present century, Morô included three social strata: an upper class of land-owning gentry, a middle class consisting mainly of independent farmers, and a lower class consisting mainly of tenant farmers. Household heads of the upper class were called *totsan*, and special honorific terms were used to address the wife of the *totsan*, his son, and his daughter. The heads of middle-class households were addressed as *tosan* by their social inferiors, while the term *ishi* was used by social superiors to address lower-class tenants and clients.

The patron-client relationships were independent of class relationships, though most of the upper-class household heads were in fact patrons. But relative class refers to relative social rank, while the patron-client relationship was contractual. A man became a client by receiving land (for faithful service to a wealthy farmer, through marriage to an upper-class girl, or through the establishment of a branch house of the lineage—but only the first of these was a common way of becoming a client; branch houses and client relationships were usually quite distinct). In return for the land and certain rights, such as the right to borrow money or grain without interest, the client was obliged to give a certain amount of annual labor service. The amount of service to be performed was negotiated at the time the land was transferred, but it was binding upon the client's descendants without the right of reduction. Some of the Morô patron-client relationships had been established more than 200 years ago, and at least in one case, some 60 days of service were required each year.

In addition to the negotiated labor service, the clients performed additional labor for debts incurred to their patrons, instead of making repayments in cash. Since most clients were also tenants, their burden of labor service was correspondingly increased. Moreover, the clients were often required to provide not only their own labor, but also that of all members of their families who were old enough to work, particularly at the time of rice planting.

We can appreciate the difficulties encountered by the lower class under these conditions, without entering into a discussion of the general inability of the small farmer in Japan to survive without supplementing his farm income (Fukutake, 1962, pp. 55ff). In the twentieth century, Morô has been torn by conflict born of the inequities described above. In the late 1920s the lower class managed to win the right to have local headmen elected from their ranks, a privilege formerly held only by the upper class. In 1943 the clients struck successfully for the abrogation of their contracts. Finally, a third conflict resulted in cash rents being charged on irrigated land, rather than rents being paid in kind. This was, of course, just before the postwar agrarian reform.

Today the honorific term *totsan* is still used toward the upper-class household heads, but the corresponding honorifics for their wives and children are practically obsolete. Likewise, the terms *tosan*, as a term of address by inferiors to middle-class household heads, and *ishi*, as a term of address to social inferiors, have virtually disappeared.

Two factors appear to underlie these linguistically marked social changes, both of which are indirectly attributable to industrialization. First, the availability of jobs in the cities, heightened by wartime production, provided young men with outward mobility. Then the availability of jobs outside the community reduced the economic dependence of lower-class families on the largely upper-class patrons. It seems likely that the increase in economic independence made upward mobility possible. At any rate, Yoshida suggests that the relative independence which came with outside jobs enabled the lower class to organize the long-standing protest that finally won them further independence.

The Morô case illustrates concomitant changes in social structure and verbal behavior, which are adequately documented and have taken place over a relatively short period of time. We will conclude this brief treatment of change through time by comparing two divergent speech communities; one of these changed its patterns drastically, while those of the other were virtually crystallized for nearly two centuries.

PRONOMINAL USAGE IN A CANADIAN MENNONITE COMMUNITY

The study of contrasting *du/Su* patterns in a Canadian Mennonite community (Howell and Klassen, 1971) began as a routine check on symmetrical and asymmetrical patterns of pronominal usage, with a particular focus on the suggestion by Roger Brown (1965) and associates that symmetrical patterns have come to prevail in Western Europe and its extensions, thus linguistically marking the change from a closed, rigidly stratified society to one that is open and egalitarian. Largely on the basis of work done in French Canada, Lambert (1967) showed that Brown's case was overstated, in that broad social changes do not uniformly influence all segments of a society at the same rate (Howell, 1968). We must then look more closely for factors that account for differential rates of change.

The Mennonite study examines two patterns of pronominal usage in a single speech community, one of which supports "the triumph of the solidarity semantic," while the other pattern denies it. The explanation seems to lie in the different histories of the two groups that comprise the congregation of the Mennonite Church in Herschel, Saskatchewan, in the Canadian prairie.

Herschel is an agricultural community with a village population of about 150 persons, most of whom are English-speaking and non-Mennonite. But there are some 55 Mennonite families on farms outside the village, and they comprise about a third of the rural population of Herschel. The Mennonite Church has a congregation of about 300 individuals, drawn not only from the immediate area, but also from other communities 20 miles or more away. English is used for business transactions, while, as Jaquith (1970) reported for Mexican Mennonites and Dawson (1936) reported for other Canadian Mennonites, a variety of Plattdeutsch is typically used for interaction in the home, and Hochdeutsch is the language of the church. Recently, however, there has been increasing pressure to use English, not only at home but also in the church; and Sunday-school classes in Herschel have been conducted in both Hochdeutsch and English for the past several years.

Among the German speakers in the Herschel congregation there are two distinct patterns for the use of second-person pronouns. A symmetrical pattern (except where an adult interacts with a child under the age of sixteen years) is characteristic of immigrants from Danzig. Among the larger group of immigrants from the Ukraine, there is a distinct preference for asymmetrical patterns. Six informants from each group (Ukraine and Danzig immigrants) were interviewed extensively regarding their use of pronouns and terms of address, and were subsequently observed interacting with various other members of the community. In addition, personal and business letters were examined in the search for systematic differences between the two groups.

The Danzig Mennonites were unanimous in their insistence that *Sie* (V) is used symmetrically by adults who are not relatives or close friends; *du* (T) is exchanged by relatives, close friends, and individuals under the age of 16 years. Individuals under the age of 16 use *Sie* to their elders, and receive *du*. Between adults, the shift from *Sie* to *du* is made by mutual consent, and is initiated by the senior party. Except in cases that involve individuals under the age of 16, there is no pronominal marking of differential status between father and son, employer and employee, tradesman and customer, or teacher and student. The pattern for such dyads is symmetrical.

There is a close correspondence between the pronoun used and the degree of formality expressed by other terms of address. First names are exchanged by people who exchange *du*, and TLN is used by people who exchange *Sie*. The pattern is modified in the case of relatives who exchange *du*: uncles, aunts, and sometimes cousins are addressed by the kin term plus FN; nieces and nephews are addressed by FN. Father, mother, grandfather, and grandmother are addressed simply by the kin term (without a name), and they use the FN in return. The Danzig Mennonites are relatively informal in correspondence, and never use the Gothic script; only the elderly had even learned the older script in school.

In general, then, the use of pronouns and address terms among the Danzig group agrees with the picture of contemporary usages offered by Brown and associates. The Ukrainian Mennonites, on the other hand, present rather a different picture. Differential social rank is regularly marked by second-person pronouns. *Sie* is used for ascending generations of kin, who use *du* in return. Employers use *du* and receive *Sie*. An age difference of about 10 years seems to require an asymmetrical pattern, with deference being paid to the elder of the two. But while senior kin ordinarily engage in asymmetrical patterns with junior kin, personal friendship and the lack of a clear age differential (to judge from a single instance) can result in a symmetrical usage pattern: a niece and her aunt, who was only two years her senior, exchanged *du*.

As might be expected, individuals who receive *Sie* also receive a title (*Herr, Frau, Fräulein*) plus the last name. Unrelated individuals who are a generation or so senior to the speaker are addressed as

Tante or *Onkel* plus the last name. Ukrainian Mennonite correspondence is much more formal than that of the Danzig group; it includes such honorific salutations as *Hoch geehrter Herr* and *hochachtungsvill,* and the Gothic script is still commonly used. Even those who have abandoned the Gothic for the Latin scripts said that they were familiar with it through their early schooling (they were taught it in Canada as well as in Russia, though it is not being taught today in the Mennonite schools used by the Herschel population).

Thus the Ukrainian Mennonites are much more conservative than the Danzig Mennonites in their linguistic interaction patterns. They still pay linguistic homage to differential rank, while the Danzig group has switched to patterns governed by relative solidarity.

There are more general differences between the two groups. The Ukrainian Mennonites, for example, show greater adherence to older forms of German and to traditional Mennonite precepts: they remain opposed to drinking, dancing, swearing, and military service. On the other hand, they are more receptive to loanwords. They have incorporated many Russian terms for foods and plants, and have adopted the English terms for common products of modern technology: car, radio, phone, and so forth. Where the Danzig group uses *anrufen* for "to make a telephone call," for example, the Ukrainian group uses *phonen,* and reserves *anrufen* to mean "shout at." Given the traditional German predilection for coining new words out of native elements, in this regard the Ukrainian group appears less conservative than the Danzig group.

As was indicated earlier, the rather different sociolinguistic patterns just described seem to arise from the different histories of the two groups. The Mennonites initially migrated from the Netherlands, in the sixteenth century, to the swampy Vistula Delta near Danzig, where they were left pretty much alone for some two centuries. Dutch continued to be the principle language of the groups for a considerable period, but by around 1750 *Hochdeutsch* had become the language of the pulpit and *Plattdeutsch* the language of the home (Krahn, 1949; Francis, 1948). The split of relevance here came in response to a pair of manifestos issued by Catherine II in 1762 and 1763, inviting non-Jewish Europeans to immigrate to Russia (Francis, 1955). According to the Ukranian group in Herschel, they migrated to the southern part of the Ukraine in the last two decades of the eighteenth century. In the Ukraine, the Mennonites settled in closed communities. Russian and Ukrainian were studied as foreign languages in the higher schools, but the lower schools relied on German, and German was the language of everyday interaction. Moreover, their textbooks, the models for formal language instruction, were the ones they had brought with them at the close of the eighteenth century. Since communication with Prussia was not maintained for long, the Ukrainian group was effectively cut off from the language changes that were taking place there. In the Ukraine the Mennonites were not only a religious minority, they were also a linguistic enclave. The use of German reinforced their Mennonite identity, and thus it may have taken on something of a religious aspect.

As their population increased, the Ukrainian Mennonites simply opened up new tracts of the abundant land. The principal occupation continued to be agriculture, and the settlements remained rural. The Mennonite families seem to have prospered; a great deal of their interaction with the indigenous peoples took the form of employer-employee relationships in the fields and the mills, and it seems likely that this further encouraged the use of asymmetrical patterns of interaction.

The Herschel group of Ukranian Mennonites (some 40 families) left Russia after the Revolution, between 1924 and 1926, because they were in danger of losing their exemption from military service, and their use of German in the schools and churches was also threatened. Their relatively conservative sociolinguistic patterns are probably due to their isolation, which also led to the perpetuation of eighteenth-century asymmetries in pronominal usage. By contrast, the Danzig group that had remained in Prussia had to accept local restrictions on the acquisition of land, and so the surplus population moved into the cities to take up nonagricultural occupations. This gave them increased contact with non-Mennonites, especially since the children were educated in the regular schools; this ensured that they would use the local standard German. The Danzig group remained a religious minority, but they were not a linguistic enclave. They were subject to those forces of urbanization and industrialization that induce wider ranges of social interaction and tend to weaken traditional boundaries. At the same time, the Danzig Mennonites were subject to the general egalitarian shift away from verbal marking of class and status differences, evidently pretty much in the way described by Brown and his associates.

The Danzig group remained in East Prussia until after World War II, when their homeland became part of Poland; they either resettled in West Germany or migrated to other countries. Thus in 1949, some 25 years after the arrival of the Ukrainian group, 10 families from the Danzig area acquired farms around Herschel.

In the Herschel community today, both groups are subject to each other's influence and to the influence of the English speakers with whom they necessarily have contact. While the Danzig group is more egalitarian in its verbal interaction patterns, informants from the group reported that they had felt great discomfort when they were first confronted with the extreme informality of English speakers. In particular, they were disturbed when FN was used without any prior formal agreement. Finding it difficult to reciprocate, they often avoided the use of any terms of address to English speakers. Now the members of both groups seem quite able to accept the use of FN in their interaction with English speakers, but they still show reticence over the use of FN in German. Similarly, the Ukrainian Mennonites preserve a preponderance of asymmetrical patterns within their own group, but are aware of the greater degree of symmetrical interaction among the Danzig Mennonites, and they accommodate themselves to this greater informality when interacting with them.

That Brown's equation of egalitarian developments and symmetrical patterns is not peculiar to Europe (where it accounts for the Danzig case) is shown by the appearance of the equation in such non-European areas as Japan (Yoshida, 1964) and Indonesia (Wittermans, 1967). We have not accounted for Lambert's contradictory findings in French Canada, but the case of the Ukrainian Mennonites suggests that there may at least be some influences in common. It is abundantly clear, for example, that the French Canadians cherish their language as a critical symbol of their identity, perhaps in the same way as the Mennonites have identified with the German language; and this may constitute a conservative influence in the preservation of asymmetrical patterns. There are other parallels, also, such as the bi- or multilingualism of the two groups; since the second language is the language of the larger society, it is seen as posing a threat to the maintenance of group identity. This line of inquiry may prove productive wherever Brown's equation does not appear to balance.

SOCIOLINGUISTIC CHANGE IN CHINA

To conclude this chapter, we are most fortunate in having some pertinent observations on how language usages have changed in China during the past 25 years, under a political philosophy that actively deplores social class differences. Fincher (1973) noted the predictable popularity of *tóng zhi* "comrade," the radical abandonment of social titles, and the strong aversion to professional and governmental titles. There is great emphasis on the role of the individual as a contributor to collectivity, and Fincher states that "circumlocutions for leadership positions abound. The society systematically deprives 'responsible authorities' of their personal titles in an effort to make them more responsive authorities" [p. 167].

Fincher (1973) suggests that various lexical changes can be grouped according to their relationship with various societal changes, such as nationalization, political socialization, and the spread of technology. One of the most interesting lexical developments is the popularization of the term *ai-rén,* "lover," as the usual way of denoting one's own or another's spouse or fiancé. It is a particularly liberated expression, and has implications for family structure. The original connotations of courtship or extramarital sex are retained outside of the Peoples Republic, which makes it a little embarrassing for outsiders to use the term, but those connotations have been lost in popular mainland usage.

Ai-rén is one of several localisms that reflect historical landmarks. It is identified with the Long March to Yenan in 1935, and was used by the Yenan community, which provided so many of the leaders of the Peoples Republic. Since Yenan has the image of a Spartan, egalitarian, but puritanical society, Fincher thinks it somehow fitting that the term lost its sexual connotations there.

Not only lexical changes, but also certain changes in grammatical constructions, were in accord with the new political philosophy. One that sounded "foreign" to Fincher (1972) appeared when she heard a Travel Service official in Shanghai talking on the telephone to a colleague in Nanking. Fincher had been reporting a sudden decision to stop there *en route* to Peking. The agent said, "I'm sorry to have made you passive" to his colleague; this was by way of an apology, because circumstances had forced him to take the initiative away from the colleague. Instead of indulging in "commandism," he should have been soliciting the suggestions of his colleague.

The actively promoted increase in bilingualism has been much less subtle, but it has had an enormous practical impact. This has been achieved by using Mandarin as the language of instruction in the schools throughout the country. At the same time, regional speech varieties are maintained with official blessings. As Fincher (1972) reports:

> At group sessions in Peking—for example, banquets—it was always a great asset to be able to pass as a native speaker of Can-

tonese and Amoy as well as of Mandarin. And while touring, speakers of Mandarin as a second language were still happy to find out I could understand and use their home dialects. But what we enjoyed with each other was our common similarity in being able to communicate with each other in *both* dialects or languages. The spread of Mandarin in a bilingual setting liberates people to enjoy their own dialects with no trace of uneasiness or inferiority. [pp. 338–339]

SOCIAL DIVERSITY AND LANGUAGE CHANGE

Traditionally linguistis have argued that we cannot actually observe language in the process of change—it is only after the fact that we can see that there has been change. But in the first chapter of this volume the suggestion was made that many of the developments in American English that seem to drive Edwin Newman and others to distraction are, indeed, evidences of language in the process of change. The great pioneer in viewing phonological and grammatical variation within a speech community as indicative of language in the process of change is William Labov (1972, most notably). Based largely, though not exclusively, on his detailed analysis of speech in the Lower East Side of Manhattan, New York (Labov, 1966), Labov correlated local values of standard /r, o, d, æ, ɔ/ with social class and ethnic groupings in the community. To illustrate with the simplest of these, the presence or absence of /r/ in preconsonantal and final position (as in fourth floor), he found consistent differences in accordance with casual and careful styles, with relative age, and with social class differences. Thus virtually all New Yorkers begin "r-less," and the lower class speakers tend to remain that way even in careful speech. The higher social classes are likely to employ the /r/ in careful speech, but virtually all New Yorkers will sometimes drop the /r/ in casual speech, especially if emotionally involved, as when recalling a close encounter with death. Drawing on earlier accounts, Labov shows that prior to World War II all native New Yorkers were "r-less" even in careful speech. Evidently the dislocations induced by the war brought great numbers of New Yorkers into contact with standard speakers, who use the /r/ of course and who tend to ridicule New York speech. Many of the New Yorkers sensitive to the stigmatized nature of their speech, including those who subsequently became school teachers, tended to favor the use of /r/ in the years since the war. So children tend now to incorporate the /r/ only after they begin school, though never with complete consistency, even in the careful style. While it is generally the higher classes that show the /r/, the greatest incidence is in the speech of lower middle class women, due in part to their tendency to "hypercorrect," or add /–r/ where it does not belong. That is, because the final /-r/ is typically missing in words such as "beer" or "fear," which are then pronounced to rhyme with the standard pronunciation of "idea," when the effort is made to add the /-r/, it is added to words that end in an unstressed vowel in the standard: thus "idear."

The variation in the values of the front vowel /æ/ and the back vowel /ɔ/ is a development within the community, rather than an imposed value, as is the case with the /r/. There is a general raising tendency in both cases, but it is most marked for the Italian ethnic group in the former case and for the Jewish group in the latter case, and in both cases is more apparent for women than for men.

Such variations are evidently motivated in part by a desire to incorporate prestige forms (as in the case of /r/) and in part by a need to mark ethnic identity (as /æ/ and /o/).

LANGUAGE AND SOCIAL IDENTITY

The previous section was directed at the subject of language exchange, but the example bears also on the subject of the way language marks social identity. In a small insurance office two women who had been chatting in English immediately switched to Spanish when approached by another worker with whom they did not want to interact (Howell, 1973). In this case, Spanish was used as a privacy system, in effect telling the other woman that she did not belong to their social group. But even routine speech differences reveal different social affiliations. The individual uses such differences

> . . . to claim and proclaim his identity, and society uses them to keep him under control. The person who talks right, as we do, is one of us. The person who talks wrong is an outsider, strange and suspicious, and we must make him feel inferior if we can. That is one purpose of education. In a school system run like ours by white businessmen, instruction in the mother tongue includes formal initiation into the linguistic prejudices of the middle class. [Sledd, 1969, p. 1307]

While some academicians, at all levels, perhaps, are able and even willing to tolerate verbal performances by students that are at the least nonstandard, either to avoid discouraging the student or because the presentation is not seen as critical to the substance of the offering, most of us show greater admiration for the student who can dress insights or observations in "good" English (or French, Swahili, and so on). This is not simply because we are part of a conscious and deliberate plot to suppress a querulous minority (though such motivation probably cannot be denied in some cases). Among the more innocuous reasons for such a preference is that in the very process of learning about history, English, literature, civics, and the like, we also learn something about the formal language through which such subjects are taught. Given the tradition of writing in formal English, whether we approve of that tradition or not, a certain range of styles come to be associated with formal learning, and we expect the "educated" person to reflect something of those styles.

To provide a very simple illustration modified from Gumperz and Herasimchuk (1972, pp. 99–100), the following three utterances may be used to describe the same event:

1. "They are holding a meeting to discuss the issue."
2. "They are getting together to talk it over."
3. "They're sittin' down to rap about it."

But they imply a progression from formal to informal, and there are restrictions on the use of styles. That is, if the term "rap" is going to be used, it would seem a bit odd in this context:

4. "They are holding a meeting to rap on the issue."

While two people can sit down and "rap" about something quite informally, the holding of a meeting is more formal, and it implies that there are two or more potentially contesting parties, probably some sort of agenda, and certain understandings about who will talk when. So a verbal expression of the event such as the following would be curious:

5. "They're hav'n a meet'n to discuss the issue."

Viewed in somewhat different terms, we may note that if the different situations in which the several styles are appropriate are considered to describe different functions of speech, then social functions may have an impact on grammar. Aside from differences in lexical selection, there are contractions in the more informal styles and the -*ing* is differently realized. The formal /-i / becomes /-in/. The point is made more dramatically by Wolff and Poedjosoedarmo (1982), who examined the use of Indonesian (Malay) by the two major groups of Javanese speakers in central Java. The Peranakan, who identify as Chinese, may integrate Indonesian quite thoroughly into their Javanese, but tend to keep such things as inflectional affixes in Javanese even if everything else is Indonesian. The switch to Indonesian forms can be made without regard for phrase structure. On the contrary, for the indigenous Pribumi Indonesian serves educated discourse, and it is important to mark the fact that it is Indonesian being employed. To this end the Indonesian is not integrated into Javanese speech, as was the case for the Peranakan, and switching follows the phrase structure of the sentence and, above all, the inflectional endings (ignored by the Peranakan) are Indonesian in these cases. Yet there are some Javanese forms which are retained in the code for educated discourse in order to mark degrees of respect. But there are times when Indonesian is employed to avoid the need to mark relative social rank; in this situation those Javanese markers are scrupulously avoided in favor of the socially neutral Indonesian forms (p. 123).

NONSTANDARD LANGUAGE AND THE SELF-FULFILLING PROPHECY

If a teacher is likely to be made uncomfortable by such relatively subtle stylistic considerations, it is not difficult to understand why even greater discomfort may be created by responses in black English vernacular (BEV), a pidgin, or any forms that are considered to be nonstandard. A dissonance is created which is hard to accommodate nonstandard speech varieties with the notion of being "educated"; and very often the evident lack of education implied by the use of nonstandard speech is taken to signify a lack of intelligence. Even if one disregards the imputation of genetic inferiority on the part of nonstandard speakers, the assumption is commonly made that such speakers are culturally and/or verbally deprived. And if a teacher makes such assumptions, lower performances may be expected from such students, who will then, in effect, learn to perform at a lower level than they otherwise might.

Lewis (1970) offers a simple illustration of how a presumably well-intentioned and presumably benevolent teacher put the process into effect. The second-grade teacher of an "integrated" class was a reserved but pleasant woman in her early twenties who, as an immigrant, had had trouble with her English; she had been discriminated against on the basis of her ethnic origins, and thus felt sensitive to problems of language learning and to the social difficulties encountered by minorities. Her class was divided into "fast" and "slow" groups, with perhaps a dozen in the former group and three in the latter. During Lewis' periods of observation only two of the slow group were in attendance (both of them were black). The teacher's way of teaching the presumably slow students to read was to deal with the sound values of individual letters, rather than of larger sequences. Later, when it was time for them to read aloud, the sentence in question was "I am a man." She asked one of the "slow" students, "Can you read that, Joe?" The youngster glanced at the picture of the beaming man to which the sentence referred, and replied "He is a man." While the child was evidently interpreting the sentence, the teacher assumed that he had been unable to read it accurately, and proceeded to take him phonetically through the first part of the sentence. The student was rather perplexed, since he understood the sentence and had been conveying its meaning.

When Lewis asked why the two black students were assigned to a slow category, the teacher said that they came from "nonliterate backgrounds," but that with special help they would be able to catch up with the other students. But her low expectation of their performance was revealed in the way she posed her question: "Can you read that"—not "will," "would," "please," or any other form that would have implied the assumption that he had ability to read. These were beginning students, but Lewis feels that the chances are good that they will learn to accommodate themselves to the relatively low expectations held for them by the teacher. The powerful influence of teacher expectations has been demonstrated even with mice. Lewis cites Rosenthal and Jacobson (1968), who showed that randomly chosen mice learned mazes more quickly when their human trainers were made to believe that they were genetically bred for superior maze-learning. On the other hand, mice whose trainers were led to believe they were dealing with animals bred for dullness performed with a corresponding lack of speed, even though there was actually no genetic difference between the two groups. Similar results have been obtained experimentally with students; that is, teachers who feel their students are relatively bright elicit better performances than do teachers who are led to believe their students are relatively slow (Lewis, 1970, pp. 12–14). Lewis cites a number of studies which suggest that the teacher in this case was exacerbating whatever problems may have existed originally by dealing with individual sounds rather than with larger contextual events. (She did use contexts with her "fast" group.)

A study that bears upon Lewis' observations was reported by Blodgett and Cooper (1973). These investigators surveyed the attitudes of 210 elementary school teachers in Tuscaloosa, Alabama, toward the BEV employed by their students. According to their results, one-third of the teachers perceive BEV as an "underdeveloped, undesirable, or uneducated manner of speaking" (p. 121), and more than two-thirds agreed with statements recommending that the school should initiate some kind of remedial program for children who speak BEV.

NONSTANDARD LANGUAGE AND "VERBAL DEPRIVATION" THEORY

Examples such as those given above are practically innocuous when compared with the thoughts of some academics who are able to influence public policy. The most extreme view of this sort maintains that for all practical purposes, lower-class black children have no language at all! Labov (1972) discusses at length the practical program offered by Carl Bereiter, Siegfried Engelmann and their associates (Bereiter *et al.*, 1966; Bereiter & Engelmann, 1966). Working with four-year-old black children from Urbana,

> Bereiter reports that their communication was by gestures, "single words," and "a series of badly connected words or phrases, such as *They mine* and *Me got juice*." He reports that black children could not ask a question, that "without exaggerating ... these four-year-olds could make no statements of any kind." ... Thus Bereiter concludes that the children's speech forms are nothing more than a series of emotional cries, and he decides to treat them "as if the children had no language at all." (Labov, 1972, p. 205)

Some of the improbable findings made by people such as Bereiter are attributable to the intimidating nature of the interview situation. Labov notes that he and his associates had to employ special techniques to tap the verbal ability of black ghetto youth under the age of about ten years. Even Clarence Robins, a skilled black associate of Labov, who was familiar with the sociolinguistic problem and with the inner city subculture, could elicit only minimal responses from an eight-year-old when he was interviewing the child. But when Robins brought along potato chips, lending a party air to the situation, and the boy's best friend was present, and taboo words and taboo topics were introduced (thus communicating the permissibility of both) into the interaction, which Robins conducted sitting on the floor of the lad's own room (thus reducing the physical intimidation), the results were quite different. The boys proved, of course, to be highly verbal (Labov, 1972, pp. 205–213).

We know that the BEV is a fully-fledged language (or dialect, if one prefers), and we know (and Labov and associates have been able to demonstrate) that black youth are highly verbal. To back up for a minute, to see what the ruckus is all about, Lewis (1970) suggests that there have been three stages in the academic and popular views of black culture in the past 2 decades or so. First came the view that there was no such thing as a black culture apart from the larger American culture, a notion that was compatible with the assimilation-integration approach of the contemporary civil rights movement. Then various liberal, sympathetic, but culturally biased white middle-class sociologists (and particularly specialists in "abnormal psychology") fostered the idea that blacks did have a subculture, but that it represented a kind of social pathology. And finally, the concept that an identifiable black culture existed which was not pathological, but in fact was laudable, developed in connection with the "Black is Beautiful" movement, which represented a conscious effort to revive a sense of pride in the heritage of Afro-Americans. At the same time (or perhaps lagging somewhat behind) came the championing of BEV as the appropriate and laudable speech variety.

The first stage involved educational policies and techniques that required no accommodation to the black subculture (which was but a minor component of the American Melting Pot). The second stage required "correctional measures" to deal with the social pathology, or the presumed cultural and linguistic deprivation, of the blacks. So programs were designed on the assumption that students who were willing and able would be brought up to snuff. But as Labov (1972) notes:

> The essential fallacy of the verbal deprivation theory lies in tracing the educational failure of the child to his personal deficiencies. At present, these deficiencies are said to be caused by his home environment. It is traditional to explain a child's failure in school by his inadequacy. But when failure reaches such massive proportions, it seems to us necessary to look at the social and cultural obstacles to learning and the inability of the school to adjust to the social situation. Operation Head Start (for example) is designed to repair the child, rather than the school; to the extent that it is based upon this inverted logic, it is bound to fail (p. 232).

Labov then goes on to note that the people who evaluate such programs are precisely those educational psychologists who designed them. "The fault will be found not in the data, the theory, nor in the methods used, but rather in the children who have failed to respond to the opportunities offered to them" (p. 232). Given that process, it is little wonder that Jensen (1969) produced his now infamous argument on the genetic inferiority of ghetto children. Since Labov (1972) has dealt with Jensen's paper in detail, we need not labor the issue here.

THE LINGUISTICS OF WHITE SUPREMACY

Under the impetus of the "Black is Beautiful" movement, the "legitimacy" of black culture in America and the BEV have been increasingly recognized as important and valued symbols of black identity. Yet this puts the linguist concerned with such problems in something of a bind. As we have indicated explicitly earlier, and implicitly throughout, any speech variety is a legitimate object of study, and as a medium of communication it should not be the subject of value judgments. Yet the realities of American social life are that those individuals who speak Standard English have a powerful advantage over speakers of nonstandard varieties. The solution usually considered appropriate these days is that we should admit the legitimacy of nonstandard varieties while trying to induce speakers of those varieties to acquire competence in SE as a second variety, to be used when socially appropriate.

James Sledd (1969) calls this sort of bidialectism "the linguistics of white supremacy," and castigates its promoters for outright hypocrisy:

> The basic assumption of bi-dialectism is that the prejudices of middle-class whites cannot be changed but must be accepted and indeed enforced on lesser breeds. Upward mobility, it is assumed, is the end of education, but white power will deny upward mobility to speakers of black English, who must therefore be made to talk white English in their contacts with the white world (p. 1309).

Sledd questions not only the motives of the bidialectists, but their possibilities for success, and even the desirability of their possible success. Programs that teach SE as if it were a second language, Sledd feels, have failed in part because the linguists concerned in effect lack the materials necessary to do the job properly (such as detailed descriptions of the relevant speech varieties, including SE) and because they probably would not know what to do with those materials if they did have them; and in part the programs fail because black children do not always (if ever) aspire to speak in the fashion of the white middle class.

It is not completely clear just what the better course would be. Sledd (1969) said that we should stop wasting money on finding more expensive ways of polluting the universe, more expensive ways of expanding the arms race, and, of course, we should, in short, cure all of our social ills. To this we must all cry "Hear, hear!" though it is clear that we are unlikely to see any crash programs designed by the government to this end. Sledd admits that it is useful to concern ouselves with more effective means of teaching reading and writing (allowing also for the reading and writing of black English). If we read somewhat between the lines, Sledd also seems to be saying that if we really believe all speech varieties to be equally valid, we should act accordingly and accept the BEV; if we hire and appoint without requiring that the appointees use SE, then the language problem may in effect take care of itself:

> We should learn from the example of the British; the social cataclysm of the Second World War, and the achievement of political power by labor, did more to give the "disadvantaged" English youngster an equal chance than charitable bi-dialectalism ever did (p. 1314).

Sledd's diatribe has been presented at length not because it has launched any movement, but because it serves as a corrective to the occasional (if not frequent) overselling of the linguistic product, and it illustrates the contradiction in the Orwellian position that all speech varieties are equal, but some are more equal than others. Among the less equal of the equal varieties are those employed by Puerto Ricans, Chicanos, Hawaiians (here this is a geographical rather than an ethnic label), and probably others whose voices have been more subdued. The speech variety symbolizes social identity, and yet it obstructs social mobility within the larger society.

The question of language and social identity, however, is far more subtle than the foregoing would indicate. For the most part, it operates below the level of awareness of the speaker. In Hemnesberget, Norway, for example, villagers who claim local descent show a powerful sense of local identification, which is marked by the use of the local dialect, even though outsiders (such as the land-owning commerical and administrative elite, who originally are largely from outside the village) consider the dialect to mark lack of education and lack of sophistication. Any local resident who spoke the standard with other locals would be seen by them as putting on airs (Blom & Gumperz, 1972). But village youth may go to the universities in Oslo, Bergen, and Trondheim, where they will become familiar with the pan-Norwegian values that are associated with the standard speech variety. Blom and Gumperz (1972) hypothesized that even though members of a former peer group from the village, who would return from the universities in the summer, all claimed to be speakers of the pure local dialect and to embrace local attitudes about dialect use, they would switch varieties when topics appropriate to the local or the broader identities respectively were discussed.

Not only was their hypothesis supported in their experimental situation (a social gathering of the peer group, in which relevant topics were introduced), but when Blom and Gumperz (1972) played the taped conversations to a linguistic informant who had been working with them, he refused at first to believe that they had been recorded locally. After he had recognized the voices of the participants, he showed disapproval of the mixing of speech varieties. Indeed, some of the participants themselves were upset when they heard themselves on the tape. They vowed not to switch away from the local dialect in future sessions, but nonetheless they did. Blom and Gumperz noted that when an argument required that the speaker should validate his status as an intellectual, he would switch to the standard forms that symbolized that status. They thus concluded that code selection rules are similar to grammatical rules, in that both operate below the level of consciousness, and may even be independent of the speaker's overt intentions.

The Norwegian example is more subtle than the matter of a Creole or BEV versus standard, but Labov (1963) provides an example of even greater subtlety from Martha's Vineyard, Massachusetts. Some members of this island community centralize the onset of the diphthongs /ay/ and /aw/, while others retained the standard southeast New England values for the diphthongs. This sort of distinction is not particularly elusive to anyone whose ear has been trained, but the local people on the island had not noticed it. Labov correlated the centralization of the diphthongs with such things as age level, occupation, ethnic group, and geography, but in the end the key to the centralization of the diphthongs was the attitude of the speaker toward the island. Those who identified with the island, who had positive feelings toward it, centralized the diphthongs, and those who had negative feelings about the island did not. The effect was found even in four fifteen-year-old boys, all of whom planned to go away to college, but only two of whom planned to pursue their careers on the island: the two who saw their futures off the island did not centralize the dipthongs.

There are other ways in which language and social identity show their relationship. Fred C. C. Peng (personal communication), for example, has noted that nasal prosody is a feature of Japanese singing, but not of Japanese speech; further, it is not a feature of all kinds of singing in Japan, but rather of the singing of traditional Japanese songs, typically while wearing a kimono, and so forth. Japanese rock singers or singers who generally perform in a nontraditional way usually lack the nasal prosody. The reason is not clear, but it is apparent that somehow the nasalization goes with "Japaneseness."

LANGUAGE AND SOCIAL RELATIONSHIPS

All of these examples deal with identity more or less in the sense of ethnic identity, but with this more general framework we can also see shifting styles and levels of politeness in accordance with more specific social identities. In Korean, for example, there are about six more or less clearly marked levels of politeness, and the way in which the speaker perceives him or herself in relation to the other party governs which level is chosen. That is, the speaker and listener enjoy a specific identity relationship, and if there are several facets to the social relationship, several identity relationships may be involved. Thus, when a Korean graduate student became the lover of his female supervisor on a research project, he was in a contradictory situation. When on the job, he had no choice but to speak to her deferentially; he was in turn addressed familiarly, and because she was his mentor and his elder, he would be required even in private to continue the interaction pattern in Korean. But the personal relationship in private was intimate and equal, and therefore could not be accommodated in Korean (where an age difference of even a couple of years requires deference by the junior), so in private they both used English (Howell, 1967).

A more detailed account of the same phenomenon, in which the verbal interaction pattern must reflect a shifting social relationship, is provided by another Korean couple (in Howell, 1968). The well-heeled son of a manufacturer was staying at a resort hotel not far from Seoul, nursing his disappointment over having failed an entrance examination to the university of his choice. One morning he was awakened by a fetching young woman whom he had noticed on the beach, but had never got around to meeting. She had noticed him, too, and because she was evidently about to leave the hotel for the city, she took the initiative and invited him out for a swim. At this stage both exchanged extremely polite language, and on the way to the water they jockeyed to see where they stood with respect to each other socially (primarily in terms of relative age). The girl was more artful than the young man: when she learned his age, she admitted to the same age, and when she learned of his recent academic disappointment she implied that she, too, had met with a similar reversal. Well, not only were there no traditional obstacles (in the way of an age difference), but they were both licking their wounds, so to speak, and the way was clear for a very personal relationship. In the course of the initial encounter (a matter of some hours, apparently), the couple shifted from very polite forms to very familiar forms. Romance blossomed for a month, until the lad learned from his friends that the girl was actually 3 years his senior—in age and in school.

The societal norm required deference on his part; the identities that were salient for him now were not those of lovers, but rather those of junior and senior. He had to symbolize that relationship by using language more polite than hers. But she was still motivated by the personal considerations that prompted her deception in the first place, and each time he raised his level of politeness she tried to match him. If she had tried to continue to symbolize the love relationship by using the more familiar forms, she would have been using those familiar forms that were her privilege as a senior. Predictably, the young man matched her politeness with yet greater politeness, which she would try to match, but soon she would simply lapse into the more familiar forms that were her privilege, and of course the romance was dead.

Korean is a particularly convenient language for such studies, because the levels of politeness are clearly marked linguistically, but even in English we have ways of indicating our social relationships verbally: cold politeness toward a former friend indicates that something has happened to change the relationship, for example. Or to take a common developmental case in American universities, if a professor who once addressed a student formally as "Ms. Y," now calls her by her given name, he implies that their relationship is at least somewhat closer than it had been originally. But these considerations will be dealt with in greater detail in the next chapter.

LANGUAGE PLANNING

The question of how to deal officially with nonstandard speech varieties in America is a problem in language planning, but it is trivial by comparison with the problems faced in many other parts of the world. In the so-called developing nations, for example, it frequently happens that no standard language has been agreed upon. In West Africa, some 500 to 1000 languages, typically divided into many dialects, are spoken in the fourteen nations that have emerged from the Cameroun Republic and Senegal (Armstrong, 1968). Of course English and French are widely known throughout the area, but they are reminders of the old colonialism, and their use favors those already in power. Similar objections exist in most former colonies around the world.

Where a few large factions are competing for the selection of their own languages as the standard, the question can get quite bloody, as it has in India. In West Africa there is not a single country in which a given language is spoken by more than a sizable minority of the population. As Armstrong (1968) points out, if one minority language is chosen, the native speakers of that language will have a great advantage in the matter of examinations for the schools and for the civil service; hence the speakers of the other minority languages would naturally object. Politically the problem is sticky, and it may be generations before widely accepted and uniform policies are developed. In the meantime some nations continue to rely on the European languages, while others name more than one indigenous language as standard. Ghana selected 9 of its 45 languages for national status, while Guinea granted national status (at least in principle) to all of its languages.

In a simpler situation, where language labels are political more than linguistic (as in Scandinavia), it is still necessary to select a speech variety as standard and to gain its acceptance. On the matter of selection, one school of thought is that the variety should be an existing vernacular, but another school feels that the variety should be eclectic, representing what amounts to a compromise among the several vernaculars. Haugen (1968) calls the first approach the unitary thesis and the second the compositional thesis. Once the choice is made, however this is done, there are problems of standardization of vocabulary, spelling, and implementation (including the preparation of schoolbooks, teachers, and so on); and after a norm has been codified and elaborated by its users, its original base may no longer be identifiable. Haugen feels it will have become "an independent artifact in the culture, one of the devices by means of which a particular group, usually a power elite, manages to maintain or assert its identity and, when possible, its power" (p. 268).

In 1948 Kroeber discussed the problem of how language spells identity in terms of ethnic revivals, or in the case of black English, "ethnic discovery" might be a more apt expression. Kroeber was writing immediately after the war that led directly to the withdrawal of European colonial power around the world, before most of the developing nations achieved that identity and developed the consequent language problem. At that time two cases seemed of particular interest, and both were seen as more or less experimental. The first was Gaelic, a dying language, and the second Hebrew, which probably had not been anyone's vernacular for 2,000 years or more. The Irish case seems established, though there is still controversy over problems of bilingualism in the educational process (see Macnamara, 1966). Gaelic was spoken at least in some rural areas when the push to make it a national language began. Hebrew was no one's native tongue, apparently, when efforts were first made in Palestine in the 1880s to revive it as a spoken language. Yet in 1948, according to Kroeber, some tens of thousands of Palestinian Jewish children spoke nothing but Hebrew. By 1961, 75% of Israel's Jewish population indicated that Hebrew was their only language for daily interaction, or at least their main one. According to Blanc's (1968) interesting account, there were still no native speakers of Hebrew in 1900, and the typical speaker of Hebrew was likely to have been East European by birth, and to have had Yiddish as a first language. He or she had to refer constantly to written sources and authorities for guidance, and freely employed other languages for purposes of communication. In 1930, the typical forty-five-year-old still was not a native speaker, but the children might be, since they were probably raised in Hebrew-language schools. At this time there were already differences in the speech of the young and of their parents, and a leveling influence appeared in the speech of the young as they interacted together.

By 1960, there was about a fifty-fifty chance that the middle-aged speaker would have had Hebrew as a first language. Whereas their grandparents had spoken Hebrew as a matter of ideology, by 1960 the native speakers were relatively little concerned with the ideological factor; they spoke it for the same secular reasons that we all speak our native languages. In the case of recent immigrants, Hebrew is spoken largely as a matter of simple convenience. In both cases, of course, this does not mean that religious considerations are completely irrelevant, but simply that other issues are important enough by now to give the language autonomy. At present there are some million native and near-native speakers; a variety of formal and informal styles have developed; and at the same time, a general standardizing process has been operating to give modern spoken Hebrew its own distinctive form.

STANDARDIZATION VERSUS SOCIAL IDENTITY

It is doubtful that a uniform standard language could be established and long maintained in a complex society. Japan, for example, long known for the conformity of its people, has had a language standardization program for about a century, yet uniformity has not been achieved. The objective of the program was not so much to get everyone speaking identically as it was to provide a means for any Japanese to communicate with any other Japanese, no matter what their native dialects. The language of instruction throughout the country is based on the speech of the people in the western part of Tokyo, until 1868 known mainly as the residential area for feudal lords and their retainers. While textbooks were in the standard, and teachers were supposed to use only the standard, the program was bolstered by the use of the standard in movies and on the radio. But the greatest advances in the standardization of Japanese seem to have taken place during the years of the Pacific War, when people were forced to leave their native areas in massive numbers (to serve with the several branches of the military, for instance, or to evacuate burned out cities), and since the war, with the impact of television and the stepped up movement toward the larger cities (about 10 percent of the population lives in Tokyo; nearly 25 percent live within commuting distance).

Most Japanese grow up knowing their local dialect and the standard, but in the different parts of the country the standard seems to be developing local features.

In Tokyo, the ideal form of the language is considered to be embodied in the speech of the announcers of the Japanese National Broadcasting Corporation (NHK), a quasi-governmental organization. The language promoted by the NHK has diverged from the original speech of western Tokyo, while western Tokyo speech has gone its own way to some extent, and in the eastern part of the city, some neighborhoods are developing or reviving locally distinctive speech which is different from the speech of western Tokyo (Howell, 1981). The link between language and the desire to mark social identity seems powerful enough to counter to some extent the active promotion of a standard language. It must be admitted that in general the standardization program has been quite successful, and the point is that there are counter tendencies that tend to undo the success of the program.

Finally, we may mention a rather unusual instance of *national* identity that depends on a writing system. To become a Japanese national, one must have a Japanese name that is written with Chinese characters. Thus when the Hawaiian sumo wrestler Jesse Kahaulua became a Japanese national in order to remain in sumo as a stablemaster after he retired as a wrestler, he took the name Watanabe (family name) Daigoro, which he writes with Chinese characters. (His professional name remains Takamiyama Daigoro.) When he retired he took a different professional name to go with his new role as stablemaster—that is standard practice. There is another side to this coin, however. Just as one must be able to write one's name with Chinese characters as a qualification of nationality, when the person is not a national but is of Japanese extraction, the Chinese characters are not used. Thus, the names Inouye and Matsunaga are very common in Japan, and are ordinarily written with Chinese characters; but those are the family names of the two senators from Hawaii, so when the Japanese press refers to the senators, their names are spelled out in the Japanese syllabary, clearly indicating that they are *not* Japanese.

REFERENCES

Armstrong, R.G. Language policies and language practices in West Africa. In J.A. Fishman, C.A. Ferguson, & J. Das Gupta (Eds.), *Language problems of developing nations*. New York: John Wiley & Sons, Inc., 1968.

Bereiter, C., & Engelmann, S. *Teaching disadvantaged children in the pre-school*. Englewood CLiffs, N.J.: Prentice-Hall, Inc., 1966.

Bereiter, C., Engelmann, S., Osborn, J., & Reidford, P.A. An academically oriented pre-school for culturally deprived children. In F.M. Hechinger (Ed.), *Pre-School Education Today*. Garden City, N.Y.: Doubleday &Company, Inc., 1966.

Blanc, H. The Israeli koine as an emergent national standard. In J.A. Fishman, C.A. Ferguson, & J. Das Gupta (Eds.), *Language problems of developing nations*. New York: John Wiley & Sons, Inc., 1968.

Blodgett, E.G., & Cooper, E.B. Attitudes of elementary teachers toward black dialect. *Journal of Communication Disorders*, 1973, *6*, 121–133.

Blom, J.P., & Gumperz, J.J. Social meaning in linguistic structure: Code-switching in Norway. In J.J. Gumperz & Dell Hymes (Eds.), *Directions in Sociolinguistics*. New York: Holt, Rinehart & Winston, Inc., 1972.

Brown, R. *Social psychology*. New York: The Free Press, 1965.

Brown, R., & Ford, M. Terms of address in American English. *Journal of Abnormal and Social Psychology*, 1961, *62*, 375–385.

Brown, R., & Gilman, A. The pronouns of power and solidarity. In T.A. Sebeok (Ed.), *Style in Language*. New York: John Wiley & Sons, Inc., 1960.

Callan, H. *Ethology and society*. London: Clarendon Press, 1970.

Dawson, C.A. *Group settlement: Ethnic communities in western Canada*. Toronto: The Macmillan Company, 1936.

Fincher, B.H. Impressions of language in China. *China Quarterly*, 1972, *50*, 333–340.

Fincher, B.H. The Chinese language in its new social context. *Journal of Chinese Linguistics*, 1973, *1*, 163–169.

Firth, J.R. The technique of semantics. *Transactions of the Philological Society (London)*: 36–72. Also in *Papers in Linguistics 1934–1951*. London: Oxford University Press; and in D. Hymes (Ed.), *Language in Culture and Society*. New York: Harper & Row, 1935.

Foster, G.M. Speech forms and perception of social distance in a Spanish-speaking Mexican village. *Southwestern Journal of Anthropology*, 1964, *20*, 107–122.

Francis, E.K. The Russian Mennonites: From religious to ethnic group. *American Journal of Sociology*, 1948, *54*, 101–107.

Francis, E.K. *In search of Utopia*. Altona, Manitoba: Friesen & Sons, 1955.

Friedrich, P. Structural implications of Russian pronominal usage. Condensed from a contribution to W. Bright (Ed.), *Proceedings of the Los Angeles Conference on Sociolinguistics*. The Hague: Mouton & Co., 1966.

Fukutake, T. *Man and society in Japan*. Tôkyô: University of Tôkyô Press, 1962.

Garvin, P.L., & Riesenberg, S.H. Respect behavior on Ponape: an ethnolinguistic study. *American Anthropologist*, 1952, *54*, 201–220.

Geertz, C. *The Religion of Java*. New York: The Free Press, 1960.

Goodenough, W.H. Rethinking "status" and "role": Toward a general model of the cultural organization of social relationships. In *The relevance of models for social anthropology*. A.S.A. Monographs 1. New York: Frederick A. Praeger, 1965.

Gumperz, J.J., & Herasimchuk, E. The conversational analysis of social meaning: A study of classroom interaction. In R.W. Shuy (Ed.), *Report of the Twenty-Third Annual Round Table Meeting on Linguistics and Language Studies*. Washington, D.C.: Georgetown University Press, 1972.

Haugen, E. The Scandinavian languages as cultural artifacts. In J.A. Fishman, C.A. Ferguson, & J. Das Gupta (Eds.), *Language problems of developing nations*. New York: John Wiley & Sons, Inc., 1968.

Howell, R.W. Linguistic status markers in Korean. *The Kroeber Anthropological Society Papers*, 1965, *55*, 91–97.

Howell, R.W. Linguistic choice as an index to social change. Unpublished doctoral dissertation. Berkeley, Cal.: University of California, 1967.

Howell, R.W. Linguistic choice and levels of social change. *American Anthropologist*, 1968, *70*, 553–559.

Howell, R.W. *Teasing relationships*. An Addison-Wesley Module in Anthropology. Reading, Mass.: Addison-Wesley Publishing Co., Inc.,1973.

Howell, R.W. Indigenous varieties of Tôkyô speech. Unpublished paper presented at the 1981 Meeting of the Western Conference of the Association for Asian Studies, Berkeley, Calif., 1981.

Howell, R.W., & Klassen, J. Contrasting du/Sie patterns in a Mennonite community. *Anthropological Linguistics*, 1971, *13*, 68–74.

Jaquith, J.R. Language use of Mexican Mennonites. Research report, *Newsletter American Anthropological Association*, 1970, *11*, No. 6, 9.

Krahn, C. *From the Steppes to the Prairies (1874–1949)*. Newton, Kansas: Mennonite Publications Office, 1949.

Kroeber, A.L. *Anthropology*. New York: Harcourt Brace & World, 1948.

Labov, W. The social motivation of a sound change. *Word*, 1963, *19*, 273–309.

Labov, W. *The social stratification of English in New York City*. Washington, D.C.: Center for Applied Linguistics, 1966.

Labov, W. *Language in the inner city: Studies in the black English vernacular*. Philadelphia: University of Pennsylvania Press, 1972.

Lambert, W.E. The use of *tu* and *vous* forms of address in French Canada: A pilot study. *Journal of Verbal Learning and Verbal Behavior*, 1967, *6*, 614–617.

Lewis, L. Culture and social interaction in the classroom: An ethnographic report. Working Paper No. 38, Language-Behavior Research Laboratory. Berkeley, Ca.: University of California, 1970.

Macnamara, J. *Bilingualism and primary education*. Edinburgh, Scotland: Edinburgh University Press, 1966.

Rosenthal, R., & Jacobson, L. *Pygmalion in the classroom*. New York: Holt, Rinehart & Winston, Inc., 1968.

Rubin, J. Bilingualism in Paraguay. *Anthropological Linguistics*, 1962, *4*, 52–58.

Sledd, J. Bi-dialectism: The linguistics of white supremacy. *English Journal*, 1969, *58*, 1307–1315, 1329.

Slobin, D.I. Some aspects of the use of pronouns of address in Yiddish. *Word*, 1963, *19*, no. 2, 193–202.

Wittermans, E.P. Indonesian terms of address in a situation of rapid social change. *Social Forces*, 1967, *46*, 48–51.

Wolff, J.U., & Poedjosoedarmo, S. *Communicative codes in Central Java*. Ithaca, N.Y.: Dept. of Asian Studies, Cornell University. Data Paper: Number 116, Southeast Asia Program, 1982.

Yoshida, T. Social conflict and cohesion in a rural Japanese community. *Ethnology*, 1964, *3*, 219–231.

Chapter 12

LANGUAGE AND CULTURE

Because language is the keystone of the cultural edifice which more than anything else distinguishes man from the rest of the animal kingdom, the ethnographer, more than most other social scientists, requires at least a modicum of linguistic sophistication. There are both pragmatic and theoretical reasons for this.

As a practical matter, when ethnographers go into the field, they must have *some* means of communicating with the subjects of their study, and unless they already have considerable competence in the relevant language, they will have to prepare themselves for that indispensable part of their field work. Thomas Rhys Williams (1967), for example, found it desirable to seek the minimum competence in Dusun (a language of Borneo) necessary to deal with the daily routine, and he seems to have drawn on his linguistic training to transcribe and analyze Dusun utterances. In the meanwhile, of course, he was dependent on an interpreter and also, apparently, on the use of Malay as a contact language. Even after he had gained some proficiency in Dusun, he frequently had to rely on his interpreters. Some possibilities for misunderstanding may be avoided that way; the interpreter is likely to know which topics require tact, and how one should apply that tact. If the investigator has a sufficient command of the language in question, he can monitor his interpreters and at least ensure that his questions are indeed being asked, and that the answers are not being edited for him.

Earlier generations of ethnographers, especially those under the influence of Franz Boas, were strongly encouraged to gather textual materials in the native language in order to develop what were in effect archives analogous, if not quite comparable, to the documentary sources for the classical civilizations (Lowie, 1937, p. 132). Today the texts are more likely to be on microfilms and tape recordings. The loss of interest in written texts, except when used for linguistic purposes, stems from a number of considerations besides the development of other media. There is less interest in "salvage" anthropology today than there was in the past, when it seemed important to chronicle preliterate cultures before they disappeared. Virtually without exception, they have disappeared, through the processes of assimilation, acculturation, and sheer extinction, and so there is less to salvage in the older sense. Further, while the earlier ethnographers tried to record everything imaginable about the cultures they were describing, the tendency these days is to enter the field with one's interests directed toward a particular problem, and thus to forego the encyclopedic inventories that were popular in the past.

LANGUAGE AS THE KEY TO A CULTURE

Among the arguments most frequently used to gain support for foreign language programs is the one which maintains that foreign languages are the key to understanding other cultures. But the case is overstated if it is taken to mean that the study of a foreign language *automatically* plugs the student into another culture in any very useful or economical way. We can learn more about Japanese history, traditions, and world view from a few hours of intensive reading in English than we can from many weeks of intensive Japanese language study. Indeed, as Frake (1981) has noted, with apparent puzzlement, some brilliant ethnographies have been written by people who did not know the language of their subjects.

Yet it is apparent that the question of language enters at some point. Even our English language books on Japan will be replete with Japanese names (Tôkyô, the Tokugawa Period, the Meiji Restoration) and labels for cultural items and ideas for which there is no ready English equivalent (Zen, *harakiri, kimono, shôgun*). And as Frake

(1981), who has been very deeply involved in the languages of the people he has studied, points out, a great deal of what people in any culture do, is talk. In other words, in many respects, speaking is the principal cultural activity and should not be ignored!

Certainly the *kinds* of cultural information that are easily available to an ethnographer will depend to some extent on his or her command of the language. But being a native speaker does not automatically enable one to describe the rules of the language and being a native of the culture does little more than assure us of the presence of the intuitive base on which an explicit descriptive statement must ultimately rest. What is critical is that we know what questions to ask and how to ask them, and that is more a matter of professional training than of the language as such.

CULTURAL LABELS

As was previously indicated, one who is reading competent accounts of another culture in English will encounter foreign words for which there is no very convenient equivalent in English. But this is just the most superficial indication that the foreign words are labels for cultural objects and events, and even these words are a distillation of the much larger word-pool that the writer could have drawn upon if he had sought greater accuracy. For, as will be discussed later, there is such a close correspondence between linguistic and cultural events that relatively few labels can be translated precisely.

We learn our labels in a cultural context. To take an obvious example, to one who has never travelled on an underground train, and knows of it only through written or verbal references to the "subway," the label will have the same limited meaning whether it is applied to the corresponding mode of transportation in New York, London, Paris, Toronto, or Tôkyô. But any New York commuters visiting Tôkyô will find the underground experience there quite different from what they are used to. Instead of riding in noisy, filthy, unreliable trains, they will be riding in clean, quiet, and highly reliable trains. The crowding during the rush hour may cause them to think nostalgically about what they used to consider an impossible situation in New York, while the sights and smells will also be different. The full meaning of *chikatetsu* cannot simply be rendered by the term "subway," and similar differences in meaning will also be found for the Paris *metro*, the London "underground," and so forth.

To take a somewhat different example, we might assume that

loanwords, at least, would have a comparable range of meaning to that of the original. But the Japanese *kimono* is essentially a formal garment, while the American use of the label (particularly popular in the 1930s) described a wrap-around woman's housecoat that corresponded more closely to the Japanese *nemaki*. To take an example in the other direction, Americans and Japanese may both regale themselves *in* a bar, but the Japanese cannot sit *at* the bar. He sits at the *counter*, which the Americans usually do only in eating establishments.

Clearly the ethnographer will do well to learn the range of meanings of the labels used in the culture he is studying, even though he will have to edit his findings in order to present an economical account in his own language.

Briefly, then, language is used in anthropology first, as a medium of communication, and next as a primary source of information about culture and society. In addition to a concern with the facts of language as such, and with the way language and society influence each other, there are at least two other areas of major anthropological interest here. The first, the study of the way language influences our perceptions, follows without difficulty from the idea of cultural labelling. The other is the question of how techniques of linguistic analysis can be utilized to reveal the structure of cultural entities. The way in which language influences perception has been most famously discussed by Benjamin Lee Whorf.

THE WHORFIAN HYPOTHESIS

When a Conference on the Interrelations of Language and Other Aspects of Culture was held in Chicago in March, 1953, virtually the whole conference was taken up, according to Hoijer (1954, p. vii), with a consideration of "the hypothesis suggested in Benjamin L. Whorf's *Collected Papers on Metalinguistics* (Washington, D.C., 1952)." The *Collected Papers* appeared some 11 years after Whorf's death in 1941, at the age of forty-four, though the principal papers on "the hypothesis" had appeared during the 2 years or so before his death, and the essential idea had been voiced a century earlier.

In 1940 Whorf described "a new principle of relativity, which holds that all observers are not led by the same physical evidence to the same picture of the universe, unless their linguistic backgrounds are similar, or can in some way be calibrated" (Carroll, 1956, p. 214). Thus the idea is known also as the theory of *linguistic relativity*. Our grammars are not simply systems for reproducing ideas; they actually shape our ideas, guiding our mental activity and our analyses of our impressions. Whorf puts it thus:

> The world is presented in a kaleidoscopic flux of impressions which has to be organized in our minds—and this means largely by the linguistic systems in our minds. We cut nature up, organize it into concepts, and ascribe significances as we do, largely because we are parties to an agreement to organize it in this way— an agreement that holds throughout our speech community and is codified in the patterns of our languages [Carroll, p. 213].

In 1929, more than a decade before Whorf offered his formulation, Edward Sapir, with whom Whorf was later to become closely associated, elaborated the idea that "We see and hear and otherwise experience very largely as we do because the language habits of our community predispose certain choices of interpretation" (Mandelbaum, 1949, p. 162). Appropriately enough, the concept is known as the Whorf-Sapir (or the Sapir-Whorf) hypothesis. Indeed, the idea is usually traced even further back, to Wilhelm von Humboldt, who is credited with stating in 1848 that man lives with the world around him principally as language presents it (Trager, 1959). The most detailed discussion (in English) of von Humboldt's view of linguistic relativity is that of Brown (1967), who shows not only that even von Humboldt had predecessors, but that his views must be culled laboriously from his works.

Before describing linguistic relativity more specifically, we may speculate briefly on why the idea was so slow to catch fire. Since von Humboldt has been translated into English only very recently and since he had a tiresome style in German, it is not surprising that his influence has only been belated and indirect in America. Sapir, of course, was wonderfully articulate, and Whorf was very persuasive, yet both were long dead before the concept of linguistic relativity became fashionable. Dell Hymes (1961) is probably correct in attributing the lag to the studied indifference (extending to active hostility) shown by descriptive linguists toward problems of meaning. During much of the 1930s and 1940s, it was an accepted doctrine that linguistic analysis should rely on form to the exclusion of semantic considerations (aside from the necessary minimum to establish contrasts).

It is not clear why interest should have been so dramatically revived. Perhaps it happened in part because the idea caught the fancy of anthropologists who were not primarily linguists. Also, it fitted an atmosphere primed by a generation of culture and personality studies, which culminated, perhaps, in Benedict's (1946) brilliant analysis of Japanese character. This drew heavily on the linguistic labelling of culturally important behavioral categories (especially the complex system of obligations).

Perhaps part of the answer lies also in the character of Whorf himself. A chemical engineering graduate of M.I.T., who became a fire prevention engineer with the Hartford Fire Insurance Company, and was eventually an executive with the firm, Whorf never received an advanced degree in anything. Yet he developed his linguistic abilities (essentially on his own) to a point of considerable professional respectability, and he served for a while as a lecturer in anthropology at Yale—never, in the meanwhile, severing his connections with his insurance firm (Carroll, 1956).

At any event, Whorf's argument has in one way or another been a source of fascination and debate for a generation, and nothing has really been settled. Fishman (1960) has written a "systematization" of the Whorfian hypothesis that has proved particularly useful. The first of four levels that Fishman discerns deals with the way in which language codifies experience. Thus we may expect to find that vocabularies will reflect culturally important categories. Since snow, for example, is very important to the Eskimos, they have many terms to describe it, and this means that in their language it is easy to *refer* to the different kinds of snow. On the other hand, the Aztecs have little need to concern themselves with cold-weather phenomena; consequently they have few terms to describe distinctions that would be critical in a different environment.

That languages codify phenomena in this way is the most widely accepted part of the hypothesis. To give a less concrete, and therefore less obvious, example at this level, Gastil (1959) has noted that the French use one term for both "conscience" and "consciousness," which means that the distinction between the two is not as readily available to the French as it is to the English speaker. On the other hand, the French do see a partial identity in our two terms that it would be hard for us to appreciate. Lindeman (1938), for example, argued that this linguistic difference has led to a greater conceptual fusion between the two usages by French philosophers than has been made by English or German philosophers.

Thus the first level discerned by Fishman (1960) concerns a language-language correspondence. The second level relates linguistic codification to its behavioral concomitants. In order to support the idea that native speakers of different languages have different mental experiences, which is the essence of the hypothesis, we must show that there is some correspondence between the presence or absence of a particular linguistic phenomenon and the presence or absence of a particular nonlinguistic response (Carroll & Casagrande, 1958).

There has been some experimental support for the hypothesis at this level. As early as 1889, Lehmann showed that to identify each of nine different shades of gray with a different number was a considerable help in discriminating among those shades of gray (Fishman, 1960). Much more recently, Brown and Lenneberg (1954) demonstrated that when a range of colors is presented to a subject, he can name those that fit into the range of a single word, such as "red," more quickly than he can label colors for which there is no single term, such as "reddish brown." These and similar experiments indicate clearly that verbal labeling facilitates the perceptual handling of events, but sometimes their implications are carried further, to suggest that people actually *see* colors in accordance with those labels. Thus we have two words, "blue" and "green," but the Japanese word *aoi* is sometimes used where we would use one of our terms, but not either of them at random. Thus *aoi* describes the "blue" sky, "green" edible seaweed, and the "green" of inexperience (our "greenhorn").

It appeared, then, that the continuum of the color spectrum was arbitrarily segmented according to various cultural conventions, and labels were assigned to those segments in ways that need not correspond from one culture to another. The members of the various cultures were assumed to perceive colors in accordance with these cultural and linguistic labels. Then, in 1970, Berlin and Kay (Berlin, 1970) announced the results of a cross-cultural study in which they had found substantial agreement among the cultures on the perception of color loci. Members of different cultures essentially agreed on the area of the bluest blue, the reddest red, and so forth, even though the *boundaries* of the color terms still showed the lack of concord that had been noted previously.

Fishman's first two levels are basically lexical. The first level concerns the fact that the number of coded categories related to a given range of events will vary from culture to culture; the second level deals with the actual behavioral consequences of those coded categories. The third level relates linguistic *structure* to its cultural concomitants. If cultural behavior has been conditioned by language, then since language has structure, we should be able to find a relationship between the structure of a language and the structure of the behavior of its speakers (Trager, 1959; McQuown, 1954). Whorf

(1940) argued that we polarize nature in our English language, dividing most of our words into noun and verb categories that have different grammatical and logical properties. Nootka, a language of Vancouver Island, on the other hand, seems to us to contain only verbs; this implies that the speakers have a monistic view of nature, utilizing a single class of words to treat all kinds of events. In Nootka, "a house occurs" or "it houses" corresponds to our noun "house." The reason the Nootka terms seem like verbs to us is that they are inflected for durational and temporal nuances. A house can thus be an enduring house, a temporary house, a house that used to exist, a house that will exist in the future, or many other kinds of house.

Inspired by Whorf, Hoijer (1954) tried in a similar vein to show that Navaho religious views were closely congruent with the implications of Navaho grammar. He stated that to the Navaho, "the way to the good life lies not in modifying nature to man's needs or in changing man's nature but rather in discovering the proper relation of nature to man and in maintaining that relationship intact" [p. 101]. The universe is given, and the Navaho must adjust to it. Similarly, Hoijer argues, the actors in a Navaho utterance are not divided into the active and passive categories— performers of action or the ones on whom actions are performed—as in English. Rather, the actors are entities that are linked to actions which have already been defined in part as pertaining to classes of beings.

Without belaboring the point, the argument is intriguing, but we can easily see that it is susceptible to endless debate. Experiments may not end debate, but they may elevate the quality of the debate. It is fortunate, then, that Fishman's fourth level, which deals with linguistic structure and its behavioral concomitants, has been examined experimentally. Carroll and Casagrande (1958) explored the differences between Navaho and English verbs, and looked for evidence of behavioral reflections of the differences.

Navaho verb forms vary in accordance with the shapes of the objects to which they refer, while English verbs have the same form no matter what the object looks like. That is, we "carry" balls, sticks, squares, and so on, without requiring that the morphological nature of the object be given expression. Carroll and Casagrande worked with two groups of Navaho children; one group had Navaho as its primary language, and the other had English as its primary language. The children were presented with two objects that differed in both color and form, and then were asked to associate one of these with a third object, which was the same shape as one of the first two and the same color as the other. (Given a white ball and a black cube, for example, a black ball could be associated with the cube on the basis of their common color, or with the other ball on the basis of their common shape.) If the children's responses were guided by the requirements of the Navaho verb forms, we should expect that objects of the same shape would be placed together, rather than objects of the same color but different shapes.

As a control group, middle-class white children of comparable age in the Boston area were also given the test. The results were in the direction we would expect from the Whorfian hypothesis, but the question did not rest there. The children who mainly speak Navaho *did* choose on the basis of the Navaho verb system significantly more often than the Navaho children who mainly speak English, but the young Bostonians were *more Navaho* in their responses than the dominant speakers of Navaho! The most likely explanation seemed to be that the Boston children were raised with toys that capitalize on a variety of shapes; this explanation seemed to gain support from a subsequent finding that Black Harlem children in New York responded more in the fashion of the Navaho children who had English as their dominant language.

While the Harlem children may not have had the variety of commercial toys that were said to account for the Boston choices, it is far from clear that they lacked exposure to a wide variety of shapes. Even the grimmest picture of a slum does not present a uniform surface: peeling paint, rats, cockroaches, and garbage all provide a diversity of shapes. It may not be the existence of shapes as such, but rather the extent to which children are encouraged to manipulate them, that is significant. Fishman (1960) suggested that the Boston findings raise the question of *degrees* of linguistic relativity. After all, we can learn to see things in unaccustomed ways, and we can usually find a way to describe events that are alien to our customary experiences. As Fishman suggested, profit lies less in efforts to "prove" or "disprove" the Whorfian hypothesis than in future efforts to delimit more sharply the kinds of language structures and nonlinguistic behaviors that do or do not show the Whorfian effect, to establish the degree to which it is effective, and to determine to what extent it can be modified.

Most recently, Fishman (1982) has called attention to another of Whorf's concerns: ethnolinguistic diversity as a worldwide societal asset. Whorf felt that we suffer in not understanding other forms of scientific thought or analyses of nature, which he felt have as much scientific validity as our own thinking habits. In some cases English is simply an inferior instrument. Whorf felt that Hopi, for instance, was a language that provides a more rational analysis of situations than does English: English is to Hopi as a bludgeon is to a rapier [Fishman, 1982, p. 8]. Writing in 1941, Whorf warned that

> Those who envision a future world speaking only one tongue, whether English, German, Russian, or any other, hold a misguided view and would do the evolution of the human mind the greatest disservice. Western culture has made, through language, a provisional analysis of reality and, without correctives, holds resolutely to that analysis as final. The only correctives lie in all those other tongues which by eons of independent evolution have arrived at different but equally logical, provisional analyses. [Fishman, 1982: 9]

THE MEANING OF KINSHIP TERMS

The anthropological study of kinship systems predated Whorf's work by many decades, but the topic is admirably suited to Whorfian notions. We may illustrate this by examining, with Lee (1950), two Ontong Javanese kin terms.

If we ask an Ontong Javanese man what he calls his sister, he will supply the label *ave*, while the corresponding label for "brother" is *kainga*. To this point it seems clear enough that *ave* = "sister" and *kainga* = "brother." As a matter of routine, perhaps, we will double-check by asking the sister what she calls her brother, and we will learn that he is her *ave*, while her sister is *kainga*. The terms are now reversed, with *ave* = "brother" and *kainga* = "sister."

We need not assume that our informants are indulging themselves at our expense. Evidently, whereas we place a premium on absolute sex in kinship labels, the Ontong Javanese label according to relative sex, so that siblings of the same sex are covered by one label, while opposite-sexed siblings are covered by another label. A male's brother and a female's sister are both *kainga*, while the male's sister and the female's brother are both *ave*. There is nothing remarkable about this; indeed, Koreans have two separate sets of sibling terms, one used by males and one used by females, which yields four different terms for "elder sibling."

But the Ontong Javanese have not finished with us yet. Now we are told that the man's *kainga* includes not only his brother, but his wife's sister and his brother's wife! And, of course, a woman's *kainga* includes not only her sister, but also her sister's husband and her husband's brother. This distressing bit of news means that sex as such has nothing to do with the terminology at issue. We have been deluded by our own terms for kinship, which are largely descriptive and tend to emphasize the actual biological relationships. Apparently the terms *ave* and *kainga* are governed by different underlying principles from those that govern our sibling terms. They are part of a different kind of semantic network.

While the Ontong Javanese system is different from our own, we should recall that our own system is not strictly biological. After all, we often call friends of the family who belong to the generation above ours "auntie," or "uncle," where no biological relationship exists, and affines of that same generation are typically given the same kinship terms. Further, the social aspect of kinship in our own system is even stronger than has just been implied. A few years ago, when David Schneider remarked to a gathering of the Kroeber Anthropological Society in Berkeley that we call someone "uncle" because he acts like an uncle, this seemed improbable enough to send us scurrying out to find a suitable local informant. We located a male adolescent, determined who his uncles were, and learned that his mother's brothers were uncles no matter what; one of his mother's sister's husbands, however, would not be an uncle any longer in the event of a divorce, but the other member of the category would remain an uncle even if there were a divorce. The difference, it seemed, was that he did not know the first affine at all well, but he was quite close to the second. This second uncle acted like an uncle.

Given this reminder that our kinship system does not depend exclusively on biological relationships, we are better prepared to understand the Ontong Javanese system. It seems that the Ontong man shares the ordinary details of his living routine with his brothers and their wives for a large part of the year. He sleeps in the same large room, he eats with them, and he jokes and works around the house with them. The rest of the year is spent with his wife's sisters and their husbands, in the same free, easygoing atmosphere. So *kainga* relax in each other's company.

The *ave* present a different picture. Inter-*ave* relationships involve great strain and propriety. *Ave* can never spend their adult lives together, though they may on rare occasions be thrown together temporarily. They can never be alone together under the same roof; they cannot chat together easily, and one cannot refer even remotely to sex in the presence of an *ave*. When the *ave* of one member of a group is present, the others must be circumspect. A male *ave* has special obligations toward his female *ave* and her children (though we are not told the nature of these obligations). *Kainga*, in short, means a relationship of ease, cheerful and informal, and filled with shared living. *Ave* means a relationship characterized by formality, prohibitions, and strain.

Even from this brief characterization, it is clear that the social reality of kinship is differently formulated and differently labelled by the Ontong Javanese and by ourselves.

SEMANTIC DOMAINS

It is not difficult to see how researchers can move from problems of labels and their meanings to problems of taxonomies, and thence to the question of semantic domains. Semantic domains seem to constitute the main interest of ethnolinguists, probably because systems of belief have proved vulnerable to the techniques of componential analysis (which are borrowed from structural linguistics).

An early classic in the analysis of semantic domains or cognitive structures is Conklin's (1955) study of color categories among the Hanunóo of Mindoro Island in the Philippines. While working on the ethnobotany of the Hanunóo, Conklin found himself puzzled by some of the ways in which items were classified with respect to color. He had been operating in terms of hue, saturation, and brightness, the dimensions of our Western color concepts, but these constituted a poor guide to the Hanunóo scheme. What did matter was relative blackness, whiteness, redness, and greenness. The largest of the four categories is *mabiru,* which includes what we generally call black, violet, indigo, blue, dark green, dark gray, and deep shades of other colors and mixtures. *Malagti*⁹ includes white and very light tints of other colors and mixtures. *Marara*⁹ includes maroon, red, orange, yellow, and mixtures in which these colors seem to predominate. The smallest of the categories, *malatuy,* includes light green and mixtures of green, yellow, and light brown. All color terms can be reduced to these four categories, which Conklin calls Level I terms, and on which there is general terminological agreement among the Hanunóo. There is a great deal of overlapping on a second, more specific level which contains an indefinite number of categories on which it is difficult to get agreement. (Of course we have the same trouble in our own system when trying to agree on whether a particular item is oyster-white, off-white or perhaps a kind of pale beige, and so forth.)

The four main categories are set up according to factors that we would not ordinarily think of as relevant for color, but these factors do have reference to important external environmental considerations. First, a distinction between dark and light is obvious in the contrasted meanings of the first two terms, but there is also an opposition between "dryness" and "wetness" in the last two terms (the "red" and "green," respectively). This latter is important in dealing with plant life: most types of living plant have some fresh, succulent, and often "green" parts. Thus a shiny, węt *brown*-colored part of freshly-cut bamboo is *malatuy* rather than *marara*?.

Besides the opposition of light and dark, and of wet and dry, there is also an opposition between deep, unfading, and thus often more desirable material, and pale, faded, or "colorless" substances. This places the "black" and "red" terms in contrast to the "white" and "green" terms. The contrasts hold not only for natural products, but also for manufactured and trade goods: red beads are more valuable than white beads, for example. Moreover, while objects tend to be regarded as aesthetically pleasing as they approach the focal points of each category, the green of natural vegetation is not prized, and green beads are considered to be unattractive and thus worthless.

What Conklin did, in short, was to isolate the principal ingredients, or components, of this scheme by seeing when different color labels were applied to substances that were being compared. That is, if the same color term were applied to a pair of substances, those substances would not contrast; they would be considered the same color. Conklin continued the search by finding out which substances elicited different labels and thus were considered to have different colors. The members of the categories thus defined by contrasts may then be examined to see what they have in common. In the present case qualities such as blackness, whiteness, redness, and greenness appear, though the range of meaning of these terms must be specified. Conklin did not invent contrastive analysis, of course, since it was well established in linguistics, and various other linguistically oriented anthropologists were developing similar approaches.

In 1956, Goodenough and Lounsbury each published componential analyses of kinship (Trukese and Pawnee kinship respectively). The idea can be conveyed if we look at the analysis of our own consanguineal (through "blood" rather than through marriage) kin terms, following Wallace and Atkins (1960). Wallace and Atkins first took the common terms spelled out in Figure 16.1, excluding "ego," of course, and reduced them to primitive kin-types. This expands the original 15 terms considerably, since "grandfather" includes both the mother's father and the father's father, "uncle" includes both the mother's brother and father's brother, and can also include the fa-

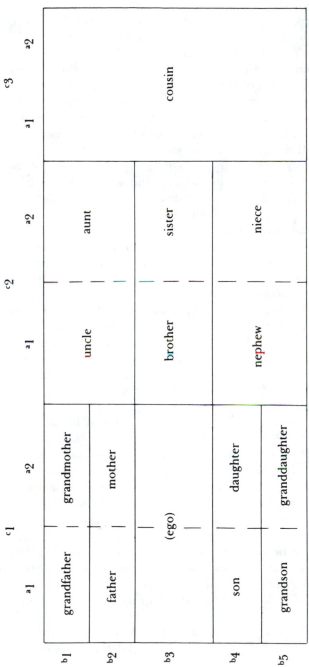

Figure 12.1. A Componential Paradigm of American English Consanguineal Core Terms. (Reprinted by permission from A. Wallace and J. Atkins, The Meaning of Kinship Terms, *American Anthroplogist*, 62, 1960.)

ther's father's brother, the mother's father's brother, and so on. The task of listing cousins is truly formidable: the father's brother's son, father's brother's daughter, mother's brother's son, mother's brother's daughter, father's sister's son, father's sister's daughter, mother's sister's son, and so on. But all of these terms except "cousin" specify the sex of the relative; some of the terms specify whether the relative is lineally or nonlineally related to the ego ("father" versus "uncle," for instance); and all of the nonlineal terms indicate whether the ancestors of the relative are also ancestors of the ego, and *vice versa* (as with brothers and sisters) or not (as with cousins).

From these observations it appears that three dimensions are sufficient to define all of the terms. First is the sex of the relative, which can be designated as (a); a_1 indicates a male, and a_2 a female. Second is the generation of the relative (b), which is here indicated by b_1 for two generations above the ego, b_2 for one generation above the ego, and so on, down to b_5 for two generations below the ego. Finally, lineality (c) is marked; c_1 indicates lineals, c_2 colineals, and c_3 ablineals (those who are neither lineals nor colineals).

There are complications that are not duplicated here, and Wallace and Atkins (1960) used the example as strictly illustrative, and made no pretense that it was an exhaustive study of American kinship. Clearly, however, the approach can be applied to virtually any semantic domain, and in addition to kinship, notable treatment has been accorded ethnobotany (Berlin, Breedlove, & Raven, 1973) and disease categories (Frake, 1961). But not all anthropologists have been carried along on the bandwagon of structural semantics.

Burling (1964), for example, has issued a useful, if harsh, criticism of the largely implicit claims for componential analysis, suggesting that it might be more appropriately regarded as "hocus pocus" than "God's truth." The point that seems to have bothered Burling, as it has bothered many others, is the idea that the analysis actually reflects the psychological reality of the members of the culture in question. It is a hard thing to be sure about, since we cannot actually see through the eyes of a member of another culture (somewhat, perhaps, as we cannot be sure that the experience of pain as felt by one individual is precisely the same as that felt by another individual). Perhaps we can gain some appreciation of the question by looking at some aspects of the semantic domain of Japanese surface anatomy.

The label *kubi* includes the head and neck, or to put it more graphically, what is lopped off when one is decapitated. This *kubi* we may designate *kubi*₁; it includes the *atama* "head" and the *kubi*₂ "neck."

That is, the simple term *kubi* may refer either to the head plus the neck, or just to the neck. This kind of dual representation recurs time and again in the discussion of Japanese surface anatomy.

The more inclusive, higher order, *kubi*$_1$, is found not only on (or off!) humans, but on most animals, including insects and birds—but not on fish. It is productive, with a number of extensions: *kamakubi* "sickle-*kubi*" describes a snake poised to strike or a "goose-neck," while *kubi*$_1$ by itself describes the neck on a bottle, the zone to which the hairs on a writing brush are attached, and the nob and stem on an alarm clock (but not on a wristwatch, because there is no appreciable gap between the body of the watch and the part of the stem that is turned—the head, so to speak); *kubi*$_1$ also describes the part of the floor lamp below the bulb(s), when the shade is removed. (The shade is a *kasa* or umbrella, so that a floor lamp with a shade and a mushroom fall into the same morphological category.)

Evidently it is the relative horizontal discrepancy of the stem and the part that appears over it which determines whether a form will be a *kubi*$_1$ or a (nonanatomical) *kasa*. An important feature of *kubi*$_2$ is its frailty, when compared to that of the *atama* "head." There are times when *atama* is used in place of *kubi*$_1$, as to describe the nob on either an alarm clock or a wristwatch, but this seems to derive from a lower-order *atama*$_2$, which designates the crown of the *atama*$_1$. The *kubi*$_1$ also appears in *chichi-kubi* "nipple," since the apparatus of the breast plus the nipple bears a resemblance to a decapitated head (though there is no evidence that any informant would spontaneously associate it with the *kubi*$_1$ of the dead human).

The lower-order *kubi*$_2$ appears in *te-kubi* and *ashi-kubi* (the place where the hand joins the wrist and the foot joins the ankle respectively). It may be worth noting that while the *kubisuji* is the term for the nape of the neck of either sex, the female nape is also called *er-ikubi*, and the corresponding anatomical zone is sexually provocative to men. (There are other terms for the nape, but here we are considering *kubi* terms.)

Theoretical Implications

We are trying to make two points here. One is that we can take something as universal as body parts, which we might assume would be divided up in pretty much the same way, no matter where we went, and we find that actually there are some interesting differences from one culture to another. We only see *kubi*$_2$ as a unit ("neck"), and we have some of the same extensions. We can refer to the neck of a bot-

tle, for example, but the shape of the head plus neck (*kubi*₁) provided other possibilities for extensions in Japanese. The whole
network of concepts built up from *kubi* constitute a rather different
entity from the network based on "neck." This also holds for many
of the labels of surface anatomy in Japanese and English. Since the
same differences could be found in many semantic domains, such as
things to eat, coins, or just about anything, the implication is that the
Japanese have a wholly different way of looking at things than the
Americans. Many of the differences are subtle, no doubt, but whether
they are subtle or gross, it would probably be difficult to gain a real
understanding, a visceral understanding, of a different cultural view
of the world. We know that bilinguals, whose two languages are essentially maintained in two cultural settings, respond to stimulus
words and phrases with different associations. It is likely that only
really coordinate bilingual, bicultural individuals can provide the answer to the way perceptions differ, and so far we have not posed the
right questions to reach an answer. There may be a difference between learning to understand events in terms of another culture and
perceiving them more spontaneously in those terms. When the
American, for example, sees the bus coming from a distance, he or
she says, "The bus is coming." The Japanese seeing the same event
says, "The bus has come." It is not too difficult to learn to translate
the present, progressive action of the English expression into the
completed action implied by the Japanese expression. But is this also
to learn to perceive the action of the bus as having been completed?
There is at least one comparable situation in American English, involving the use of *got* or *have got*. Someone going for a fly in baseball
or in response to the ringing of a telephone is likely to call out "I got
it!" Or "I've got it." In either case, suggesting that the action has been
completed even though it has not been. Do we perceive the event as
having been completed when we call out? Probably not. Yet this sort
of treatment of events is common in Japanese, much less common in
English, and takes a bit of getting used to even with the advantage of
a few similar examples in English. We cannot dismiss the hypothesis
on the basis of this example, and consider the visceral effects of some
expressions. Those of us who have led sheltered lives may wince when
we hear our earthy Anglo-Saxonisms, but can the foreigner who
learned English as an adult be induced to wince at the same expressions even if he or she also led a sheltered life?

The second point to be made on the basis of the Japanese example of the *kubi* is the notion of a dual representation. Is there a
perceptual difference between a system that lacks dual representa-

tion and one that draws on it heavily? The Japanese term *te* can mean "hand," but it can also include the whole appendage from the shoulder to the fingertip; the *ashi* may describe the whole leg or more specifically the foot, and so forth. Is there a perceptual difference between the Japanese and the Americans? Or is the concept really so different? Is there anything in English that is similar? As a matter of fact, there is at least one analogous example: "hair." This term may refer to a single strand, "a hair," or to all of the hairs at issue: "Your hair is turning gray." Grass is physically similar, but we cannot say "*a grass," when meaning "a blade of grass," or even "a joint of grass." (The latter, facetious example is not appropriate, because the shape of the commercial pot is too unlike hair.)

At any rate, we find it difficult to perceive the difference between hair and grass in Whorfian terms, and yet we feel that we should be able to if the Whorfian hypothesis were correct.

We can get into the same trouble if we worry about the fact that Japanese does not ordinarily distinguish between singular and plural, while English does. At first blush we would think that this should be important, since we are obliged by our grammar to indicate the distinction, and at times we may even feel uncomfortable if we do not know whether an object is singular or plural (as when we are obliged to translate from a language such as Japanese). We cannot point to our own zero-marked plurals, such as "deer" and "sheep," because we usually have other markers to tell us whether they are one or many. But if we examine the "many," we can see that we are not much concerned that we cannot know, when a plural form alone is used, just how many are involved. In other languages, on the other hand, the person may be singular, dual, trial, or plural. How would a speaker of such a language analyze English? Would he or she count our plural as a neutralization of dual, trial, and plural?

While Frake's (1962) componential analysis of our category of "something to eat" and Conklin's (1962) analysis of the terms we use to designate our everyday units of monetary exchange (nickel, quarter, and so on) seem intuitively valid, the question of psychological reality has not really been answered. In other words, to skip back to *ashi* as "leg" and *ashi* as "foot," is the dual representation different from our lumping together of trial and plural? We have no comfortable answer, but the hypothesis would seem to require one.

Michael Agar (1982) has provided a recent assessment of cognitive anthropology. On the one hand, cognitive anthropology blends with an emerging interdisciplinary concern with "cognitive science," which draws on people in cognitive psychology, artificial intelligence, philosophy, neurophysiology, sociology, and anthropology. On the other hand, it overlaps with another emerging field: discourse analysis, which is largely concerned with stretches of naturally situated talk. Citing Hutchin's (1980) study of discourse involved in public land litigation in the Trobriands, work by Fillmore (1981) and Kay on the kinds of information available to children in dealing with reading tests, Quinn's (1982) study of key words as linguistic anchors for the organization of background understandings, and his own ongoing work with Jerry Hobbs on the life history of a heroin addict to find a way to specify the knowledge that provides the inferential wherewithal to understand stretches of discourse, Agar describes several changes in cognitive anthroplogy.

First of all, the data taken for analysis consist of stretches of discourse, rather than related sets of lexemes. Second, the older taxonomic or componential representations were pretty well limited to superset/subset or conjunction relationships, while the current schematic representations permit a more holistic presentation of knowledge. Third, the schemas that are being constructed today come from a mix of a general sense of the group, intuition, and things that the people say and do. This contrasts with the older preoccupation with elicitation strategies. Agar feels that there was an older bias favoring the presentation of a static world of conventions, while there is now more concern with the intentions of the actors who move through that world. Finally, today theoretical pointers are sought to mediate between the local, detailed, analysis of transcripts and the broader statements about a group that ethnographers hope to make.

In brief, the new look preserves the focus on language as the prime path to the understanding of group life.

> However, by shifting to discourse and schemas, by decreasing concern with mechanical elicitation strategies, and by beginning to worry about the relation of knowledge structures to actor's intentions and broader cultural themes, this more recent version adds breadth and depth, retaining the old strengths while enabling it to confront other issues of ethnographic concern. [Agar, 1982, p. 85]

THE GRAMMAR OF CULTURE

Somewhat in the way grammar consists of rules for the generation of utterances, a grammar of culture consists of rules for the generation of patterns of behavior. It is necessary, of course, to determine the components of cultural patterns, just as it is necessary to determine phonemes, morphemes, and the like. But a mere inventory of components does not constitute a language, any more than a listing of culture traits constitutes a culture.

Goodenough (1981) has mentioned forms, beliefs, and values as the points of reference for behavior. The behavior itself, whether obvious or not, is purposive: purposes and goals give coherence to action, and we interpret the actions of others in terms of the purposes and goals that we impute to them. Goodenough puts it thus:

> All meaningful behavior is in this respect like speech behavior. The communicational intent of an utterance provides the focus around which words and grammatical constructions are selected and arranged syntactically into coherent sentences. Similarly, the intended consequences or purposes of other kinds of behavior provide the foci around which people, things and acts become organized syntactically into coherent activities. [pp. 81–82]

Goodenough suggests that for most recurring purposes, people develop recipes or formulas. Thus there are recipes for ways to dress, for conducting parties, for seeking favors, for wooing members of the opposite sex, or, less overtly perhaps, members of the same sex.

Goodenough distinguishes recipes from routines and customs. Recipes refer to ideas and understandings about ways to do things, while in his terminology, routines and customs refer to the execution of the behavior. We may develop highly personal routines. We have recipes for setting a table for dinner, but except perhaps for the requirement that the tablecloth (if one is used) be placed first, there is no special order for performing the individual steps in the routine. That is, we tend to develop our own routines for setting out dishes, chopsticks, and other paraphernalia. Where people bring their individual routines into group activity, one routine may become the standard and thus part of the recipe itself, in that there will now be a "right way" to perform the routine. This is how Goodenough (1981) sees customs:

> Unlike routines, which arise from habits of executing particular recipes, customs have to do with habits of choice among alternative recipes and alternative developed routines. . . . A custom, then, is a recipe or a routine for executing a recipe that is regularly resorted to . . . in preference to alternative recipes or al-

ternative routines for executing them. Customs arise when the choice of recipes or routines for given occasions has itself been routinized. [p. 86]

Goodenough carries his discussion to successively higher levels of behavior, but to follow him further would be to depart too far from our language orientation.

METHODS OF ANALYZING CULTURAL PATTERNS

If we can speak meaningfully about "a grammar of culture," we should be able to apply methods of grammatical analysis to the analysis of culture patterns; this has been done to get at the cognitive structures, as already discussed, though we have not actually gone through the analytical processes whereby we arrived at the structures. We have also noted that we need rules for the sequencing of events. Goodenough has commented on some of the kinds of sequences, but has not actually tried to write the grammar. (See also Berne, 1964).

Here we would like to offer a hint as to how the problem of sequencing might be approached; we are using some of the concepts developed by Sidney M. Lamb (especially as described in 1964).

One of the basic notions in Lamb's system is that an event on one level or stratum is realized on the stratum immediately below. Thus the plural morpheme (on the morphemic level) will be realized in various ways on the phonemic level, depending in part on the phonetic context. After the unvoiced stop at the end of "dock," the plural is realized as /-s/, but after the voiced stop at the end of "dog," it is realized as /-z/. In baseball, a "ball" can be realized in several ways: outside a fairly clearly defined space, determined by the location and width of the plate, or by passing inside that space in the direction of the batter, or by passing within the space, but either above or below a height that is fixed by the dimensions of the batter. The extent to which the ball misses the target area is not relevant; what is relevant (emic) is whether the umpire decides that the ball did or did not pass through the space in question. The actual realizations of the "ball" correspond to the so-called free variations in the realization of a phoneme.

The "strike" is a little more complicated. It may be realized by the passage of the ball through the area that the "ball" did *not* pass through. In this case, and in the case of the "ball," the realization depends on the batter's not making any attempt to contact the ball with his bat. If the batter swings at the ball and misses, that is a "strike," no matter where the ball passed. A "strike" may be realized if the batter contacts the ball with the bat and it subsequently passes somewhere other than into that part of the field which is designated "fair" territory, so long as no opposing player catches it before it touches the ground. In each case there is permissible variation, such as catching the inside corner, the outside corner, right down the middle, and so forth; or the ball may be fouled either to the right or left of the playing field or directly behind the plate. For the execution of the "ball" and the "strike," it does not matter whether the batter stands to the right or left of the plate, but he is obliged to remain in the appropriate "box."

These low-level examples of realization show another important feature of Lamb's model, *diversification*. Diversification refers to the existence of alternate realizations, on a given stratum, of the events of a higher stratum. Thus the "strike" is a higher-order event than either the swing-and-miss or the alternate realization "called strike."

Another important feature of realization is *neutralization*, which is in some ways the opposite of diversification. It involves the common realization of events that are different at a higher stratum. For example, /ð ə dágz/ is ambiguous, because it may mean either dog-plural, dog-possessive, or even dog-plural-possessive. At the morphemic level the plural and the possessive are separate, but they sometimes show up in the identical form on the phonemic level. Similarly, the intentional and the unintentional walk are the results of different decisions at a higher level; in the latter case the decision was to "pitch to" the batter, while in the former case the decision was to "put the man on" base, usually for tactical reasons, such as to facilitate the execution of a double play, or to be able to force him out later. Both decisions, though, are realizations of a still higher-order decision, to "retire the side" by getting three men out.

A *composite realization* is one in which an event is realized by a combination of events at the stratum immediately below. Thus the "intentional walk" is realized by a sequence of four balls. The opposite of composite realization is *portmanteau realization;* the most famous linguistic example of this may be the French /o/ as a realization of *á*+ *le*. A good example from baseball would seem to be the "home run," which is simultaneously a "hit," "a run scored," and "a run batted in."

In the last example, incidentally, it should be noted that the "home run" is on a lower stratum than each of the events for which it constitutes a portmanteau realization. The home run is only one of several realizations of "hit," of "a run scored," and of "a run batted in," though it is the only portmanteau realization of all three higher-level events.

Zero realization may be illustrated linguistically by the absence of a plural marker for "sheep;" in baseball it occurs as the third out when the home team breaks a tie in the ninth inning, since the game ends without a final out having been made, though the higher-order rules call for three outs to retire a side.

The opposite of zero realization is *empty realization*. A linguistic example would be the "it" in "it's raining," since the "it" lacks any referent. In baseball, every uncaught foul after the batter has made two strikes would appear to be an empty realization of the "strike," since it does not advance the game. That is, it seems to represent nothing at a higher stratum.

Anataxis is the last feature of realization that Lamb deals with. This means that the order of units of one stratum differs from the order of their corresponding realizations on the lower stratum. In ordinary linguistic parlance, anataxis is called metathesis, and refers to the interchange of two phonemes. Some English speakers, for example, pronounce "ask" as if it were "ax" (aks). An example of this in baseball might be the case in which a pitcher is removed from a game with a man on base, when that man later scores. The run in this case is charged not to the current pitcher, but to the man who has already left the game.

Lamb's concepts provide various ways of getting from higher- to lower-order events, though one must also spell out the tactics in order to describe the sequencing of events. In a way these are spelled out in considerable detail for most games, and, as Goodenough (1971) has indicated, they are also spelled out by individuals such as Dale Carnegie and Emily Post for certain kinds of social behavior. But for the most part, anthropologists have described sequenced patterns without showing sufficient explicit concern for what is emic and what is etic in their descriptions.

Finally, a very brief illustration from Ervin-Tripp (1969) can give us an idea of how sequenced behavior might be approached from the generative viewpoint. The ritual is that of "leave-taking." Leave-taking (LT) has two parts for two actors. Thus:

Leave-taking——————[is rewritten]→LT 1 + LT 2

This means that leave-taking consists of two parts. The LT 1 can then be expanded to

$$LT \ 1 \rightarrow Goodbye + CP$$

Here the second component is a courtesy phrase of some sort, which can be represented in various ways:

$$CP \rightarrow \begin{cases} \text{I am glad to have met you.} \\ \text{I hope to see you again (soon).} \end{cases}$$

The brace includes alternate expressions, and the parentheses indicate optional elements. Then

$$LT \ 2 \rightarrow \ Thank \ you \ (+ \ yes, \ we'll \ have \ to \ get \ together \ again).$$

Obviously the ritual has descriptive possibilities that are only hinted at here. A much more detailed study, of sequencing in telephone conversations, has been produced by Schegloff (1972). In the nonverbal area, Goodenough (1971) has made a first step in this direction; he shows a similar point of view, though he has not reduced the analysis to the linguistic-type notion.

It is far too soon to proclaim this the wave of the future in ethnographic description, but the devising of more formal approaches to description and analysis will undoubtedly continue.

REFERENCES

Agar, M. H. Whatever happened to cognitive anthropology: A partial review. *Human Organization*, 1982, *41*, 82–86.

Benedict, R. *The chrysanthemum and the sword.* Boston: Houghton Mifflin Co., 1946.

Berlin, B. A universalistic-evolutionary approach in ethnographic semantics. *Current Directions in Anthropology*, 1970, *3* (Part 2), 3–18.

Berlin, B., Breedlove, D., & Raven, P. *Principles of Tzeltal Plant Classification.* New York: Seminar Press, Inc., 1973.

Berne, E. *Games people play.* New York: Grove Press, Inc., 1964.

Brown, R. *Wilhelm von Humboldt's conception of linguistic relativity.* The Hague: Mouton & Co., 1967.

Brown, R., & Lenneberg, E. A study in language and cognition. *Journal of Abnormal and Social Psychology*, 1954, *49*, 454–462.

Burling, R. Cognition and componential analysis: God's truth or hocus-pocus? *American Anthropologist*, 1964, *66*, 20–28.

Carroll, J. B. (Ed.). *Language, thought, and reality: Selected writings of Benjamin Lee Whorf.* Cambridge, Mass.: The M.I.T. Press, 1956.

Carroll, J. B., & Casagrande, J. B. The function of language classifications in behavior. In E. Maccoby, T. H. Newcomb, & E. L. Hartley (Eds.), *Readings in Social Psychology.* (3rd ed.) New York: Holt, Rinehart & Winston, Inc., 1958.

Conklin, H. C. Hanunóo color categories. *Southwestern Journal of Anthropology*, 1955, *11*, 339–344.

Conklin, H.C. Comment [on Frake, 1962]. In T. Gladwin and W. G. Sturtevant (Eds.), *Anthropology and Human Behavior*. Washington, D.C.: The Anthropological Society of Washington, 1962.

Ervin-Tripp, S. M. An analysis of the interaction of language, topic and listener. *American Anthropologist*, 1964, *66* (Part 2, no. 6), 72–85.

Ervin-Tripp, S.M. Sociolinguistics. In L. Berkowitz (Ed.), *Advances in experimental social psychology* (Vol. 4). 91–165. New York: Academic Press, Inc., 1969.

Fillmore, C. J. Ideal readers and real readers. Paper presented to the 32nd Annual Georgetown University Round Table on Languages and Linguistics, Washington, D.C., 1981.

Fishman, J. A. A systematization of the Whorfian hypothesis. *Behavioral Science*, 1960, *5*, 323–339.

Fishman, J. A. Whorfianism of the third kind: Ethnolinguistic diversity as a worldwide societal asset. *Language in Society*, 1982, *11*, 1–14.

Frake, C. O. The diagnosis of disease among the Subanun of Mindanao. *American Anthropologist*, 1961, *63*, 113–132.

Frake, C. O. The ethnographic study of cognitive systems. In T. Gladwin and W. C. Sturtevant (Eds.), *Anthropology and Human Behavior*, 1962, pp. 72–75, Washington, D. C.: The Anthropological Society of Washington.

Gastil, R. D. Relative linguistic determinism. *Anthropological Linguistics*, 1959, *1* (no. 9), 24–38.

Goodenough, W. H. Componential analysis and the study of meaning. *Language*, 1956, *32*, 195–216.

Goodenough, W. H. *Culture, language and society*. An Addison-Wesley Module in Anthropology. Reading, Mass.: Addison-Wesley Publishing Co., 1971.

Goodenough, W. H. *Culture, language, and society*. (2nd ed.). Menlo Park, California: The Benjamin/Cummings Publishing Company, Inc., 1981.

Hoijer, H. (Ed.). *Language in Culture*. Chicago: University of Chicago Press, 1954.

Hutchins, E. *Culture and inference*. Cambridge, Mass.: Harvard University Press, 1980.

Hymes, D. H. On typology of cognitive styles in language (with examples from Chinookan). *Anthropological Linguistics*, 1961, *3* (no. 1), 22–54.

Lamb, S. M. The sememic approach to structural semantics. *American Anthropologist*, 1964, *66* (Part 2, no. 3), 57–76.

Lee, D. Lineal and nonlineal codifications of reality. *Psychosomatic Medicine*, 1950, *12*, 89–97.

Lindeman, R. Der Begriff der Conscience in Franzosichen Denken. Leipsig, East Germany: Jena, 1938.

Lounsbury, F. G. A semantic analysis of the Pawnee kinship usage. *Language*, 1956, *32*, 158–194.

Lowie, R. H. *The history of ethnological theory*. New York: Rinehart & Company, Inc., 1937.

McQuown, N. A. Analysis of the cultural content of language materials. In Harry Hoijer (Ed.), *Language in culture*. Chicago: University of Chicago Press, 1954.

Mandelbaum, D. C. (Ed.). *Selected writings of Edward Sapir*. Berkeley, Cal.: University of California Press, 1949.

Quinn, N. "Commitment" in American marriage: a cultural analysis. *American Ethnologist 9*: 775–798.

Schegloff, E. Sequencing in conversational openings. In J. J. Gumperz & D. Hymes (Eds.), *Directions in sociolinguistics*. New York: Holt, Rinehart & Winston, Inc., 1972.

Trager, G. L. The systematization of the Whorfian hypothesis. *Anthropological Linguistics*, 1959, *1* (no. 1), 31–35.

Wallace, A. F. C., & Atkins, J. The meaning of kinship terms. *Amer. Anthropologist*, 1960, 62: 58–80.

Whorf, B. L. Science and linguistics. *Technology Review*, 1940, *42*, 229–231, 247–284.

Williams, T. R. *Field Methods in the Study of Culture*. New York: Holt, Rinehart & Winston, Inc., 1967.

INDEX